D0070687

This is the ultimate guide to running social in a medium or large organization. Practical, current, and indispensable!
Jay Baer, Founder of Convince & Convert and host of the *Social Pros Podcast*

Full of strategic wisdom and practical experience.
Lisa Shepherd, President, Mezzanine Growth

Outlines the process for the beginner and expert alike and sets a new baseline that others will now need to reach.
Tim Hughes, Co-founder and CEO, DLAignite

Social Media Marketing for Business

Scaling an integrated social media strategy across your organization

Andrew Jenkins

KoganPage

Publisher's note

Every possible effort has been made to ensure that the information contained in this book is accurate at the time of going to press, and the publishers and authors cannot accept responsibility for any errors or omissions, however caused. No responsibility for loss or damage occasioned to any person acting, or refraining from action, as a result of the material in this publication can be accepted by the editor, the publisher, or the author.

First published in Great Britain and the United States in 2022 by Kogan Page Limited

2nd Floor, 45 Gee Street
London
EC1V 3RS
United Kingdom
www.koganpage.com

8 W 38th Street, Suite 902
New York, NY 10018
USA

4737/23 Ansari Road
Daryaganj
New Delhi 110002
India

Kogan Page books are printed on paper from sustainable forests.

ISBNs

Hardback   978 1 3986 0371 4
Paperback 978 1 3986 0369 1
Ebook   978 1 3986 0370 7

British Library Cataloguing-in-Publication Data

A CIP record for this book is available from the British Library.

Library of Congress Cataloguing-in-Publication Data

Names: Jenkins, Andrew (Social media consultant), author.
Title: Social media marketing for business: scaling an integrated social
    media strategy across your organization / Andrew Jenkins.
Description: London; New York, NY: Kogan Page, 2022. | Includes
    bibliographical references and index.
Identifiers: LCCN 2021058696 (print) | LCCN 2021058697 (ebook) | ISBN
    9781398603714 (hardback) | ISBN 9781398603691 (paperback) | ISBN
    9781398603707 (ebook)
Subjects: LCSH: Marketing–Social aspects. | Internet marketing. | Social
    media.
Classification: LCC HF5415 .J46 2022 (print) | LCC HF5415 (ebook) | DDC
    658.8/02–dc23/20211215
LC record available at https://lccn.loc.gov/2021058696
LC ebook record available at https://lccn.loc.gov/2021058697

Typeset by Integra Software Services, Pondicherry
Print production managed by Jellyfish
Printed and bound by CPI Group (UK) Ltd, Croydon CR0 4YY

CONTENTS

ACKNOWLEDGEMENTS

You are reading this because many people and organizations have been kind, generous and supportive of me at some point in time and, in some cases, unendingly. Many opened doors, made introductions or connected me with people with the intention of mutual benefit. Whenever possible, I have tried to reciprocate. I would not be running my company or writing these words without their willingness to take a chance on me or help me, in some cases even before I asked.

Let me begin by thanking some of the people who were instrumental at the early stages of my journey. You did not know what you were going to inspire when you showed me something as innocuous as a thumbnail picture (nor did I necessarily know it at the time) but, Lincoln Stewart, you gave me an entrepreneurial epiphany for which I am eternally grateful.

First, I want to express my gratitude to Roland Harwood for the opportunity he gave me while at NESTA that changed my life and the path of my career. I wouldn't be doing what I am doing now and writing this book if it weren't for Roland. I have valued our collaborations over the years and look forward to the opportunity to collaborate again in the future.

My connection with Dick Rempt reminds me and should remind all of us that we are part of a global community. Social networks have enabled a sense of belonging to that global community. That was certainly the case when Dick and I first connected. What began as a social exchange has become a friendship. Over the years we have collaborated, supported each other and provided updates on our respective entrepreneurial pursuits, challenges and successes.

This book came about because of the generosity of Tim Hughes in making an introduction because of a goal I shared with him. My goal became a reality because Tim chose to pay it forward. It may have seemed like a simple or easy thing to do for Tim at the time, but it is a big deal to me. He was also kind enough to share advice about writing based on his experience writing two books of his own. I look forward to sharing what comes because of writing this book.

Many others have played a role in my success to date. Let me pre-emptively apologize to anyone that I may have missed. It was not intentional.

They may not have known or realized it but each of them extended kindness and generosity to me whether through an introduction, a referral, advice or some other form of support. They include, in no order and so as not to hurt any feelings, David Alston, Sionne Roberts, Jaime Stein, Laurie Dillon-Schalk, Alexa Samuels, Michael Smith, Ferg Devins. Joanne Jacobs, Sabaa Quao, Anita Windisman, Scott Wambolt, Jim Little, Howard Morton, Gary Jarosz, Susan Diaz, Lindsay Bell-Wheeler, Martin Waxman, Alison Garwood-Jones, Eden Spodek, Diane Begin, Mary Pretotto, Gord Kerr, Rosalina Lin-Allen, Steve Mast, Randy Matheson, Hessie Jones, Dave Fleet, Joel Marans, Sulemaan Ahmed, Jo-Anne Wallace, Teresa Ho, Stewart Hayes, Rod Lohin, Mark Bowden, Michael Bungay-Stanier, Andy Paul, Jeremy Miller, Louis Trahan, Roger Pierce, Bruce Tatters, Chad Williams, Jon Ferrara, Jonathan Soon-Shiong, Tim Rooney, John Bromley, Gavin McGarry, Chloe Perelgut, Gregg Tilston, Karim Kanji, Aaron Polmeer, David Basskin, Susan Walsh, Nabil Harfoush, Rahaf Harfoush, Justin Kozuch, Alexander Manu, Alex Osterwalder, Michael Dila, Chris Thompson, Todd Grierson, Virginia Brailey, Lucas Chang, Brandon Moore, Albert Luk, Chris Case, Katie Tingley, Janine Harris, Adam Green, Alan Smith, Allan Booke, Greg Cormier, Derek Lackey, Lorne Solway, Andrea Wojnicki, Mark Evans, Andrew Sinclair, Aran Hamilton, Bruce Runions, Bruce Simpson, Chris Mildon, Brian Cook, Mike Orr, Blair Currie, Bilal Jaffery, Baron Manett, Baris Akyurek, Brian Deck, Craig DesBrisay, Cyrus Mavalwala, Dani Gagnon, David Jones, David Mahr, Frank Eliason, Tara Grant, Guy Avigdor, Helen Androlia, Jason Dojc, Jed Schneiderman, John Huehn, Bret Leech, Leigh Mitchell, Peter Flaschner, Peter Reitano, Tim Burrows, Greg Vissers, Steve Sheather, Ujwal Arkalgud, Fariba Anderson, Carlos Paz Soldan, Robert Luke, James Morris, Roisin McNamara, Javier Burón, Kate Chernis, Rachel Ott, Mark Schaefer, Charlene Li, Chris Messina, Cat Martinez, Heidi Tsao, Frank Eliason, Mark Orlan, Scott Newlands, Suzanne Merrett, Daryl Ching, Jay Baer, Lisa Shepherd, Lee Odden and Patrick McCaully.

Organizations that I want to thank include the Rotman School of Management, the Michael Lee Chin Family Institute for Corporate Citizenship, the University of Toronto and the School of Continuing Studies, George Brown College and the Innovation Advisory Board, Seneca College, OCAD University, the Royal Bank of Canada, Royal Canin, Bladder Cancer Canada, Campbellford Memorial Hospital, the Geneva Centre for Autism, Red Cloud Securities, Aviso Wealth, the Response Marketing Association,

Vissers Sales, Score Statistical, Sharman's Proper Pies, Delvinia, Audiense, Rival IQ and Lately.

I also want to thank the Volterra team whose work with clients, content and strategy played such an important part in what ultimately ended up in the book and for keeping things running smoothly while I took time to write the book.

I have likely missed acknowledging and thanking several people and organizations. I am sorry. It was not my intention. I have had a 25 year-plus career working with a multitude of people and organizations that have all impacted me in some way. There are too many to name but know that I would not be who or where I am without you.

Finally, and most important, I want to thank my family for their immeasurable love and support. Teaching, building my business and writing this book have meant time away from you. Your unending patience and understanding are truly appreciated. I also want to say that I know and understand the true cost of my absence and will be focused on making it up to you in the years to come.

Introduction

My first tweet had a typo. My second tweet was an apology for the typo in my first tweet. A friend and one of my first followers tweeted back to me to just relax. I have come a long way since that first tweet 13 years ago. Frankly, the social media landscape has come a long way too.

Before Twitter, I was already on Facebook and LinkedIn. The latter was just getting rolling when I was finishing my MBA and I ended up being one of the first 200,000 members. I have seen that platform as well as many others come, go and, for those that remain, evolve in order to remain competitive and relevant.

However, my online experience predates social media. Nearly 30 years ago, I was finishing film school (an example of my eclectic background that informs the work I do in social media every day but more on that later), and one of my classmates, Lincoln Stewart, who had been dabbling in web design, showed me a thumbnail picture of a shirt online. He clicked on it and it got bigger. We take that for granted now, but it was an epiphany for me at the time.

I had spent my high school and university years working at a menswear store. The thumbnail image epiphany inspired me to start my own e-commerce company selling menswear online in 1995. 1995 BG – Before Google.

Unfortunately, solutions like Shopify, Squarespace, Wix, PayPal, Square or Stripe did not exist then, which meant everything had to be built from scratch. Furthermore, banks and customers were reluctant to trust an unknown entity that was just set up. I was based in Canada and Canadians were very reluctant to trust e-commerce, but ironically I was getting inquiries from the US, Scandinavia and Japan. Sadly, the logistics of shipping and customs at that time made transacting with those regions prohibitive.

After persisting for over a year, I wrapped up the business and parlayed my experience into working for my first start-up, coincidentally an e-commerce start-up targeting the kind of small business that my e-commerce company had been. It was there that I witnessed the prevailing appetite of the US marketplace for early adoption of technology. It is no wonder that the dominant social networks began there.

I won't bore you with my start-up experiences, the dotcom boom and bust or my time at business school. Let's fast forward to 2007. I had landed my first job post-MBA in 2004 at one of Canada's largest telecom providers, but they shut down my department and I was laid off. While I was investigating my next move, I was doing some research on LinkedIn and made a discovery that would change my life for ever.

I owe my career to LinkedIn

During my MBA, I was introduced to the concepts of integrative or design thinking and innovation. The idea of solving complex problems with fresh and/or counterintuitive ideas with the freedom to fail intrigued me. I was looking for people and organizations that had those same beliefs.

My research led me to find Roland Harwood, then at NESTA, the National Endowment for Science, Technology and the Arts. I sent him a message through LinkedIn to see if he would be open to chatting. I told him that I was interested in learning more about the work that he did and about NESTA. We chatted soon thereafter and continued to keep in touch in the months that followed.

I ended up being in the UK for a job interview some months later and arranged to meet Roland in person, further strengthening our business relationship. I returned to Canada and began establishing my business focused on strategy. A few months after my UK trip I reached out to Roland in the early part of 2008 to see if he knew of any companies interested in outsourcing professional services or management consulting to Canada given the exchange rate at the time. He responded that, coincidentally, they had a project and they had me in mind for it. That is when everything changed.

NESTA was exploring whether or not the emerging social networks were reflective of cities and the communities within them and whether social networks would indeed become the new city or city of the future. Looking at social networks by comparing them to attributes of cities, I began my research in earnest.

I examined all of the social networks that I was currently a part of and joined all of the predominant and competing ones at that time. I often note to people that in 2008 Facebook was not the number one social network. That position was held by Myspace. Unfortunately, like many other platforms, Myspace fell out of favour and a select few remained standing.

I joined Second Life, Bebo, Orkut and many more. Most are gone now. Some, like Bebo, were acquired for an exorbitant amount of money only to disappear and be reacquired by their founders for a fraction of the price that they sold it at. Bebo claimed to be relaunching a new social network in 2021 but as of the writing of this book remains in private beta.

I looked at all of the social networks from the perspective of where and how they were similar and different to cities. I looked at their demographics, governance, commerce, etiquette, culture and more. I looked at how communities formed and how trust was established as well as lost. While the overall conclusion was that social networks exhibited many city-like qualities, the prospect of them becoming the new city was unlikely. Having said that, there were numerous signs that showed the unique qualities (i.e. followers) and inherent behaviours (i.e. like, comment and subscribe) of social networks would continue to evolve and grow as these virtual communities continued to grow and interact.

With the NESTA research project completed, I now had a wealth of social media knowledge on which to build. I have spent the years since growing a social media-focused company, going from a solopreneur to a team supporting a growing number of clients. Additionally, I have had the good fortune to teach social media strategy at the University of Toronto for the past seven years.

It was a social network that enabled me to make a connection in another country that would change my life irrevocably and for the better. That is why I am confident in saying that I owe my career to LinkedIn and, more importantly, Roland Harwood, someone who has not only been a valuable connection but has become a friend and someone with whom I continue to collaborate.

More valuable connections

Not long after I completed the project for NESTA in 2008, someone posted a question in one of my LinkedIn discussion groups asking which social network would end up being the overall winner. Fresh off my NESTA project with a head full of facts and statistics, I responded by saying that there likely would not be a single clear winner but that a number would coexist, serving different groups with different wants and needs.

The person who asked the question was a fellow entrepreneur named Dick Rempt. That exchange sparked an ongoing dialogue that led to being hosted in his home near Amsterdam when I was there for an event. We have been friends for over a decade, all because of social media and, more specifically, starting a conversation on LinkedIn.

That highlights what I have experienced over the last decade-plus working in social media – having valuable conversations. While advertising gets a lot of air time when it comes to social media discussion, it still comes down to valuable conversations with your community, whether B2B, B2C, government or non-profit.

One of my most recent high-value conversations was with Tim Hughes of DLA Ignite. He and I had connected on LinkedIn, Facebook and Twitter because we shared many mutual connections and interests such as LinkedIn and social selling. While we had been connected virtually for quite some time, it was not until last year that we had the opportunity to meet in person. During our conversation I expressed a desire to write a book as one of my professional goals and that I already had an idea for what kind of book it would be.

Hearing my goal, Tim volunteered to introduce me to his publisher with whom he had written two books. Fast forward a few weeks and an intro was made. The pandemic delayed things a bit, but here we are writing a book for the very publisher to whom I was introduced by initially a social connection who has become a friend.

Do you see a pattern here? Social connections become valuable connections and I am not just saying they are valuable in a monetary way. They are valuable because we provide value to each other. It is not just a one-way street. As much as social media has grown, we mustn't lose sight of the fundamental fact that it is 'social'. We are social beings and we crave connection, even if they are virtual. This has proven to be all the more important as we dealt with major events such as the pandemic.

Organizations that can genuinely and transparently combine being social with their objectives can achieve success but they must not do so at the expense of the valuable connections they have with their community. The saying goes that it is easier to retain an existing customer than acquire a new one. The same can be said of a community member.

Focus and learning

Suffice it to say that the social media space is dynamic with players entering and exiting depending on the appetite of users and investors. As I write this in 2021, Clubhouse and the idea of social audio is hot. Many platforms such as Twitter and LinkedIn are alluding to audio features to compete with Clubhouse. It is hard to say who will emerge victorious. Clubhouse is well founded and growing in popularity every day. Twitter and LinkedIn already have vast user bases familiar with how they work so new audio features might be easily adopted.

Alternatively, people might get caught up with the bright new shiny thing like the latest hyped social media platform that is Clubhouse. Early signs show that there is momentum building for Clubhouse downloads and activity. As with other new platforms, they take time to establish themselves, and those trying to establish a presence will have to work hard to build and maintain thought leadership.

When it comes to social media, thought leadership is an often overused phrase. So is the word influence. However, the underlying sentiments of those terms, providing value, informing and educating are still some of the key factors for success in social media. You have to earn the right to be seen as a trusted thought leader who has subject matter expertise and is influential within an industry or sector. There are no shortcuts.

Much of this book will focus on where and how companies can establish a social media presence, grow it and engage their community over time. We will look at a variety of organization types and industries. I will share my own experiences as well as those of some of my clients. I will reference case studies that warrant your attention and bring home the point I am trying to make about social media and related strategies.

You will gain insights into tools, methodologies and best practices from our own experiences working with clients, and from other practitioners whose input I solicited. While tools are important to manage and scale social media management and the execution of strategy, they should serve your objective rather than being your primary objective.

Whether you are the only social media resource or part of a team, you will learn what it takes to set up an operating model for social media and how to devise and execute social media strategies that go beyond likes and follows to actually help achieve your corporate objectives. You will learn what risks and potential pitfalls exist and how to mitigate or avoid them altogether.

You will gain an understanding of what is involved in reputation management from a social media perspective and the importance of social listening and monitoring for brand protection, customer service, community engagement and sentiment analysis. You will also learn the strengths, weaknesses and nuances of the major social networks, as well as some of the emerging ones, and their relevance to your organization and objectives.

01

You're in charge of social media, now what?

So now you find yourself responsible for your organization's social media success. Whether you were asked or you actively sought out the opportunity, you still have to sort out a number of things to ensure that success, even if you are very familiar with the organization, how everything works and who does what.

Are you a born project manager? Do you like checklists or to-do lists? Regardless of how you deal with projects and tasks, let's keep it simple. Here are some things to ask or consider to help get your oriented and progressing towards your social media objectives as soon as possible.

Role and responsibilities defined

If you are new to the role as an internal or external hire, are the role and its responsibilities sufficiently defined? Are you clear on what is expected of you? Do the measures of success seem reasonable to achieve?

Often we find ourselves in a role where the job description is a bit vague and management, when pressed, isn't always able to provide clarity or fill in the blanks. You want to confirm what is expected of you and document what success looks like from the perspective of your key stakeholders. Furthermore, does everyone want the same performance metrics or do they differ depending on the stakeholder group?

You also want to be careful that you control as many of the factors impacting your performance metrics as possible. The last thing you want is to be held accountable for outcomes whose influencing factors are outside your span of control or tied to someone else. For example, imagine being tasked with improving community sentiment but paid social media campaigns managed by another group were causing an increase in negative comments on your social media channels, thereby increasing the negative sentiment being captured through social media listening. Those overseeing the paid campaigns don't have to answer for the negative sentiment but you do. That's not the greatest position to be in.

Make certain that your executive sponsor is on the same page as you in terms of your role, responsibilities, and measures of success and is prepared to defend you to other stakeholders if your efforts are ever questioned. If you are not careful, misunderstandings can make their way through the organization and unrealistic or incorrect assumptions can be made about you.

You may find yourself having to defend yourself against questions being asked from misinformed stakeholders. I was heading up a social media team and other business units thought we were an internal agency set up to serve them and potentially compete with external agencies on retainer. That was absolutely not the case, but it is hard to change perceptions if they have already become entrenched. Hopefully, your executive sponsor can help properly socialize your mandate with key stakeholders to avoid potential confusion.

Find out who else has similar objectives or whose success is intertwined with yours and ensure that you make an ally of them and their team if need be, as quickly as possible. Foster collaborative relationships as much as possible to ensure you are all working towards common goals rather than creating friction that could prove counterproductive.

Resources and support

In your new or current role, do you feel that you have the right resources, people, tools and otherwise to achieve success? Do you even know what you need, or do you need to conduct research and evaluate solutions? How much will you be overseeing and how much will you actually be doing yourself? Do you have to make a business case to get what you need?

Sometimes it can feel like you were thrown in the deep end, and you are busy just trying to tread water. Demands and expectations can differ with each stakeholder group. One group's excellent is another group's good. Some prefer speed of execution over quality while others scrutinize everything and seek the input of many. If you are being asked to do more and/or better than before then you want to make sure you are clear on what more and/or better looks like to those key stakeholders.

How you address stakeholder needs and expectations will dictate the resources and support you need. What parts fall to you and where will you need help? What tools and resources are currently available? In the case of the tools, do you need time and/or training to familiarize yourself with them? Are there people available to you who already know how to use them? Will one or more tools or service providers, such as social media management tools or content providers, help deliver what is expected?

There are quite a number of free and inexpensive tools and service providers available that enable a modest budget and individual or small team to accomplish a lot with just a little. From free management and analytics tools to artificial intelligence (AI) based tools that help create multiple social posts from a single blog, organizations can now scale their social media activities to meet the consistency and frequency that social media demands without overburdening existing resources.

Who has your back?

One of the most overlooked things about social media is change. Scaling social media strategies for an organization means change. Organizations and the people within them are resistant to change. That is why it is critical to have an executive champion who will back you up, communicate your role and responsibilities to others and help garner budget for tools and resources to help make the changes necessary for social media success with as little friction as possible.

I was hired by the Chief Brand Officer of one of Canada's largest banks. I was hired as a consultant to help establish and build their social media team and operating model. During one of my early presentations to him I showed him some social media examples from other financial services firms from around the world, to inspire his thinking and inform our strategy discussion. He asked me what I would do and I answered, 'It depends on how bold you want to be.' He then told me that he had promised the board that the bank would be a leader in social media within five years.

That was enough support for me to move ahead. He had the ear of the board and had made them a promise – one I was to help him keep. Unfortunately, he resigned a few months later and when the new executive took over the social media portfolio, they had no interest in social media and, over the next year, proceeded to dismantle everything that had been built or was in progress, leaving very little behind before retiring. It just goes to show you the importance of an executive champion and their support.

The politics unspoken

As mentioned previously, rolling out social media within an organization means change and sometimes that change means office politics can be involved. They can prove to be very disruptive or downright impossible to overcome. Acknowledging the possibility that they exist and trying to navigate them delicately can help mitigate the risk that they may impede your ability to achieve your mandate.

Once I was working with a company that had acquired another company, but both organizations were operating under separate brands with the eventual merging of the two brands planned. Until that merger was completed, they still seemed to operate as two distinct companies with two distinct cultures. It was the culture of the acquired company that proved to be an obstacle.

The acquired company had such an entrenched culture that, for example, they had their own graphic designer who was not allowed to talk to the graphic designer from the company that acquired them for fear of tainting their brand and design, even though the merging of the brands was inevitable.

This entrenched culture made itself evident when I conducted stakeholder interviews with key people from the acquiring and acquired companies. Some of the people from the acquired company were subtle while others were more overt about their disdain for social media and the fact that they had no intention of providing support for any social media efforts involving their business.

I knew then that any strategic recommendations I would make were at high risk of failure. Add to that the fact that I was seeing challenges within the organization about who did and did not want to own the execution and ongoing operations of social media and you had a recipe for disaster. Ultimately, the acquired company coalesced once the brand merger happened and resistors adapted or self-selected out of the organization, like so often happens after a merger or acquisition.

Another political scenario worth looking out for, especially if you are new to a role, is to learn if anyone you are working with or that is working for you was passed over for the role. In one instance, I was always suspicious that one or more people were resentful about being passed over for the roles that I and a colleague had. We were both brought in from outside the group while many on the inside had been there for some time.

You may ask yourself, 'What do politics have to do with social media?' Sadly, the answer is a lot. Sometimes social media can be a political hot potato that nobody wants to touch. In other instances, it can be a turf war where multiple groups are fighting for control, to be the pointy end of the spear.

In one instance, the company I was working with had a presence on social media, but the origins of the social accounts were fraught with scandal. Internal resources and an outside agency had gone rogue and established social media accounts without the express permission of the company. Eventually, the contract with the agency was terminated and the employees responsible were moved off into other roles.

What developed afterwards was a situation where the largest single business unit with the greatest amount of political clout took ownership of the social accounts even though the mandate for the channels was to be enterprise-wide and not just that of this particular business unit. What ended up happening was other business units had to coordinate with and seek permission from the business unit to get their content on the company's social accounts. Even if other business units had greater organizational power, they lacked the political power to usurp control of the social accounts.

Tread lightly and watch for any potential political landmines sitting just below the surface. I am not trying to sound ominous here. It is just that we have all experienced office politics, and it is no different when it comes to social media.

Where are you starting?

Are you starting from zero or are you taking over established channels and activities? Depending on your answer, you are going to have different considerations and requirements. There will be a lot more work upfront if you are starting from scratch as you won't have any performance history to learn what has and hasn't worked in the past. Sometimes that can work in your favour, but you can't always count on that.

Taking over established social media activities means you have historical data at your disposal, but potentially you have added the pressure to commit to objectives that surpass past milestones without knowing how reasonable those expectations are. You will want to determine what past success looked like and the factors that drove that success in order to properly benchmark your efforts going forward.

You need to see how performance is tracked and reported. Is data readily available or is there a lot of manual compilation before insights can be derived? Who receives reports and how often? Is the organization good at tracking and reporting on its performance, not just for social media but in general? Assuming they are good at that, how have they done in the past when it has come to setting and achieving their objectives? Do they consistently meet or exceed them? If not, why not?

You want to make sure that the tools and procedures are in place for you to track your performance, compile the data and report on your achievements to the stakeholders to whom you are accountable. Falling victim to incomplete or vague data or guesswork is probably not what you signed up for. If you need to establish the performance metrics, tracking and report procedures and possibly supporting tools, then call that out as soon as possible to buy yourself time. Include your stakeholders so that what is to be tracked and reported on is established collaboratively. That way everyone is set up for success.

KPIs and the feel-good forecast

Once you have determined where the company has been, you are going to be asked where you are going to go, and probably to commit to that. We've already talked about getting everyone on the same page when it comes to expectations but perhaps breaking it down further will help. Consider dividing your activities into three buckets or categories – Community, Content and Conversion – what I like to call the three Cs of social media ROI. Let's examine each one more closely.

Community

Vanity metrics such as fans and followers are important, but they are not the only social media metrics of importance. We have been asked to predict how many fans and followers we will reach in a given period of time. There are two ways to answer that question. I can be snarky and say give me your credit card and I can buy ten thousand followers for you. That will give you the follower optics you want, but it will dilute your metrics, and your followers will be a mixture of fake accounts, bots and other irrelevant players.

Alternatively, I can say that we will need to conduct paid campaigns on the channels that allow them and rely on organic efforts on the ones that don't. That means we are at the mercy of fate and subjectivity when it comes to organic and paid growth. Regardless of how an account gets presented to a potential follower, it still comes down to whether or not they see value or become interested in becoming a follower. You need to convey value so they see what is in it for them very clearly.

Content

Social behaviour varies from platform to platform and what works on one may not work on another. Furthermore, content performance can vary, and subjectivity can influence interest and engagement. Without historical data, you may find yourself just guessing at potential future outcomes. That's not ideal but you may not have any other choice.

Likes are the easiest type of engagement to get, but you don't want to stop there. Ideally, you want to see additional indicators that your content is resonating such as comments and shares. Those require more effort and commitment, but if you are able to solicit those types of responses then it would indicate you are producing content that is engaging your audience.

Predicting what content will engage and to what degree is challenging. As mentioned before, without historical data, you are just guessing. The more data you can compile over time allows you to determine trends and to get a sense of the content types and formats that garner engagement.

Hopefully, your stakeholders will give you a bit of latitude to try different topics/themes and experiment with formats and scheduling to see what does and doesn't work for engagement. Social media requires constant testing and measurement to inform adjustments to strategy.

Conversion

Fans, followers and likes are fundamental metrics for social media success, but ultimately conversion is the metric most closely aligned with business objectives. A conversion is basically an action taken by a person in response to your call to action. That could be asking someone something, such as registering for your webinar, signing up for your newsletter or actually buying something based on your prompting. The goal of organic and paid campaigns is to drive a response to a call to action that results in a desirable outcome for the organization such as newsletter signups, content downloads or webinar registrations.

I often get asked whether or not social media has ROI. My answer is yes, but I qualify it to say that it just has to be designed into your strategy. That is why you need to have clearly defined corporate objectives that you can align with your social media strategies and tactics. Work back from the desired outcomes to determine where and how social media can play a role.

If you are fortunate to have historical data, you still want to be careful about committing to outcomes that are unreasonable. If past performance showed a particular percentage such as a conversion rate of 10 per cent and you are expected to achieve a stretch goal of a 25 per cent conversion rate with everything else remaining unchanged, then you are going to be in trouble. Like Einstein said, 'The definition of insanity is doing the same thing over and over again and expecting a different outcome.' If you are tasked to perpetuate the same strategies and tactics but are accountable for a different outcome then, again, you are going to be in trouble.

You also want to make sure you all agree on the definitions of what you are measuring and how. For example, metrics can vary from platform to platform; you want to determine metrics and definitions common to all so that it is an 'apples to apples' comparison. We were tasked with measuring engagement across LinkedIn, Facebook and Twitter. We chose to go with engagement rate by impression, which was common to all three platforms.

Sometimes you can fall victim to trickle-down KPIs and pressure to produce what some call a 'feel-good' forecast. These are metrics built on guesses that will likely never materialize, unless you are extremely lucky, but give comfort to the stakeholders asking for them. Unfortunately, you are only buying yourself some time until, inevitably, you will be asked why they were not achieved.

Hopefully, you will be able to provide stakeholders with reasonable and valid KPIs and forecasted outcomes but preface them with assumptions and caveats that explain conditions and factors that will likely play a role in the likelihood of those KPIs and forecasted outcomes being achieved.

Don't force the fit

For a book about social media, we sure are talking a lot about things like culture, politics, operations, stakeholders and change. We need to talk about those things because they are some of the most overlooked factors influencing social media success within larger organizations. In some ways, executing

FIGURE 1.1 Social media stakeholder bell curve

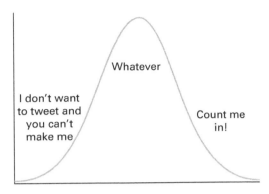

SOURCE Andrew Jenkins

social media strategies isn't hard. Navigating the political and cultural land-scape within every organization is hard and this is why I am flagging them here at the beginning of the book. Be patient. We will get to social media but we need to have a frank discussion about the organizational challenges you are likely to face.

As with any change initiative within an organization, you are going to have keen, early adopters that get on board with things right away. You will have the largest proportion of the organization falling in the middle, the neutral zone, where they are not against the change but they are not exactly raising their hands enthusiastically to show their support for it either. Finally, you will have the laggards and naysayers who oppose the change and are resistant to your efforts. Don't waste your energy on them. You already have the early adopters on your side so focus on the folks in the neutral zone. With their added support you end up having the majority of the organization on your side.

Be mindful of people you will be relying on to help with the roll-out of your social media strategies and supporting operation model. Are you asking more of them? Are you changing their role and/or responsibilities? Are you adding new performance measures for which they will be accountable? While some will be keen to be a part of your social and digital efforts without expecting much or anything in return, you need to ensure that you are not steamrolling your agenda over them. You want to make sure they are willingly accepting any changes, that they felt consulted about it all and any potential resentment is avoided.

In order to ensure the desired change happens you want to focus on a few key success factors. They include communication, environment, milestones and vision. Let me explain how they ladder up to the desired change for the organization.

Communication

When was the last time you or someone you know complained about an organization communicating their mission, vision or values too much? Pause for dramatic effect. That's what I thought. Never. Usually, it is the opposite. Organizations go through their strategic planning efforts every so many years, document them and then file them away until the next strategic planning period, leaving the key elements of their strategic plan collecting dust.

It is critical that stakeholders be regularly reminded of what the organization is trying to accomplish and the role they play in helping the organization achieve those objectives. The more time that passes between strategic planning periods the more likely organizational memory can wane.

Erring on the side of over communicating will ensure that organizational memory remains clear and current. Regular reminders of what is required and why will help retain the momentum for change. How many lengthy projects have you been involved in where it feels like no one seems to be certain of the reasons you are doing what you're doing or what success looks like? You want to be able to survey the key players periodically and have them be certain of their mandate.

Environment

As you familiarize yourself with how the organization and your specific area are configured, you want to avoid the mistake that some people often make, which is forcing the change. In the case of social media, that means forcing the organization to adapt to social media rather than the other way around.

Any attempt to bend the organization to social media's whims will likely fail. Bend social media to the organization instead. You need to understand and respect how the organization is configured, how communication flows and how things get done and by whom, and then layer social media on top. This will ensure greater alignment and be less disruptive to the day-to-day operations.

Over time you can make tweaks to the environment (i.e. incremental changes to processes, introducing new tools and/or methods, leveraging insights from reporting to inform and justify changes, adding or changing how resources are allocated) to support your social media efforts, but tweaks won't feel like shocks to the organization's systems. You want to make small changes and adjustments over time that avoid disruption but move the organization closer to social media business as usual.

Make frequent touchpoints with key stakeholders to make them feel heard and to learn from them what is working and what isn't so adjustments can be made that they had a hand in making. This will foster greater support for change because they were instrumental in defining the change rather than having it dictated to them.

Milestones

It's easy to tell people what they need to do, but it isn't necessarily easy to get them to do it. You will likely find yourself telling stakeholders what needs to be done to achieve social media success, but how do you get them to buy in and stay bought in? You need to enable some early and frequent wins to help them build and maintain momentum.

While you may have conveyed the long-term objectives for social media within the organization, if successfully achieving those outcomes seems too far in the future, you will need to break things down into smaller increments, a series of milestones that build on each other and provide a sense of progress toward the organization's social media objectives.

These frequent and early wins should be celebrated and illuminated to the rest of the organization so they see change happening and the associated success that it is driving. If people see their colleagues being and driving the change and it is working then they will be more likely to align themselves with the change. The Heath brothers, in their book *Switch*, referred to this as finding the bright spots. Find examples of the change already happening and working, and celebrate across the organization.

While change may be a marathon, people need to feel that sprints from milestone to milestone are doable. With every milestone achieved, the organization is closer to its goals and the state of change required for sustained social media success.

Vision

When we are working it is very easy to find ourselves head down and churning through our inbox. If we are not careful, we can lose track of our priorities and what warrants our attention. We may have been told what the long-term vision is for the organization's social media efforts, but we don't necessarily keep that vision front and centre in our mind. Over time we can forget what we are working towards.

If you have conveyed the social media vision for the organization then you want to make sure you frequently remind people of that vision and where and how what they are working on serves that vision. Too much time passing from when they first heard your vision puts things at risk. Tell them their contribution is important and make it tangible to them. If they feel invested and see impact from their efforts, they will be all the more likely to stay the course.

They need to feel that they are a part of pursuing the collective vision for social media for the organization rather than simply doing a task to serve someone else's vision. The former means a greater likelihood of success while the latter means you may have people just 'phoning' it in and looking elsewhere for opportunity.

Change doesn't need to happen first

I have talked a lot about culture, politics and change. You may have the impression that because so much of this chapter was devoted to those topics that they should take priority over social media and developing strategies for the organization. That is not the case nor is it my intention to suggest that.

I needed to discuss them because they are important, possibly critical, to keep in mind when developing and executing a social media strategy. However, they should not stand in the way of you getting started. They can be dealt with in parallel to your development of your social media strategies and implementation plans.

It is about bearing them in mind and being cognizant of where and how they may impede or potentially derail what you are trying to do and accomplish. Remember you are going to be held accountable for certain outcomes so you need to take action and move forward, even if it feels like you are hitting headwinds.

Resistance to change will always exist even if this organization is successful. People are human. Everyone is supportive of change as long as it does not mean the change is happening to them. That is a nice sentiment but not the reality we face in our work life. You will never eliminate this resistance entirely so you need to accept it, embrace it and manage around it on an ongoing basis.

Start with a light day

When I was studying film production at university, I was working on one of my group projects, and we were about to begin production. My professor offered some advice that applies beyond film. She said to make the first day of production a light day. That meant making it a short shoot day and light on workload. A light day allowed the crew to become accustomed to working with each other, to get into their groove without too much pressure. It also allowed for any issues to be dealt with before we got too deep into production when the stakes would be higher and time more costly.

Applying that same thinking to social media is worth considering. Moving too fast or too aggressively can backfire. Get clarity on the timeline you are to follow, and map your milestones onto it but be reasonable. You may want to set stretch goals for the organization, but you do not want to set it up for failure.

Like a light day, start modestly. You will still have to do some heavy lifting and some upfront work setting tools, systems and procedures, but avoid overwhelming them with high volumes of content. We worked with different lines of business of a financial services company, and we didn't do any posting initially. They wanted to know more about our planned approach before letting us move ahead.

We defined a preliminary posting volume and cadence that was manageable for everyone involved and took into account the organization's existing content and ability to produce more. We identified existing content that could be leveraged and what sources for new content were available within the organization. Over six months, posting volume, content curation, content production and reporting activity increased.

With every month that passed, we ran analysis on every social channel to determine which channels were experiencing growth and increased engagement. We examined what type of content and format performed best. We shared insights with key stakeholders to show our progress, slowly garner their support for more content and mobilize key employees as advocates to amplify corporate messaging.

Now we are into a groove with a populated content calendar that tells every stakeholder what to expect but leaves some slack in the system to respond to content opportunities such as media mentions of subject matter experts who are spokespeople for the organization. We have a strong sense of the content that performs best and the topics that resonate with the target audience, but we continue to test, measure and adjust.

What worked three months ago may not work tomorrow so we must continue to be agile. Thankfully, social media can provide vast amounts of data from which we can derive insights to inform our strategy. We have constantly reviewed optimal days and times for posting and experiment with new days and times in pursuit of greater engagement and reach.

Everything we have learned from supporting one line of business is now being applied to another. The first focused on the B2B audience while the second was more B2C. Their audiences may differ but much of what we learned still applies and we can apply the learning from one to the other. Furthermore, fundamental principles of social media such as providing valuable content that educates, informs and helps people accomplish their goals still apply regardless of whether the audience is B2B or B2C.

Where do we go from here?

My hope is that in reading this book you will be left with new insights to help you navigate change, manage disparate stakeholders, build a roadmap to social media success, manage a brand's reputation and gain the confidence to develop a scalable social media operating model including best practices, policies, procedures and governance.

That may not sound as inviting as making content that goes viral, but that is not what most organizations are focused on. I often joke, when asked about making something go viral, that if you have puppies in your content then you increase the likelihood of going viral. That shouldn't be the goal. That's like saying your goal is to capture lightning in a bottle.

Focus on the practical. Commit to what you can manage. Produce content that informs and educates. Seek to engage and influence. Align your actions to your corporate objectives. Track your progress and adjust where needed.

In subsequent chapters, I will still reference parts of this chapter, where applicable, but let's embark on a social media journey that will take you through getting your grounding, developing and executing social media strategies, establishing and maintaining a manageable operating model and what to look for in terms of emerging social media platforms and behaviour.

Let's get you started.

02

The who/what/where of your social media and content audit

Usually when people hear the word audit, they think that it is something unpleasant done to you by an accountant. That is not the case when it comes to a social media or content audit. The goal is to learn and to extract insights – not to find out you owe more in taxes than you anticipated.

In this chapter we are going to discuss the process of a social media audit, where to focus, what you can learn and how all of that will inform your ongoing social media strategy. We will also discuss a content audit as a subset of the overall social media audit – but a critical component nonetheless, because content drives social media engagement.

For the purposes of this chapter, we are going to discuss a social media audit from two perspectives. First, we are going to look at conducting an audit for and on the organization that employs you. Second, we are going to look at competitors, peer organizations and other industry players for benchmarking.

Where you start a social media audit is really a personal preference. Given the two perspectives mentioned above that will guide an audit, we are going to start from the inside and work our way out to the competitive and industry landscape. However if, after reading this chapter and based on your own experiences, you want to take your own approach then that is your prerogative.

The basics

You will want to start with the simple stuff. What information can be gathered quickly and easily? What are the obvious or known things versus what needs to be researched? What is the depth and breadth of your audit, and how does it affect what you can gather and how?

Capability and capacity

Part of your audit needs to be a review of the organization's current social media capabilities and capacity. What are they doing internally? What services do they get from outside vendors? Are social media and digital resources centralized or decentralized? How are resources configured? Will you need to collaborate across teams, departments or business units? If the mandate for social media is growth, then are there sufficient resources in place? Do the current resources have the necessary skills? Will you need to hire and/or provide training?

We will delve more deeply into this when we get to the SWOT analysis later in this chapter as well as in the section on outsourcing in chapter 8. Regardless, you will want to identify areas that need closer examination to ensure objectives can be met and whether there are any gaps or impediments that would severely hinder your ability to meet those objectives.

What have you got?

What kind of social presence do you have? What accounts exist? How active are they? When were the last posts? How did they perform? These are just some of the preliminary questions that should be asked.

The social platforms that your organization has may vary based on the kind of organization you are. A consumer packaged goods company trying to reach consumers may put emphasis on Instagram, Snapchat or TikTok. A B2B professional services company may have a presence on platforms that are typically B2C while focusing more time and energy on platforms like LinkedIn.

Regardless of what your type of organization, each social platform will serve you differently, some better than others. Each one has strengths and weaknesses that you need to keep in mind as you develop your social media strategy and execute it. Also, what is working now may not be working as well six months from now.

While they are considered vanity metrics, they still play a role in terms of establishing an engaged community that can amplify your message and content to their social graph. That is why you should start quantitatively with your audit. How many fans or followers do you have on each channel? What is the posting frequency? How does your content perform? What kind of engagement does it get? Does the type of content affect the performance?

What's in your toolkit?

Scaling your social media presence is essentially impossible without tools to create content, curate content, manage it all and analyse the results. With that in mind, what social media-related tools are already being used? Is it a situation where you have an all-in-one management tool or a collection of more purpose-built tools? Survey current users to find out if the current toolkit is meeting their needs and what is on their wish list.

It has been said that a fool with a tool is still a fool so you may want to take the opportunity during the audit to rationalize the tools currently being used and determine if some need to be replaced or dropped altogether. It is not unusual for us to discover clients under-utilizing tools or not using some at all for which they paid dearly. If they are not saving you time, money or providing actionable insights then you may want to rethink what tools you have and what tools you need.

Will your current toolkit help you conduct the audit? Can you extract the quantitative data you need and organize it easily to derive actionable insights? You may find that engagement on Facebook has gone up by 10 per cent since the previous month but what is the 'so what?' of the increase? What caused it? How does that differ from the previous month or the same month last year? Data in isolation does not say much. An audit and the necessary tools to conduct one will provide the context for the data and, hopefully, the 'so what?'.

Fans and followers

After you have tabulated the number of fans and followers for each channel, you will want to dive a little deeper. How long has the channel been in existence? Is it currently being managed? We have been in situations where we have inherited channels that we allowed to go dormant for a long period of time so the initial focus was on rejuvenating them.

What kind of growth rate have they experienced? Was that driven by organic efforts, paid campaigns or both? You can build followers on Twitter and Instagram by proactively following others in hopes that they reciprocate. That organic method cannot be applied on Facebook or LinkedIn. We have typically used paid campaigns to build followers on Facebook and leveraged the connections of employees to build a following for a company page.

One key consideration when examining friends and followers is to determine, if possible, how many of them are employees, people seeking employment, competitors, partners and existing customers. We can often fall into a false sense of success based on the number of followers. If they are all 'friendlies' that, while supportive, will never buy our product or service, then how valuable are they as a follower beyond sharing our content? Having Mom and Dad like your Facebook page is nice but it doesn't put money in the bank.

When examining fans and followers you will also find that the majority of your followers or community members are 'net listeners'. They lurk. They like. But they do not comment much, if at all. A lot of the community engagement is carried by a select few within it. They make themselves evident as the most talkative and/or active on your feeds. This is one of the key qualitative aspects of fans and followers that should not be overlooked. You want these advocates on your side and the onus is on you to nurture them.

You will also come to find that some of your followers are influential. Not Kardashian influential but influential in their own way. Influencer marketing is on the rise but more specifically micro-influencer marketing. Celebrities might be influential, but their followers are not necessarily following them for sincere reasons. Furthermore, a celebrity influencer may have millions of followers, but that does not translate into action taken when the celebrity promotes a brand.

A micro-influencer, on the other hand, who has a deeper, more trusted relationship with their followers, has a greater likelihood of getting them to take action based on their recommendation. Your goal should be to ensure that you are the referred or the recommended.

Channels

We posed some questions earlier about which social platforms your organization might be on, but let's take a closer look. You have mapped your channels. You have compiled the number of followers. You have an initial sense of engagement. Now what?

Get into the specifics going channel by channel. Is each channel supporting corporate objectives? Do the types of posts suggest that there is a strategy? Are they 'on brand' and, if not, how far off are they? Does each channel show the necessary consistency and frequency for posting of content? There are tons of social accounts out there with huge gaps between posts and/or the posts seem to have been done with no rhyme or reason for day, time or purpose. Are there gaps on your channels?

TWITTER

Channels like Twitter require higher volumes of content and greater frequency of posts. The shelf life of a tweet is approximately 15 minutes. Furthermore, a social post is never seen by your entire audience. In order to cumulatively reach your entire audience, you need to post more times per day and more days per week, using analytics to guide those efforts.

A tweet at 10 am on a Monday morning will likely be seen by a different portion of your audience than a tweet posted at 4 pm on Thursday. That means you have permission to post the same thing more than once but at different days and times because you are reaching different audience members each time. This is certainly the case if your followers span time zones.

INSTAGRAM

Twitter may allow for higher posting volumes and repeated posts but best practices for channels such as Instagram suggest fewer posts per day and per week. More thought needs to go into the posts and consideration needs to be given to how the images will look on the account itself and not just the feed of the viewer. By that I mean some accounts are highly curated and the image collections show planning and a thoughtful approach to the content. Instagram only allows for rich media (i.e. images or video) while many of the other channels provide more latitude when it comes to content types. This puts added pressure on you regarding creation and curation for the channel.

When you look at your Instagram account or that of others to whom you are comparing yourself, what do you see? Is posting happening consistently? Is there an obvious aesthetic? Is it well designed? One of my favourite examples is Instagram.com/SymmetryBreakfast. They do one thing and do it very well. The aesthetic is obvious, well designed, consistent and led to a book deal.

Some companies like to use Instagram to convey company culture and an employer brand – kind of like a portal into the organization. Does your account reflect that and, if so, is it resonating with the target audience? Does it show a 'day in the life' of an employee within the organization? Are there video testimonials from employees? Does it suggest that employees are well treated and enjoy coming to work? If not, you may want to have a chat with key people about employee engagement and how that could be reflected in social media.

FACEBOOK

While I am describing certain steps to take as part of a Facebook page audit, these steps should apply to the audit of all of your social channels. You want to make sure that it is 'on brand' and the company information is up to date including address, website and contact information, etc. If there is a post pinned to the top of the page, is it current or an old post that has been forgotten?

As with other channels, is there consistency and frequency with posting? Do the posts reflect a theme or cohesive strategy? How much third-party content is there, if any? Is the branded content directing people to the corporate website or elsewhere such as YouTube? Facebook and the other platforms give preferential treatment to native content rather than content that sends visitors off the platform to other destinations.

Leverage Facebook's ad library to see past campaigns and marry that with a review of the ad manager to see historical campaign performance. Use the ad library to examine campaigns from peers, competitors and those you aspire to match or surpass. It will give you a good idea of the campaign activity, the creative for the campaigns and whether or not they are running variations of the same campaign with different creative or in different languages.

LINKEDIN

LinkedIn saw substantial activity growth during the pandemic as people relied more and more on virtual networking and sales prospecting. Those types of activities are person to person, one to one, rather than brand or company to customer. As much as I love LinkedIn and I owe my career to it, company pages just do not perform to the level they could or should. It has been my experience that most of the value to be derived from LinkedIn by companies comes from the proactive use of the platform by employees nurturing their existing connections and making new ones. That is why a channel audit of LinkedIn needs to go beyond just the company page.

I am not saying you should ignore a review of the company page and any showcase pages that may have been set up. You still need to review them for posting volume, consistency, engagement and whether or not they are current in reflecting the corporate brand. Then you need to go further to see how employees are extending the reach of the page, pages, to their respective networks. This employee advocacy can pay tremendous dividends for companies that empower and enable employees to share corporate content with ease. Your audit should examine if employees are so enabled too.

LinkedIn does not have an ad library like Facebook to look at competitors, but it does provide for ad transparency. You just need to go to the company page you are interested in, click on posts and then click on ads. You will see recent promoted content by that particular page. If you want to get more granular and examine a specific post's performance then click the three dots at the upper right and copy the link to the post. Paste it into a new browser tab and you will see the number of likes and comments it received. This won't give you all the information you might be looking for, but it is still a good gauge of what other pages are doing.

Content

Do the channels suggest that the organization is overly self-promotional? Do they provide educational and/or informative and helpful content? Is there any curated content from third-party sources? Is it all selling all the time? That can get tiring really fast. Unfortunately, it is a natural tendency to sell and promote. You have to fight that tendency. You will get the chance to sell but there are other considerations that should take precedence.

Organizations need to lead with value when it comes to their content. Jay Baer of Convince and Convert asks, 'Is your content so good that people would be willing to pay for it?' If you do not feel that strongly then you may need to examine the quantity and quality of the available content that you have planned.

They say that people buy a drill because they want a hole and not because they want a drill. They want an outcome. They want help to complete a job. They want to learn and be changed for the better by your content. Can your content help them? If it can then over time you can earn the right to market to them because you have built a relationship based on value and trust.

We will examine content and stakeholder needs in greater detail when we discuss the content audit. In the meantime, let me share one example of providing helpful and valuable content based on the diverse needs of stakeholders, which in this example are stakeholders touched by cancer.

For several years we managed social media for a cancer charity. You can't operate as a charity without asking for donations. However, your social media channels cannot be consumed entirely with donation requests and promotions to drive donations. Again, you have to earn the right to market or sell.

For example, if somebody came to their Facebook page on Monday and they were asked to donate and then they came back Tuesday only to be asked again, and every day afterward, they would stop coming because they were conditioned to expect it. What we did to help them was focus on curating helpful content from complementary sources that would appeal to the different stakeholders they served and eliminate the possibility of being overly self-promotional.

We curated content that discussed topics such as dietary considerations during chemo, cancer and the family, responsibilities of a caregiver, how to talk to someone with cancer and related news such as drug trials and awards of research grants. Cancer touches many different people, and our efforts provided resources for the various stakeholders.

SWOT

STRENGTHS

If you have been with the organization a while then you should be able to get the list of social media-related strengths going rather easily. Many should be top of mind or obvious. However, if you are new to the company, then your audit will help you determine those strengths. In either case, you are going to want to go as far as you can to identify not just strengths but proprietary or unique strengths that the organization has that could potentially differentiate it from competitors. You may want to categorize your strengths into two categories – unique and replicable – because the strengths that are replicable highlight a potential threat from competitors.

What are you doing on your social media accounts that is working? Are you seeing audience growth? Is engagement increasing? Is it consistent? Are there specific activities and/or content that are resonating with your audience? Is rich media such as images and video garnering the most engagement? Is a solid audience foundation already built? Are you maximizing reach and engagement based on posting times? Is your audience listening? Are they conversing with your brand?

What is your organization inherently good at? Some organizations have a number of thought leaders that can write or can be leveraged for content. Other organizations are better at producing rich media such as images, infographics or video. Is resourcing a strength? A social media team that has substantial resources can produce quality content quickly. Your competitors may be too lean to compete on every platform or with every type of content.

As you compile your strengths, you need to consider what may be required to sustain them. Does your brand have greater recognition than your competitors? Do you have a substantial lead in terms of audience size and growth rate? Are you outperforming your competitors in terms of content production volume and/or quality? Strengths can wane if you become complacent. The social media space is not static. It is constantly changing. You are fighting for people's attention. You are trying to stop the scroll. What worked last quarter may be showing signs of diminishing returns or may have stopped having any impact altogether. That is why you need to review your metrics regularly to track ongoing performance and adjust accordingly. We'll explore this in more depth later.

Keep a swipe file of what your competitors and other sources of inspiration are doing in social media to inspire your thinking and provide examples to colleagues if you want to get them onside to experiment with some new content ideas and tactics. Hopefully, your organization allows for experimentation and innovation. Without it, you will be challenged to maintain your lead over your competitors.

To achieve this, look for examples outside of your competitive circle and perhaps even your industry to see what others are doing. Look at other channels too. Carousels performed well on Instagram and became a similar performing type of content for LinkedIn, taking a proven tactic from a predominantly B2C social media platform and migrating it to a B2B channel and finding success. Even memes can be repurposed for business applications, using proven content trends to foster engagement. Look at how companies are using inherent features and functions of the various social platforms, and think about how they might be used by your organization on the same channel or a different one. It is hard to keep abreast of these developments, but innovative strategies and tactics are happening on every channel, every day, that you can learn from, that can benefit your organization and that can maintain and build your social media strengths.

WEAKNESSES

Just as with strengths, if you have been with the organization a while then you already know where your weaknesses lie. Many should be at the top of the mind or obvious. They have probably been an ongoing issue or annoyance. If you are new to the company then your audit will help you determine them but you may find that people are reluctant to admit the weaknesses or failings of the past. You may need to tread lightly with stakeholders to bring this out into the light.

Is the organization experiencing consistent success on all of the social platforms where it has a presence? If not, then which ones are underperforming or are experiencing complete failure? These types of insights may guide the rationalization of what channels and related activities to continue versus which ones to suspend. It is better to have success on a few platforms than spread yourself too thin trying to support too many channels. Every channel you open has to be resourced with people and content without a guarantee of success.

You will want to leverage data from longer periods of time to see performance trends and to diminish the effect that anomalies and outliers from campaigns might have. Generally, what type of content is letting you down? What channels just aren't doing it for the organization? Are there times and days when posts are going out that could be part of the problem? Your organization may have formed some habits that could be hard to break but will be necessary if progress is to be made.

BLOG CONTENT

For a long time, blogs were the way to build thought leadership and help your SEO. According to Google, blogs need to be a minimum of 400 words to be properly indexed. Increasingly, blogs got shorter to be easier to write and consume. The listicle grew in popularity as a blog format because they were easy to write, each item on the list could be social copy for social posts so you could get more social posts from a single blog post and the reader could easily scan them.

As with everything, things change. A study by Buzzsumo found that longer-form written content (1000+ words) outperformed shorter articles. The sweet spot seems to be 1000–2000 words. To add insult to injury, even though longer-form articles perform better than shorter ones, video is outperforming written content. That is not to suggest that your corporate blog should be abandoned. It has a role to play but if it ends up on your organization's list of weaknesses due to underperformance then a closer examination may be required to determine where and how to turn it from a liability to an asset.

Are your social media weaknesses related to your organic efforts, paid or both? Maybe you're doing great with organic but you have little to no success with paid. To be fair to your organization, maybe you have not had access to even a modest budget to experiment with some paid campaigns. If you are setting up a social account like a Facebook page from scratch then it will be challenging to get any traction without doing some paid campaigns to grow your audience. Furthermore, as each platform grows, visibility for your content becomes more challenging and competition for engagement increases. Paid campaigns have increasingly been the remedy for those challenges.

Is the social media team configured and resourced for success? Can it handle growth and scale accordingly? I have often heard the phrase 'managing social media off the corner of my desk', which means when I have time to deal with it on top of everything else I have to deal with. That does not instil confidence. I have had to explain numerous times to clients and others that social media isn't necessarily complicated but that it is incredibly hard work. It is always on. It is relentless. If you are not properly resourced to meet its demands then that is a glaring weakness that needs to be addressed.

OPPORTUNITIES

The social media audit is going to illuminate opportunities. Current activities can be improved, changed or eliminated. New channels and/or tactics could be introduced. Maybe your organization does not have a presence on TikTok but, with its exponential growth and widening user base, it may be worth considering. The long-established blog could be complemented with embedded videos or animations based on the blog content. Spinning and repurposing old content would give it new life and lessen the burden of producing new content.

Whether it is improving on the old or introducing something new, it is change and change is typically met with resistance. Leverage the insights gathered during the audit and/or industry reports to support your recommendations for the opportunities you wish to pursue. People won't support a feeling as readily as they will support a conclusion based on data. Prove to them what is or isn't working based on metrics. Share industry trend reports that help make the case for introducing new content ideas, new tactics or the establishment of a presence on a new platform.

Moving forward in pursuit of these new opportunities may have support based on data but it is still travelling into uncharted territory in some cases. You are experimenting with new content. You are trying something new in a new way. You are setting up shop on a new social platform without being certain about whether it is going to suit your organization or if your brand will find a welcoming audience there. Be sure to track performance from the outset so you can gauge your success. Be patient. Ask senior leadership for support and latitude to experiment as well as patience.

We have been asked by clients to predict the future in terms of engagement and audience size by a particular time in the future. I know it sounds evasive or like I'm passing the buck but the predictions are usually more of a guess than a prediction. Granted, these opportunities are being pursued based on accumulated data and insights but that does not guarantee specific outcomes. We are still 'trying something new'. Furthermore, there is an element of subjectivity. By that I mean we may believe that we have created the greatest piece of content ever, only to see it flop with our target audience. Just think about how many movies get released with blockbuster hopes only to fizzle out over the opening weekend.

Pursue as many opportunities as you and your team can manage to hedge your bets. Watch for early signs of success and failure. How quickly you cut your losses will depend on how patient you and/or your executive sponsors are willing to be. For example, building thought leadership in a particular field or category of content does not come with the flick of a switch. Many in the digital space emphasize six months as the time frame that it takes to succeed. How much time have you been given? Even if you have six months, you will still want to find early signs of success that show progress towards your goals.

THREATS FROM THE COMPETITION

We often only think of our competitors as threats but circumstances beyond our control can also prove to be threats to our success. Social media platforms are constantly changing the features, functions and terms of use, which can have serious implications for your social media success. Many platforms have become increasingly closed when it comes to their Application Programming Interface (API), which means data cannot be extracted to third-party tools for analysis, impeding the ability to make informed decisions.

We use Rival IQ for ongoing analysis and performance measurement for our clients. We also use it for competitive analysis. It is fantastic for providing competitive data for Facebook, Instagram, Twitter and YouTube. Unfortunately, LinkedIn only releases data for pages that have been connected to Rival IQ by the page administrator. There is no ability to analyse a competitor's LinkedIn company page in the same way Rival IQ allows you to with a Facebook page or Instagram account. You can only gauge a competitor's LinkedIn page by eyeballing it or looking at their ad history. You won't be able to identify the level of threat they are on LinkedIn as much as you can on Facebook or the other platforms.

You and your competitors have many of the same tools when it comes to the available social media channels. It is a level playing field. We can all have LinkedIn, Facebook, Twitter, Instagram, YouTube, Reddit, etc. if we so choose. Where we and our competitors can diverge is what we do on those platforms and what kind of content we produce for them. How much we or our competitors spend, if anything, on paid social media campaigns may also be a potential threat. If you work for a David competing with a Goliath who can outspend you then you might have a problem.

Facebook's ad library and LinkedIn's ad transparency enable you to see the campaigns being run by competitors, but you do not get a sense of spend, duration or outcomes. All you know is that they are advertising and what they are advertising. That is still worth knowing, especially if you have to formulate a response. Look at the campaigns closely. Are they using video? Are they awareness or conversion campaigns? How good is their copy? Are they A/B testing? Are they advertising more than you?

In addition to the advertising efforts of your competitors, you are going to want to know what channels are performing best for them. What content is working best for them? Are they on channels that you are not? How big or different are their audiences? What kind of content are they producing and in what formats? How often are they producing new content? For example, how often do they post new videos to their YouTube channel if they have one? How often do they release new podcast episodes? How consistently and frequently are they posting content? What is the mix of third-party content to their own? Are they predominantly self-promotional? What are they doing well? Poorly?

Some competitors may be market leaders that you pursue or at least attempt to emulate while others are more likely on par with you and therefore pose more of a direct threat. Be careful not to lose sight of your closer competitors while pursuing the market leader. The gap between your closer competitors may be small and more easily overcome in a shorter period of time than it will take to supplant the market leader. Furthermore, keeping close competitors at bay will be enough to keep you busy.

Existing content audit

As previously mentioned, the content that may have performed well in the past may not continue to perform. The taste and preferences of your audience will change over time so your content must change too. The onus is on you to also produce content in different formats to appeal to the consumption preferences of your audience. Some want to read your content in a quick scan while others will want to read substantive research. Others won't want to read at all, preferring to watch or listen to your content, assuming you have it in video or audio format.

Those preferences will direct your content audit. I want to add that the audit should not be seen as a single event. While it will be a more involved process, initially, if you are new to the role, it should be something that happens somewhat regularly to keep improving your content. People are hungry for your content and you do not want to serve them something stale. If you have gone to the trouble of producing a piece of content only to have it garner zero engagement or reach no one then there could be something fundamentally wrong.

Begin with the content you have. If there is a company blog then take a look at all of the historical blog posts. Identify which ones are outdated that could be salvaged with a refresh or a few updates. Check to see if there are any that are still relevant and require little to no change before being able to recirculate them. Are there any based on their title or content that are outdated or only usable at certain times of the year or during particular marketing campaigns?

If you have a YouTube channel or podcast, how many pieces of content do you have already posted? What is in the queue for production or posting? Is the current production schedule sustainable? If there isn't a consistent production schedule and setting up a YouTube channel or launching a podcast was one of the opportunities identified, then what kind of production schedule can you handle?

Clients often share their desire to establish a YouTube channel. I ask them a clarifying question about how often they plan to produce content for the channel. This usually determines whether they have seriously considered the commitment. If they are just going to store videos on the channel when they get around to producing them, and sharing them on other social channels and embedding them in their website, then that is fine. If they envision having a vibrant channel with lots of subscribers then that means they have to produce content consistently. I ask them about the kind of frequency they can commit to and they begin to realize that they may not be up to the commitment a YouTube channel demands.

It is the same with a podcast. Look no further than iTunes or Spotify to the many podcasts that have been started with tremendous energy only to peter out over time. Many of the top podcasts began nearly 10 years ago and began with the intention of having conversations among friends. Nobody was making money from podcasts back then. Nobody was sponsoring them. Only through perseverance did they build an audience. Do you have it in you to take 10 years to build something?

Beyond your blog, what other content assets do you have? Videos, whether on YouTube or not? How long are they and can they be cut up into smaller clips? Infographics? Do you have any still current e-books, research or reports that can be used for lead generation? Can they be leveraged at least for excerpts for smaller pieces of content? How did these content assets perform in the past?

I often refer to it as 'wearing your content hat'. It means that you are constantly looking for opportunities to leverage what you already have to produce content. For example, there are solutions like Lumen5 that can read a blog and using artificial intelligence (AI) to produce a video based on the contents of that blog. Another solution, Play.ht, can produce a podcast recording of a blog in a voice and accent of your choice from the AI-based menu of voices they provide.

Lately uses AI to take videos, podcasts and blogs to create or 'spin' multiple social posts from the original content. We use Lately regularly to cut podcasts and videos into short clips to squeeze more out of every piece of content. Jay Baer of Convince and Convert refers to this as 'atomizing' content. We also use Lately to spin multiple social posts from blog posts by pulling excerpts from the body of the blog. Too often, organizations take the 'one and done' approach with their content. Just think about how much time and expense is tied to one blog post. Then ask yourself, 'Was it worth it?' and 'Did it deliver value for the organization?'

Compile a list of all of your available content assets. Categorize them based on the level of work required to make them usable. Prioritize them based on your strategic objectives and implementation plan. Leverage solutions such as Lumen5 and Lately to help you repurpose and reformat content to appeal to the preferences of a broader audience. AI is making it easier and easier to work smarter rather than harder when it comes to content. Don't fear the content audit. You may discover a treasure trove of content that you do not have to recreate.

THIRD-PARTY CONTENT

Don't overlook third-party content that your organization used in the past. Assuming it is still relevant, consider sharing it again. If anyone from the organization was a speaker or panellist and there is content from that which can be reused then reuse it. It is social proof of their thought leadership so leverage it. Beyond content from the past, as part of your audit, identify the preferred and potential new sources for third-party content and identify where and how to incorporate it into your content calendar plan.

Flag any planned and potential speaking or panel opportunities to ensure no content opportunity goes unnoticed. Leverage the content of partners and cross-promote. They will reciprocate and, in so doing, help you reach audiences beyond your own. Offer speaking and panel opportunities to others too and draw in their audiences. You do not always have to be the only one producing content. Many hands make light work.

03

Social media governance and policy development

A lot of organizations find themselves in need of a social media policy when something has gone wrong, such as an employee doing something intentionally or unintentionally that puts them and/or the organization in a difficult position. How should they deal with this situation and what must they do to avoid similar situations arising in the future?

In this chapter we will explore the options available to organizations when it comes to developing, implementing and maintaining social media policies and procedures. We will also discuss best practices for social media governance, including such things as managing access to social media accounts, the approval process for content and the escalation path for issue resolution.

Policy philosophy

You may never have thought about philosophy when it comes to a social media policy but hear me out. Organizations need to be clear about their philosophy regarding the social media policy and do everything possible to ensure that it is properly communicated across the enterprise. There is no single version of a social media policy that suits all organizations. A consumer packaged goods company will not have the same policy issues as a highly regulated organization in financial services or healthcare. Those differences should be reflected in the construction of their policies.

Draconian or empowering

Before going any further, I should make a fundamental distinction. Some organizations have policies while others have guidelines. Both are appropriate but those who created them need to be clear about their intention. By that I mean are they laying out rigid, bordering on Draconian, regulations in the vein of 'thou shalt not do this' and 'thou shalt not do that' or are they providing empowering guidelines that suggest to employees that if they are going to do something then they are given the best practices and methodologies to be successful while still avoiding social media missteps for them and the organization?

Dell took the social media guidelines route and positioned their approach as helping employees avoid mistakes. They went so far as to develop the Social Media and Community University (SMACU) so all employees would be trained and become familiarized with social media within the context of Dell and, where applicable, their own individual roles. Dell referred to it as getting SMAC'd.

There were three levels of training at SMACU. The first was designed to explain the social media landscape to everyone, even if they were not using social media as part of their job. The second level focused on people who used social media in their respective roles such as customer service, technical support and marketing. Finally, the third level was for official media spokespeople representing Dell in a variety of mediums, including social media.

Dell was an early adopter of social media out of necessity. Journalist and author Jeff Jarvis documented poor customer service experience with his Dell laptop and the media fallout made Dell realize the need to be more proactive regarding social media. This led to SMACU and their social media command centre for social media monitoring, which they invited visitors to check out.

While Dell is a consumer- and business-oriented brand, the Mayo Clinic is one of those highly regulated examples I mentioned previously. While all organizations have to maintain certain privacy standards, organizations in healthcare face even more stringent privacy requirements as well as restrictions about what can and cannot be said publicly on social media channels, such as anything related to symptoms, diagnosis or treatment.

Despite those constraints, the Mayo Clinic has become a leader when it comes to social media in healthcare and developed its own social media university too. However, they did not keep the university and its curriculum just to themselves. They have made the university available for others in the industry to attend with the objectives of sharing best practices and bringing together other practitioners from across the industry to share and learn. Provide knowledge and you elevate everyone.

Missteps

Just because it's a social media policy it does not mean that the only people involved in its development work in social media. They might be driving the initiative but they mustn't do it alone. They must seek input from other stakeholders such as HR to ensure that the policy is properly constructed for everyone it might impact. Everyone in the organization needs to know what they can and cannot do when it comes to social media in relation to their work and what the implications are for them personally if they do not adhere to the social media policy.

There are numerous examples from the media of employees saying or doing something that gets shared on social media and leads to disciplinary action or even termination by their employer. However, some of those same people who were disciplined have taken legal action against their employer and, leveraging the fact that there was no social media policy in place or if there was that it was too vague to properly inform their behaviour, they were able to reverse the disciplinary action, get their employment reinstated and/or receive financial compensation for their troubles.

That is why having a social media policy in place is critical. It isn't just about protecting the company from legal action. It should help employees know and understand what is expected of them with respect to social media, whether they are at work or not. Like it or not, the behaviour of employees outside of work can no longer remain disassociated from their employer. They are inextricably linked and both parties face the possibility of a back-lash and figuring out how to navigate their way out of a PR nightmare.

One of the most infamous examples of an employee misstep was the trending hashtag #HasJustineLandedYet. In 2013, Justine Sacco was having a layover at Heathrow Airport while on her way to South Africa for the holidays. She was tweeting about her travel experiences but for unknown reasons chose to tweet this before boarding the 11-hour flight to Cape Town:

Going to Africa. Hope I don't get AIDS. Just kidding. I'm white!

While she slept through the flight, things were blowing up online and #HasJustineLandedYet became a global trending hashtag on Twitter. It was causing a furore and people began their detective work to identify who Justine was and who her employer was – in her case it was IAC, which at the time, owned the Home Shopping Network and other media properties. One Twitter user went so far as to go to the Cape Town airport to document her arrival and confirm that Justine had indeed landed.

Despite deleting her account and the offensive tweet, she could not delete the retweets and screenshots that would remain as historical evidence of her mistake. The media caught wind of her tweet and that is part of the reason it blew up like it did. First, people wondered if her account had been hacked because it seemed unlikely that Justine, being a PR and communications professional, would tweet something so offensive. Unfortunately, previous insensitive tweets on her account only proved that this behaviour was not unusual.

People were watching this play out online with a bit of a sense of humour but that quickly turned to anger and disgust. They started calling her out for her racist tweet and the verbal attacks escalated to the point of calling for her to be fired. Colleagues from IAC and the company itself distanced themselves from her and ultimately terminated her employment.

The irony here is that Justine was a PR and communications professional who should have known better. This is further evidence that common sense is not that common. I am not defending what she said or where and how she chose to say it. Many people feel the urge to share what they think and feel, even if it may offend others. Just because you want to say something doesn't mean it should be said. Having keyboard courage does not make you courageous. It just means you felt safe enough to say something behind the guise of your online persona or avatar but the angry online mob won't stand for it.

Even more ironic is the fact that Justine was hired again by IAC to oversee communications for their Match Group, but in the news about her being hired the original story about her firing is brought up again. It's important to remember that in the online world your digital footprints cannot be erased. They will follow you forever and your infamy is just one Google search or trending topic away.

I'm not sure whether a social media policy would have saved Justine Sacco from being fired. We will never know. However, Justine's story can certainly help inform companies and employees about what not to do or say. Sadly, there are still examples that indicate not everyone has learned from Justine's example. It seems like every week we hear about another company and/or person finding themselves in hot water online. It has been said that every day someone or some organization becomes 'it' on Twitter, where they are a trending topic for either good or bad reasons. The goal for everyone and every organization is to avoid being 'it' because it usually isn't a good thing.

Burger King learned the hard way that being 'it', even with good intentions, is not the kind of attention you want for your brand. In an effort to put a spotlight on the fact that the catering industry is dominated by men, Burger King chose International Women's Day to put a twist on the 'women belong in the kitchen' cliché. Unfortunately, the context of what they were trying to do was lost on readers. People did not read past the headline of 'Women belong in the kitchen' to understand what Burger King was actually trying to do. Conveying irony, sarcasm or subtle humour via text is hard and often impossible. Burger King definitely knows that now.

In the absence of a social media policy, does your organization have a code of conduct that can be referenced? Can an employee's behaviour be examined through the lens of the code of conduct? What employee actions warrant disciplinary action? Can that argument be made and defended? Is there a gap between what the code of conduct covers and the employee's actions?

I'm not trying to put the focus on disciplinary actions towards employees. The goal is clarity for all concerned. If there isn't a code of conduct or, ideally, a social media policy, you are left with one big grey area where neither party knows what can and should be done. Generally, companies and employees are not intending to do anything malicious when it comes to social media. It is just that their intentions can be lost and momentum can build online that can't be slowed or reversed easily, if at all.

A well-constructed policy provides clarity for everyone involved. It's an opportunity for an organization to define how they will support their employees, what is expected of their employees, what employees should do if they are unclear about what they can and cannot do and how situations that arise will be handled.

Specificity vs openness

While being involved in the development of a social media policy for the bank, I learned that changes to their code of conduct was a year-long process and that its certification happened at the board level. Such was not the case for a social media policy but, at times, it felt just as onerous a process.

While input from stakeholders is necessary to ensure that employees are protected and properly informed, a policy has to be specific enough so people know what they can and cannot do on and with social media in the role and away from work. Furthermore, a policy has to be written in an open or flexible way to anticipate what may happen in the future.

Social media is nearly 20 years old, but, in those nearly two decades, we have seen social platforms and technology come, go and, in some cases, take over huge chunks of our spare time. No social media policy could have anticipated what has happened or address what might still be to come.

At the time of writing this book, Facebook is the dominant player while TikTok and, more recently, Clubhouse are garnering momentum and attention. I can't predict what will happen and neither can your social media policy. It has to be written to sufficiently address the current social media landscape but still anticipate, as best as possible, where things may shift in the future.

It was not that long ago that the idea of going live on social media came to be. With that, a myriad of issues suddenly appeared for organizations. While audiences loved the idea of the immediacy it provided, organizations had to give thought to the implications for them. For example, going live means you are 'live'. No cuts. No edits. No second takes. No opportunity to delete.

What if an employee wanted to fire up Facebook Live on their phone and walk around the office without any forethought to what might be revealed in the background? They could risk revealing confidential information on a blackboard, someone in the background interviewing for a job who's supposed to be 'off sick' from their current employer or someone from a company whose mere presence in the office might mean something to the stock market. You can see just how serious it can become if people are not careful.

Right now, audio social media is hot. Podcasts have been growing exponentially. Fortunately, podcasts are recorded and go through some degree of post-production. In the case of Clubhouse, it is live and unfiltered. Hosts can moderate but that is where things pretty much stop. If you represent an organization then you have to be conscious of what you say and who might be in the virtual room to hear it.

Clubhouse isn't even a year old so it is perfectly understandable that social media policies written last year or later might not speak to it. LinkedIn, Facebook, Twitter, Slack and others have released or will release competitive responses to Clubhouse and, as a result, existing social media policies may need to be updated. New policies will need to speak to emerging platforms and associated behaviour.

While it may prove daunting, I often suggest to organizations to treat their social media policy as a living document that can be revisited and updated regularly. The social media landscape is constantly evolving. No social media policy will ever cover it all perfectly. The best that can be hoped for is to be as comprehensive and current as possible. In fairness to every organization, just because something like Clubhouse is hot, it does not mean that it will become a mainstay.

As part of your policy development, you will need to speak to the broader landscape and, where necessary, speak to specific platforms and networks and the kind of behaviour and etiquette that is to be expected, as well as that which will not be tolerated. It will be challenging to strike a balance between specificity and openness but it is absolutely necessary for mitigating risk.

Employee dos and don'ts

A social media policy will inform employees about what they shouldn't do with regards to social media. Social media guidelines empower and direct employees on how to do the right things on social media. Having social media policies and/or guidelines in place doesn't necessarily guarantee that employees will avoid mistakes, missteps or any potential risks for themselves or the organization.

You need to organize or categorize key elements of the policy. Start with the most serious ones – the ones that are the most impactful to the employee and the organization. Which ones could mean legal trouble, fines, termination, business disruption, customer dissatisfaction or brand reputation risk? In some cases, an employee and/or employer could face a combination of these.

Privacy

An organization and its employees are expected to maintain a certain standard of privacy when it comes to information about employees, customers, stakeholders and the organization itself. From something as basic as a customer's name and address to proprietary information that, if revealed, could diminish the organization's ability to compete, privacy is paramount.

Facebook is the largest social network globally. With power comes great responsibility. Unfortunately, they continue to find themselves in difficult situations regarding privacy. The Cambridge Analytica scandal didn't do their reputation any favours and since then they have told the media that they have been improving policies and procedures to address privacy concerns only to have examples revealed by the media where they have fallen short of their promise.

Despite their continued haphazard approach to privacy and poor attempts to appease the media, they continue to beat revenue estimates and maintain dominance for time spent online. The duopoly between Google and Facebook means that advertisers are forced to do business with only them if they want to reach consumers. If consumers want tailored experiences and ads then they have to be willing to share a certain amount of data on which those experiences and ads can be based.

It has been said that if you are not paying for the product then you are the product. We are handing over a tremendous amount of data to Facebook, Google and others, which means they have provided us with a sense that our personal information is safe. Unfortunately, Facebook has had trouble instilling people and the media with confidence about their management of personal data.

While you can't control what the likes of Facebook does or doesn't do with personal information, you can control what you and your organization does with it. For example, organizations need to move customers to private channels such as direct messages, email or phone as soon as possible when it comes to sharing personal information such as account, medical or financial information, depending on the organization.

Disclosure

Employees have to be careful about how much information they can share in social channels, especially if they use something like forward-looking statements that could impact the stock price of a publicly traded company. For example, Reid Hastings, CEO of Netflix, posted on Facebook about how excited he was for the coming months at the company. He didn't say anything more than that – just that he was excited. That was enough to cause concerns by regulators that his remarks were too suggestive and he was reprimanded. He got off easy when it could have been much worse.

Reid Hastings is well known enough that he doesn't necessarily have to disclose where he works. That isn't the case for most employees. Social media policies or guidelines need to stipulate that employees disclose where they work even if their bios say that the opinions expressed are their own. Even that kind of disclaimer doesn't necessarily make them exempt from scrutiny. They can't hide behind an anonymous profile or avatar and go on an online tirade against competitors or some other entity. Compelling them to disclose their employer makes it difficult for them to feel like they can say and do anything and provides a bit of a failsafe mechanism.

Some people have chosen to create anonymous or fictitious profiles so they can troll people and/or organizations. In one instance, someone created a profile on Reddit to participate in conversations about a competitor and say disparaging things. The target of their remarks took legal action forcing the revelation of the user's true identity. This led to their dismissal by their employer and the potential for legal action against them in future. There is nowhere to hide online.

Copyright

From the very beginning of the internet, technology has always outpaced policy. At the leading edge of technology it is a bit like the Wild West, where there are few or no rules, leaving people and organizations to navigate their own way. This can lead to intentional or unintentional uses of copyrighted material like images and music.

Solutions like creative commons and licensing have addressed many of the copyright issues, but they have not eliminated them. We still have to ensure that we provide proper attribution if we are incorporating the work or content of others. We need to pay the appropriate licence fees for commercial use of images or music. I tried to use a Led Zeppelin song for a video I created and YouTube did not allow it to be viewed because it recognized that the video contained copyrighted material. You won't always have something like YouTube checking your work so the onus is on you to respect copyright.

Copyright has to be honoured even when it's close to home. Employees might be asked to disclose the name of their employer, but they must also ensure that they do not do anything to infringe their brand. When I first joined the bank, the person who oversaw where and how the bank's brand was being used was dealing with a growing issue of employees using the bank's logo in their social profiles. This was a definite 'no-no' but the social media policy was still being developed so there wasn't anything that they could point to reign in this rampant rogue behaviour. Mortgage specialists and financial advisors were flogging the brand to elevate themselves. Some of them were not actual employees but merely independent agents affiliated with the bank, which only exacerbated the situation.

Finding every instance of this rogue behaviour and getting those responsible to be compliant was definitely a challenge. It was a bit like the 'Whac-A-Mole' game for kids, where just when you dealt with one, another popped up in its place. It was not going to be possible to eliminate the desire of employees to use social media so a remedy had to be found and I took it upon myself to find one.

What was needed was what is referred to as a compliance solution – something that allows employees to use social media but in a compliant way. This was especially important for financial advisors and mortgage specialists. After in-depth research, a number of vendors were selected to participate in an RFP and eventually there was one winner.

Once the winning solution was implemented, financial advisors and mortgage specialists could post to social media, having their posts checked for objectionable words, copyrighted content and other criteria before their posts were published. Additionally, the posts were archived for auditing purposes, similar to how the bank recorded calls and archived emails.

Governance

For some, governance is a serious or ominous word that can rob social media efforts of fun and agility but it is absolutely necessary. You can't fly by the seat of your pants when it comes to dealing with social media and stakeholders. They want and expect grown-ups to be in charge, able to deal with different situations as they arise with little to no disruption to day-to-day operations.

Administrative hierarchy

Whether you set up the social media accounts for an organization or you have been given access to them, you will be expected to honour the administrative protocols that are in place. You mustn't share the login credentials with others unless required or permitted to do so. Furthermore, if you are a master administrator but others have lower administrative rights then that hierarchy must be maintained. Too many people having too much authority can mean the potential risk of accounts being deleted or disrupted, or having access denied.

If protocols do not exist for how administrative rights and password credentials are to be managed then they need to be developed. The number of people and their different levels of administrative authority will have to be determined. Will everyone know the passwords or only a select few? Can solutions like password managers or social media management tools reduce the number of people who know the passwords? What happens when an employee leaves who knows such information? Are there contingency plans for just such events where the passwords get changed to avoid the risk of former employees logging in after they have left?

Some organizations put everything into a centralized document for key people to access. Governance does not have to be over-engineered. Even a spreadsheet stored securely in the cloud or on a corporate network will suffice. You may want to go so far as to create standardized formats for emails and passwords to ease overall management. For example, socialmedia@companyname.com with a select group of people having access to that inbox reduces the risk of social accounts being tied to one person's email address. This is especially important if that person leaves the organization. You may also want to involve IT to see if they have suggestions or requirements to ensure network integrity and if they have governance policies already in place related to emails and passwords.

Crisis management

In the chapter on brand monitoring and social listening we discuss reputation management and social media crises. Your social media policy and governance framework should reference social media crises, their causes and speak to how the organization and employees should respond.

A crisis doesn't necessarily apply to the organization. There could be something dramatic happening in the world that is being covered by the news media that, when juxtaposed with what you might have planned for social post content, makes you look tone deaf or worse. Do you have some sort of 'kill switch' to stop any posts from going out that could make you look insensitive and reflect poorly on your brand?

We were working with an experiential marketing agency, and it was around the time of Remembrance Day. We recommended that they not post anything on their social channels that day or at least for the morning. It would come across as disrespectful and in poor taste to be marketing at a time meant to be honouring veterans and those we had lost. Posting something to pay tribute would be fine but, again, the goal was to avoid having it look self-promotional. Our main point of contact at the company agreed.

Unfortunately, our recommendations did not get passed along to others within the organization. At 11:10 am on the eleventh day of the eleventh month, the company posted a job posting. Thankfully, it was not posted at 11:00 am because that could have really caused a backlash. The company does not have a household name brand-wise so it managed to avoid being called out. We took a screenshot of the post and shared it with our client as a reminder of our recommendation and a bit of a 'I told you so'. The goal wasn't to shame them but to illustrate just how close they came to harming their brand.

Scaling social media operations, managing content and scheduling, and dealing with stakeholders are time-consuming and require planning, but the more you plan in advance the easier it becomes for you to lose sight of what has been planned and scheduled. You could be inadvertently setting the stage for a social media crisis. That risk never goes away so you must be vigilant regarding your content planning and calendar.

In 2012, there was a shooting at a theatre in Aurora, Colorado, during a screening of the Batman film *The Dark Knight Rises*. The next day, a previously scheduled tweet from the *American Rifleman*, the official journal of the National Rifle Association (NRA), went out saying, 'Good morning, Shooters! Happy Friday! Weekend plans?' The backlash was swift and furious. People were calling attention to the post and calling them out for their poor taste and insensitivity. It took hours before the tweet was deleted but the damage was done. The pressure grew to the point that the account was deleted too.

Had protocols been in place to pause or delete scheduled posts, the *American Rifleman* could have avoided the backlash and eventual demise of their social presence. To be fair, the organization's association with the NRA likely exacerbated the situation. Most organizations can fly below the radar and enjoy a life free of controversy. However, that does not mean you should be complacent. You need to be prepared. Periodic scenario planning would help test your governance framework and protocols.

Stakeholder management

While it is important to seek input from key stakeholders such as HR when it comes to the development of a social media policy and governance framework, it isn't just about their input. You want them to be on your side rather than opposed to what you are doing or at least posing some degree of impediment to your agenda.

When Frank Eliason was leading social media at Citibank, he made a point of getting support from legal. He made fostering a collaborative relationship one of his goals in the role. Many would assume that the job of the legal team is to say 'no' because it would mean risk is being avoided.

However, Frank described his dealing with legal differently. He shared that they wanted to find a way to say 'yes'. They did not want to be seen as adversaries. Could a compromise be found that meant the social media agenda could move forward while mitigating risk in such a way as to give comfort to the legal team?

Who are the stakeholders that could be potential roadblocks? What do you need to do to build alignment? You all work for the same organization and it is safe to assume that you all share the common goal to make your employer more successful. How do you ensure that you are not working at cross-purposes? Can you make their work easier? For example, what can you do to create a faster and simplified workflow for compliance to get the necessary approvals?

My first meeting at the bank was with risk management, so that definitely set the tone for my engagement. We continued to meet regularly and we would provide updates on our progress as well as flag anything that warranted their attention and possible input. The relationship was collaborative. I was familiar with the bank, but I was not familiar with every aspect of risk management. I learned to respect what risk management was trying to do and where my efforts fit within that. While they certainly input into what we were trying to achieve, they didn't stand in our way. They were supportive but needed to ensure that we were respecting their mandate for the sake of the bank.

Identify which stakeholders you need to involve as quickly as possible. Befriend them early. Foster collaborative working relationships with them. You have goals in common so figure out a way to work together to achieve them without impeding each other. You want to avoid hearing 'You can't' or 'That's not possible'. Instead, you want to hear something like 'You can provided that...' Then what remains is to focus on the 'how' and garner support to figure it out.

Updates

The governance framework and protocols that might be in place today may be outdated in a year. The organization and departments or teams within it may change or evolve. Roles and responsibilities change. There could be growth, contraction or unanticipated circumstances like a global pandemic that impact the way we work. That will likely impact workflow and the stakeholders that need to be managed.

Furthermore, the social media landscape changes rapidly. As current platforms update their functionality or new players emerge, a review of the current social media policy, governance framework and protocols will be necessary. In the past, organizations would not have had to address social audio platforms like Clubhouse. As they become more prevalent and organizations feel the desire or necessity to use them, they will need to define their approach and the implications for employees.

Keeping watch on what is happening in social media and the broader world and reflecting that onto the social media policy, governance framework and protocols will hopefully illuminate gaps or key aspects that warrant refinement to properly address the current social media landscape and associated behaviour. Test proposed changes through scenario planning with the input of stakeholders. This doesn't have to be a weekly or monthly process, but it should be done with some regularity. A steering committee composed of key stakeholder representation will not only help develop a social media policy, governance framework and protocols but also help oversee the ongoing application and updates as required.

Embrace boring

Nobody likes to be told to eat their vegetables or be reminded to floss. It's the same with a social media policy. It is necessary but many would rather have root canal treatment than devote time and energy to developing a social media policy. Why fight what can't be avoided? Reframe your thinking and begin to see it as necessary to achieving your objectives. Rally stakeholders around your common goals. Embrace the boring and get excited by the mundane. Before you know it, stakeholder input will make easy work of policy development and you will all be aligned on how to govern your social media efforts.

04

Content! Content! Content!

Just as nobody likes to face a blank page when tasked with writing, content marketers do not want to face an empty content library or calendar. The goal should be to always be ahead with content planned, content in production and content being distributed. Scrambling for content puts quality at risk and increases the likelihood of making strategic mistakes.

In this chapter we will take a content marketing journey. We will begin with mapping a content strategy. We will then move on to where a content audit ends, reviewing existing content assets. Then we will move into content development and curation. We will take a closer look at developing a content calendar that takes some of the guesswork out while leaving some slack in the system to respond to media events and other content priorities as they arise. Finally, we will talk about executing a content marketing strategy and measuring success.

Mapping a content strategy

Whether you are leveraging existing content, creating new content or curating third-party content, you need a well-defined strategy first to guide those efforts. You need a 'why' for what you are doing. You need to ensure that your approach to content is aligned with your corporate objectives, is on brand and built for the long term.

Are you clear on your corporate objectives? How does your content marketing or broader social media strategy align with your company's strategic plan? Are the measures of success clear? Will your content marketing strategy support the organization's mission, vision and values? What current messaging themes are being prioritized? For example, is corporate citizenship or corporate social responsibility (CSR) one of your organization's communications pillars? If so, the content marketing strategy will need to reflect that kind of messaging.

Organizations need to be cognizant about the stance they take online through their content. They will need to be transparent and prepared for criticism. Increasingly, stakeholders want to see organizations publicly share their position on subjects such as CSR and how they are giving back to society. This should be reflected in their content. It can also serve as a countermeasure to any online conversation that could be critical of the company. It is not a quick fix, but over time the organization's CSR messaging could dominate the online conversation, drowning out the critics in the process.

Being clear about who your content is intended for will help guide your strategy. Who are you trying to reach? Have you identified the personas? Xtensio has a persona tool that can help get everyone on the same page in terms of who you are targeting. What are they interested in? What do they talk about? What content do they consume and share? Is it popular or niche? Trending or established? What are your editorial priorities based on those personas and their content habits?

Using a combination of social media listening, keyword research and content research tools like Buzzsumo, we can determine popular and long-tail content topics and the best formats for engagement while still aligning everything with the personas and interests we have identified. Buzzsumo can tell you if topics have matured and are seeing a drop in interest. It can also tell you whether what, how, why or listicle content is performing the best. It will also tell you the optimal length for the articles and when to publish. That's a lot of insights to inform your content strategy before you have written a single word.

Map your content across the coming weeks, months and quarters. If you want to plan longer so you can establish placeholders on your calendar for recurring campaigns or events then that is fine. Perhaps you always plan particular content for major holidays or there is an element of seasonality that you adhere to.

Add items to the calendar that have already been decided upon. Basically, start with the known and confirmed. Then add placeholders for things that are going to happen but still need further development. For example, you may have a blog planned and even the subject for the blog, but it has yet to be written. You will still want to have it in the calendar, so you can work back and plan its production.

Flag all the repeating events that happen regularly. Every week has Thursday in it so what can you plan in advance for Throwback Thursdays (#TBT)? What other days of the week can you apply preplanning to? Motivation Monday? Tuesday Tips? Wisdom Wednesdays? You get the idea. Look how quickly your calendar can get populated with content ideas planned in advance. That blank page doesn't look so daunting anymore, does it?

Make it easy on yourself and include slots in your calendar for repeating content and leveraging different formats derived from the same anchor piece of content. One blog post could be the basis of an infographic, a couple of quotes with graphic backdrops and multiple social posts with different copy extracted from the blog. Suddenly, a blog post lasts for weeks and even months rather than dying in a day or so.

Identify milestone days for the coming month and quarter that could be important to the organization. Are there any important anniversaries that will be reached by the company in the period being planned? Will they be celebrating a certain number of years in business? Is a particular product or service having an anniversary for a certain number of years in the marketplace? This doesn't just apply to the organization. Are there employees that can be celebrated for their years of service or other accomplishments?

See if there are any national days of some sort that are happening in the coming weeks that could be tied to content being planned. Sites that tell you things like This Day in History are always popular for inspiring content when done well. Are there any awareness days related to causes that align with the organization? Be careful, you want to be genuine in your support in raising awareness for the cause rather than appear to be hijacking it for your marketing agenda. Ideally, it's a cause you support throughout the year and give special attention to on awareness days. You don't want to come across as opportunistic.

Being thorough with your content planning and populating your calendar extensively will help you stay ahead of things, reduce stress and ensure greater success for your social media strategy. Having said that, you shouldn't fill up your calendar completely. You should leave some slack in the system. Leave slots empty or with flexible placeholders so you can react to changes in your audience's preferences, content underperforming or performing beyond expectations or media trends that when juxtaposed with your content could make you look tone-deaf. Remember my Remembrance Day or NRA examples? You get the idea.

You can complete a lot of your plan and calendar with these tactics but everything still has to tie back to the themes and topics that you decided will make up the bulk of your content marketing strategy. It isn't content for content's sake. You want people to come to expect a certain type of content from you. A spray and pray approach won't work and will only tell your audience that you are trying to figure things out at their expense. Devise your strategy. Execute it. Measure the results. Evolve your content strategy as needed.

Start at the end

Upon completing a content audit, you should have a good sense of your available assets and their formats. You will want to organize the content in order to make the most of what you have. The goal should be to work smarter and not harder. However, there will be work involved, especially when it comes to repurposing content.

Organize

Review the content you already have and start with existing content that requires little or no effort to make use of it. Organize it around your calendar. Select what should be used right away and organize the rest to coincide with your content plan and any other factors such as seasonality or campaigns.

Confirm that you have content that can be used with absolutely no updating. If that isn't possible then organize the existing content based on the amount of updating it requires. A content audit is intended to identify all of the content you have and its various forms. You may not have an exact idea of how much updating is required until you review each piece of content.

One of our clients is going through a website refresh and is doing an inventory of their blogs. Some of the existing blogs were planned to be used for some social posts but they discovered, during the inventory, that some of the key elements of the blogs were outdated and, as such, the social posts we had planned could no longer be used.

All written material will have to be reviewed to ensure that it is not outdated. This is especially important for content that is based on research or tied to information from other sources. If those sources are no longer current then neither is your content. In the case of your online content, you will also want to ensure that links to your sources or other external links still work.

While time-consuming, all of your video content should be watched to determine if there is anything out of date. Past webinars, presentations or interviews may no longer be relevant. They may contain or be led by people who no longer work for your firm, further highlighting that they are out of date. This kind of detailed review will also help identify potential excerpts that can be leveraged for more stackable content. Working smarter rather than harder again.

Make sure that everything reflects your current branding and corporate information. Is there any legalese from compliance, risk management, legal, etc. that needs to be updated? You may be surprised to find outdated 'About' sections or incorrect corporate information. Now is your chance to clean all of that up or to at least flag it with whoever needs to know.

Categorize your content into ready to use, ready with a few changes, requiring modest changes, requiring substantial changes and not usable anymore. Based on your calendar and overall content plan, prioritize the content that requires changes and get working on the changes so that no calendar deadlines are missed. Work as efficiently as possible. For example, if graphics need to be updated, but you can get the copy revised and approved ahead of time, then do that to avoid any unnecessary delay.

Repurpose

Now that you have categorized your content by the number of changes required, let's talk more about what is possible. Let's use an old blog as an example. Maybe it just needs a few changes to maintain its relevance and be deemed to be current. We don't have to stop there. Yes, it will be used in its blog form but with this and every other piece of content, we need to think about what else can be derived from it and what forms they could take.

We have to wear our content hat again and think in multiples. A blog should never just be a blog. It should be a blog plus a graphic quote, an animated gif, a short video clip or audio clip. Content consumption preferences are changing and old content needs to be made available in different ways to appeal to your audience.

Consider fewer topics or themes as your foundation but then layer on the content variations to expand on those topics or themes without overburdening yourself. When I was at the bank their economist would regularly release a substantial report. There were many people who wanted to read the entire report. For that reason, it could be used to capture people's contact information in exchange for access to the report.

I suggested that we build on that report by interviewing the economist and capturing it on video. There would be a longer video and perhaps a few shorter clips. In the video, the economist would be asked a series of questions to summarize the main points of the report. The answers to those questions could form the basis of a blog, used as 'pull quotes' that would be posted with a visual or graphic backdrop to make them stand out on social feed or used as copy for social posts pointing to the blog, the video or the report.

Do you see what is possible? One foundational or anchor piece of content results in a multitude of other content pieces. Not every piece of content is going to spawn half a dozen pieces of content but you should strive to extract as many variants as possible. This will address the aforementioned changing preferences of your audience and have you producing more content with incremental effort.

Collaborative content

Hosting webinars, podcasts or live sessions on different social platforms is definitely work for the purposes of creating content but it doesn't have to fall on your shoulders alone. Guests take the burden off you and offer your audience the opportunity to get more value from you and your content. You can't be the only expert promoting yourself. Leverage the thought leadership of others to complement your own.

Soliciting the help of others for your content doesn't just have to apply to webinars, podcasts and live sessions. Consider a guest blogging program. Give people an outlet for their expertise and you get the benefit of traffic to your site and potential redirection to your own content. You would certainly promote their content for them, but they will do the same and your site reaps the reward.

I have been a guest blogger for numerous sites. While it isn't necessarily monetarily rewarding, it certainly helped my credibility and personal brand. I had social proof of my expertise from other sources. They amplified my thought leadership to their audiences. They kept my blogs in rotation and put me in good company with their other contributors. The rising tide lifts all boats. It was a fantastic partnership.

One of my favourite examples of leveraging the thought leadership of experts was something the Content Marketing Institute and TopRank Online Marketing did for Content Marketing World. It is not exactly a guest blogger-type example but it certainly relied upon a number of contributors to make the content marketing initiative such a success.

They conceived of the theme 'Top Secret' and identified key thought leaders in content marketing as 'secret agents' who had secrets to share. The goals of the campaign focused on discovery, consumption and engagement. People needed to be able to find it, consume it and share it easily. Content was discovered through social media, email, blogs and search. The content would be made available for consumption as downloadable PDFs, a SlideShare presentation, long-form interviews online and as single graphic images. Contributors engaged and amplified the content. Users downloaded and subscribed to content and shared it too. Most importantly, the campaign drove attendance to the conference.

What I love about it is that the concept was so simple. They asked each thought leader 'secret agent' for one secret to content marketing success. They used their answers for content. They took headshots, bios and their quotes and created individual pages for each thought leader and collated them into an e-book of content marketing secrets. They only had to design it and compile the information. The secret agents did all the work.

They interviewed a subset of the group and turned those long-form interviews into blogs. Depending on the secrets being promoted, they positioned the secrets as tools for content marketing success or B2B content marketing tips. This helped with discovery through search and targeted different audience interests.

In less than a week, they generated 43,000+ views on SlideShare, 1000+ PDF downloads, 5000+ visits to the long-form interviews, 100+ inbound links and 3,300+ retweets. One simple idea, incorporating the cooperation of thought leaders to create a substantive foundational piece of content, created the foundation for a very successful content marketing campaign. What ideas do you have that could mobilize the thought leaders in your orbit?

Be the best answer

Having thought leaders as contributors is nice but you may not always have that option nor should you rely on it too much. You will need your content to stand on its own at some point too. Your content needs to provide value, inform, educate and persuade. It needs to make the consumer aware of your product or service, provide sufficient information for their consideration and to influence their preferences.

At each stage of their journey down the marketing funnel, the consumer must be met with more substantive content that will eventually cause them to take action and make a purchase. However, your content efforts do not stop there. Your content must also play a role in retaining them as loyal customers and ultimately turning them into advocates for your brand.

One example of providing content that influences a consumer's journey is River Pools. They specialized in backyard pools. These are luxury items typically paid for with discretionary income. They were founded in 2001 and experienced growth until the 2008 financial crisis hit and people started cancelling their orders. They weren't sure what to do.

After reflection, River Pools decided to focus on pool building and less on retail. That also meant a shift in marketing to more of an online emphasis. With that in mind, their goal was to become the most educational fibreglass pool website in the world by 'being the best answer'.

FIGURE 4.1 Marketing funnel

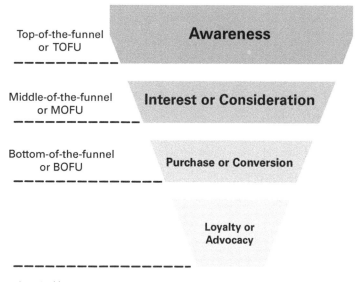

SOURCE Andrew Jenkins

They worked with the salespeople to identify the most common questions and objections during sales calls and meetings. They used that information to inform their content strategy for their blog. They didn't pitch. They informed. They educated. By taking that approach, their prospects were better qualified before they were spoken to. River Pools wasn't the cheapest but their content educated the consumer to explain why cheaper wasn't always better. One of their blog posts was responsible for $3.5 million dollars in revenue.

The River Pools site is now the most visited pool site in the world with over 600,000 monthly visitors. Marcus Sheridan, who led their content marketing transformation, is now known as the Sales Lion and he works with organizations on their content marketing, helping them provide their best answers.

Tools of production

There are numerous tools available now that make it easier to extract more from every piece of content. We are all familiar with Zoom. I used it to record conversations and interviews that could then be posted as video to YouTube and to iTunes and Spotify as podcasts. Zoom provides separate video and audio files after your session so you already have the raw material ready to work with. You can transcribe the audio with something like Fireflies.ai to use the transcript as supporting material for the podcast and as content in the form of a blog or social posts.

Tools like Lately enable you to take video and audio files and, with the click of a button, create multiple short video excerpts or audiograms from the original file. We have used this with numerous webinars to cut some of the most interesting parts into short clips to derive more from the original asset and keep the social channels populated with content from us that already has a built-in audience. Take a look at Gary Vee's Twitter feed (@garyvee) to see how he has used Lately to cut provocative sound bites from his keynote presentations.

Don't get hung up on production value. If the COVID-19 pandemic taught us anything about content production, it is that we will forgive production value for access. Think about all of the shows we watched where the hosts were in their homes rather than in a studio. We just accepted it as the new normal. This may have been one of the factors that gave rise to the phrase 'send it'. Being fast and relevant is better than slow and irrelevant.

I am not suggesting that shaky handheld video from your phone is what you should standardize on. Lower production value does not mean lousy production value. There's a difference. It is now relatively inexpensive to set yourself up with podcast mike, an HD webcam and tripod or gimbal to hold your phone steady should you choose to do a walk and talk. Look no further than TikTok to see all of the people using ring lights to improve their videos. Mine was less than $50. I can now shoot higher-quality imagery and edit it on my phone than what I could do at film school with an entire building filled with the state-of-the-art equipment for its time 25 years ago.

Lumen5 can take your blogs, read them and compile stock video clips and images to turn your blogs into short videos. If you don't like the images or clips they used then you can swap in your own or just use the animated text. Play.ht reads your blogs and turns them into podcasts. You can be a team of one and become a small-scale media production company with the tools that are available today.

Content extraction

Every time you are conceiving of a piece of content or have a piece of content available to you then I want you to think about extracting other content from it. Tools like Lately will scan a blog post for you and 'spin' or extract multiple potential social posts from that one blog post. One blog becomes a half a dozen or more social posts. You get the added benefit of testing what copy garners more engagement. Was it the original title or an excerpt?

If you are starting with written content like a blog then you need to think about spinning different social posts from it like I just described. If the blog is a listicle, then each of the key listed elements can be a social post. Listicles also make for great video animations using solutions like Lumen5 so now you can add video to your content considerations when you are starting with written content. Depending on the written content, it may make for a great podcast created using AI to read the text.

What excerpts, quotes or data points within the article would make for a great visual graphic or animated gif? Wealthsimple created an animated gif that looked like a spiral staircase built out of numbers forming the number 4 billion to convey their milestone of achieving $4 billion dollars under management. A simple concept that brought text about the achievement to life.

If you are starting with longer-form video then there is the potential to cut it up into shorter clips with distinct ideas being conveyed in each clip. If the clips do not have them already, can you add captions or subtitles to make them more accessible and to address the growing trend of watching videos without audio? At the time of this writing, 80 per cent of videos are watched without audio. You need to make sure your message is coming across without relying on audio to get it across for you.

Long-form video has its place but our attention spans are getting shorter and platforms like Facebook are saying that video ads shouldn't be longer than 15 seconds. Instagram videos are only a minute in length before you get redirected to IGTV. That is all the more reason to take your longer-form video and cut it up. This also makes for more content to share over longer periods of time without having to create new content.

Just as we moved from written content to video and podcasts, consider moving from video to written content and/or podcasts. Can the audio from your video be ripped to make podcast material or is it too reliant on the visuals that were presented? If it was just people talking then you have the potential for a new content asset as a podcast. Furthermore, can the discussion be transcribed and turned into a blog or long-form interview? Were there visuals from the video that could be static images or animated gifs to be shared as highlights?

No matter what form of content you are starting with, you have a number of different directions you can take to extract and build repurposed content. Content production has only been growing but you don't need to produce only entirely new content from scratch. That is difficult to sustain, especially if you have limited resources and budget. Hopefully, what has been suggested here gives you the confidence to leverage what you already have and get more from it.

Contrarian content

Whether you are thinking about how old content can be repurposed or you are trying to develop the content calendar for the next quarter, consider taking a contrarian approach. By that I mean, while competitors or peers might zig with their content, why not zag? Let me share a few examples that I love to explain the concept.

Karina Longworth has a podcast that focuses on old Hollywood but she takes current pop culture references and gives them an old Hollywood spin. For example, she did a series of episodes called Star Wars but the series was not about the Star Wars movies we all know but about stars during the war and what happened to their careers during and because of the war. You don't always have to copy the same approach to content as everybody else.

One of my other favourite examples does not involve social media but it is still a fantastic example of looking at the same subject matter as others but coming at it from another or opposite perspective. In November 1963 President John F. Kennedy's funeral drew numerous members of the media to cover it for their respective organizations. One of those members of the media was Jimmy Breslin who at the time was writing for *The New York Herald Tribune*. Instead of covering the funeral procession and related ceremony, he chose to go to Arlington National Cemetery to interview Clifton Pollard, the man who dug the President's grave.

Breslin's article related to the same event that everyone was writing about but it was written from an entirely different perspective, and it was richer for it. With no disrespect intended toward President John F. Kennedy, it was common for him to turn his focus to the common man rather than those considered more newsworthy. This approach endeared him to a much wider audience of common folk.

Taking the contrarian approach gives you more options and freedom regarding your content. You can revisit old content by taking a new angle with the subject matter. With new content you can differentiate yourself from peers and competitors and compete with niche or long-tail content rather than the high-volume search topics. You do not have to take this approach with every bit of your content, but consider this approach when you are stumped for ideas or challenged to bring new life to old content.

Content bible

If you don't already have a brand bible or document that defines your brand design guidelines then you will need to define and get approval for your approach to branded content. What tone do you want to establish and maintain? We have talked about content themes or topics but is the goal to establish thought leadership or brand recognition related to just a select few topics? Where, if at all, will humour fit? Will you remain politically neutral? What causes, if any, will you be supporting and how will that be reflected in your content? If you have defined audience personas then include them in the guidelines so others know for whom content is being written and developed.

Those are high-level considerations, but as part of your playbook or guidelines, you will also need to consider more practical things like how long your blogs, videos or podcasts will be. Will you have one or more branded hashtags and will you strive for standardized social post formats in terms of character counts and hashtags? Copy for social posts is getting shorter so you will need to revisit this regularly. The same goes for video length. Our attention spans keep getting shorter. This doesn't take into account changes on the different social platforms or the social media management tools that connect to them that can adversely affect our efforts.

Some social media management solutions allow us to manage the personal social accounts of the CEOs of some of our clients while others do not. Even the solutions that make this kind of management possible do not allow us to upload video directly to their accounts so we have to do it natively by logging directly into their accounts. It is not that big of a deal but it impacts workflow and disrupts the standardized processes we have in place. With that in mind, make sure the content guidelines you have in place are reasonable to maintain and be sure to review them with key stakeholders to ensure alignment.

Measuring success

You have completed your audit. You have categorized your content. You have developed your content plan. You have built your calendar. Finally, you have begun distributing your content. How do you know it is working? What will you tell management? What have you promised to include in your reporting? How often are you to report on the results of your content strategy?

Generally, you will have defined the metrics by which you will measure the success of your content marketing strategy at the beginning. This will likely include engagement, reach, formats and more specifics around engagement such as likes, comments and shares. You should be providing sufficient information for context and to provide actionable insights but avoid being too dense with data so as to confuse your stakeholder audience.

When I was at the bank, we were often tasked to create our analytics reports to be 'board ready', which meant that when they reached the board they were written in such a way as to be self-explanatory. If we had to be there to explain them then they weren't simple enough. It was a hard lesson to learn but one that has stayed with me. Social media is rich with data and you can overwhelm people with analysis and insights when they may only need a select few data points to make informed decisions.

If you are lucky, you will get to determine what you report and when. Sometimes you will have stakeholders that need time to determine what they want and need to know. For example, we worked for at least six months with one enterprise client where we reported on social media performance metrics every month. We discussed audience growth and engagement by channel. We also discussed the top-performing content for each social channel and what formats were getting the most engagement.

We kept refining what was important for them to know every month, but we kept getting ad-hoc requests for insights. Some of those requests got rolled into the monthly reporting. Now the client has essentially locked the reporting format for each month and our metrics meetings focus on noteworthy insights from the month and how they relate to strategy. The monthly reports are now in a format that can easily understand and prioritize questions related to how strategy ties to their business objectives.

Be prepared to evolve your metrics over time as needs and priorities change. We were tasked to come out with forecasted KPIs for one client with 6- and 12-month horizons. Based on early performance, we were tracking ahead of our projections and were subsequently asked to adjust our forecasts. You may also have to shift priorities in terms of content types and channels of distribution based on the results of your efforts.

You may come to realize that not all channels are performing equally or that certain content does better on certain channels. Those insights are going to help you rationalize where to devote time and energy related to content. It may also indicate which channels to simply maintain or abandon. While it may seem like a failure or like you are giving up, what is the point of pumping out content on a channel if the content isn't resonating or the channel's audience is inactive?

Use metrics to track engagement over time. What kind of engagement are you getting? What kind of content is getting the most engagement? Does it vary by channel, time of day or day of the week? A friend of mine who was leading social media for a sports organization found that even what was an acceptable tone for their content varied by channel. They could be edgier on Twitter but that was not welcome on Facebook. These sorts of insights will come in time with regular measurement.

There is still a debate amongst social media practitioners regarding native uploads versus sharing from other platforms. Social platforms give preferential treatment via their algorithms to content shared natively on their platforms rather than content shared from elsewhere via a link. That means a platform like Facebook gives preferential treatment to a video uploaded directly to their platform rather than a video uploaded to YouTube and then shared to Facebook via a shareable link. To be safe and to ensure the algorithms are working in your favour, post natively whenever possible. If you are not certain then feel free to test it both ways and let the metrics tell you the difference.

The platforms themselves provide analytics for you to assess your progress, but I recommend leveraging the analytics that social media management solutions like Sprout Social or Sprinklr provide or use analytics-only solutions like Rival IQ so that you can have more control over your analysis, especially when doing historical comparisons or competitive analysis.

Establish standardized reporting and automate what you can in terms of data compilation but be prepared for ad-hoc or manual analysis to meet stakeholder needs. There will likely always be questions that come out of left field that you didn't anticipate that require you to 'look into it and follow up later'. Just roll with it. Hopefully, you have a measurement system set-up that makes it easy to compile the data and provide the insight that the stakeholder wants.

However, if you know they are asking for something that can't be provided then tell them. Inform stakeholders what you can and cannot report on to better prepare them and so that their expectations are properly set for the future, alleviating any burden for you and your team. For example, we often get asked about competitive analysis on LinkedIn but it is a closed platform that limits our abilities or makes it impossible to compile insights about competitors.

Case study with permission from Audiense

The World Wildlife Fund (WWF) was established in 1961 to secure the funding necessary to protect places and species that were threatened by human development. As the world's leading conservation organization, WWF works in nearly 100 countries. At every level, we collaborate with people around the world to develop and deliver innovative solutions that protect communities, wildlife and the places in which they live.

Challenge

During the United Nations General Assembly (#UNGA74) in September 2019, the WWF wanted to encourage the world leaders who were attending to publicly address nature loss and acknowledge that bold action was required to secure a #NewDealForNature & People. The main challenge was to target relevant key messages to the right audiences while making this high-level policy meeting relevant to a mass audience and decision makers.

Solution

During #UNGA74, the WWF had a series of events to engage external partners. They used Insights from Audiense to identify key audiences from the events. This enabled the WWF to create content such as videos and different key messages to relevant profiles and influencers, and effectively raise awareness of the goal of creating a #NewDealForNature & People.

The WWF also uses Connect from Audiense to create tailored audiences on Twitter to target relevant key messages and CTAs for different audience sets with Twitter ads. The social conversations surrounding #UNGA74 and #NewDealForNature & People and content performance were monitored.

Results

- Total Twitter impressions
  - #NewDealForNature: 5942 Tweets*
  - #VoiceForThePlanet: 6826 Tweets*
    *Hashtag data from 17–26 September 2019
- Best performing tweet
  - Impressions: 1,063,877

- Ability to divide the influencers list into five categories
  - Heads of state
  - Ministers of environment
  - Celebrities
  - Business leaders
  - Directors of CSOs.[1]

Endnote

1 Audiense (2021) How WWF used audience intelligence to deliver key messages to relevant stakeholders, resources.audiense.com/case-studies-how-wwf-used-audience-intelligence-to-deliver-key-messages-to-relevant-stakeholders?hsCtaTracking=bc3aa2be-352b-40aa-8509-572dd1ce2e83%7C5e9e4e24-ea64-4e3b-9f09-7a1d4b3835fa (archived at https://perma.cc/P8DY-QHN6)

05

Training

One of the key factors for success in rolling out social media across an enterprise is training. From understanding what the social media policy is talking about to role-specific skills, training will be critical. In this chapter we will discuss the different types of people that will need training and what type they will need. We will also discuss different approaches to training and considerations for building versus buying a training program. There is no wrong path. It will all come down to choosing based on needs but we will discuss that further later.

The why of social media training

With the growth of social media, organizations face increased risks regarding brand reputation, employee safety and stakeholder management. Unfortunately, technology moves faster than policy so many organizations have found themselves trying to catch up and stay current. For many, social media sucks up time and increases costs in certain areas leaving some to wonder, 'Why bother?'

Well, you need to bother. Social media isn't going away. It is only getting bigger and taking up more of our time. It can't be ignored and, as an extension of that fact, neither can training. In order to mitigate risk, organizations need to ensure that every one of their employees has been familiarized with social media to protect themselves and their employer. Any public-facing role needs to know what can and cannot be said and done via social media for the sake of reputation and stakeholder management.

People are required to review their employer's code of conduct every year so it is not unrealistic to think that they should be required to complete social media training too. It may sound draconian but it is meant to protect them. It will help them avoid any potential missteps and the possibility of disciplinary action. From the employer's perspective, it will give them some comfort that risks are being mitigated but if an issue arises then training, the social media policy and, potentially, the code of conduct can provide clarity and referenceable material to navigate through the situation.

Spectrum of knowledge

If you find yourself tasked with having to develop a training program, it is probably for one of two reasons. Either you were asked to do it or it became very apparent that the familiarity and/or skills of the staff were lacking in some or all aspects of social media. Regardless of how you came to having to develop training, you need to assess your staff and determine the spectrum of knowledge within the organization regardless of whether they will be using social media in their role or not.

Consideration needs to be given to elevating everyone's familiarity with social media so that they can clarify the expectations the organization has when it comes to staff understanding and honouring the social media policy. It is unfair to hold someone accountable to the terms of a social media policy if they don't understand the basics of social media. If the policy says not to retweet certain types of content but the employee does not know what a retweet is then the employee and the organization have a problem.

Generally, you are going to find that employees will fall into three categories. First, you will find the people who have grown up 'digital'. They have never known a world without the internet and, further to that, are very accustomed to social media and living their lives online and through their phone. One caveat I should add is that they know social media from the standpoint of 'being social' in their everyday lives, but they may be less familiar or unaccustomed to using social media to serve corporate objectives.

The second category includes people who came to digital and social later in life but have adopted it out of necessity and/or interest. They became more digitally savvy as their organizations adopted new technology. The introduction of the internet was where it all began for them. That was certainly the case for me. I didn't get my very own personal computer until long after graduating from university yet you can't go to university without a computer today and I have been teaching online for the University of Toronto for years.

While this second category adopted technology rather than grew up with it, their knowledge, experience and related skills are extensive – but there will still be different levels. We live in a world where most have to have some basic digital skills to live and to do our work but that doesn't mean that we all have the deeper digital skills that roles in social media require. There will be some in this second category that have the necessary skills, but there will be others that need to upskill to meet the organization's needs and to continue along their path of personal development.

The final category are the resistors or naysayers. These are the people who may not need social media training for their role but, if given the choice, would elect to pass on training anyway. There are some that, for whatever reason, do not wish to become familiar with social media or, more broadly, digital. Some of them are content, even blissful, for never having allowed social media to permeate their lives. Maybe they are onto something. Regardless, this category is going to present some challenges, especially if they have to be trained, even to a modest level, to ensure alignment with the organization's social media policy and code of conduct. Be prepared and be patient.

Assessments

While some people will make it blatantly apparent which category they fall into, for most others you are going to have to determine which category they should be assigned to. Consider developing an assessment, survey or quiz. Leverage existing ones if they are available for use for free or via a licence fee. The goal is to identify the baseline of knowledge as well as subsequent skill levels specific to social networks, best practices and related technology and apps.

You want as many people as possible to complete some form of assessment so try not to make it feel like an exam. The goal is to acquire information quickly and with little disruption to the day-to-day work lives of staff. This is especially important when it comes to the resistors. If you push too hard at this early stage then it could mean trouble for you later. You need to try to get the support of as many people as possible.

Once you have completed assessing knowledge and skill levels, you will be able to divide people into the three main categories. Once you have done that, you can begin designing a training program to meet the needs of each category and support the pursuit of your corporate objectives. There is likely not going to be a 'one size fits all' kind of approach to training so be prepared to tailor your training curriculum and methods of delivery to meet the different learning preferences of your staff.

Curriculum design

Training for people who grew up with social media and only know a digital world will start at a more intermediate level of curriculum. While you won't have to familiarize them with the social media landscape from a personal use point of view, you will need to guide them on where and how the organization is and will be using social media. Furthermore, if they will be using social media in their role to support corporate objectives then they really need to understand the implications of their behaviour on social media, potentially speaking as the organization or on its behalf as an employee advocate.

They need to know the organization's overall objectives and how social media strategies and tactics align with those objectives. Measuring progress and performance will be critical so they will need to know what is being measured, why and, potentially, how to explain the ongoing metrics and what they mean to the overall strategy. They may need to be able to extract actionable insights from the data compiled and explain them in such a way that is easy to understand for stakeholders that are not working in social media on a daily basis. Training should focus less on technology and more on strategy and performance metrics.

Training for people like me who came to social media and technology later in their lives may have to be the most diverse because this category spans novices to experts. I certainly didn't learn about the internet or social media at school. Thankfully, I had a natural curiosity that has served me well over the years. That isn't the case for everyone.

There are going to be people who know their way around the internet and technology but are still unfamiliar, to some degree, with social media. There are going to be people who know social media from a personal use perspective but, like those who grew up digital, still need to understand where social media fits within the organization and perhaps within their role. Some within this group will be keen to be trained, others may have some trepidation and everywhere in between.

The curriculum will have to span some sort of social media that explains the social media landscape, social media strategy and measurement, tools and technologies, and related best practices. We are talking about moving people from unfamiliar to novice, novice to intermediate and intermediate to expert. That is going to require an expansive training curriculum to address the needs of each subset within this category.

Finally, even the resistors will need training. However, the goal is not to turn them into productive members of the social media team. That is likely too lofty a goal. You should be focused on minimizing or eliminating their influence on your social media mandate. You want to try to get them on your side or at least to a degree of agreeableness where they won't stand in the way of your efforts.

Some of their resistance is likely based on fear of the unknown or wanting to avoid something they do not understand. They may think that the opportunity to understand has passed them by. They may think getting up to speed will be hard and/or take too much time. You need to keep that in mind as you develop and deliver curriculum. It has to be accessible and address their concerns and fears. They need to be welcomed into your social media world.

I have found humour to be a great bridge for reaching people in this category. When I have conducted training for groups of resistors. I tell stories and humorous anecdotes. I try to reach them emotionally because they will remember it more and it won't feel like training. It will be time well spent for them because they enjoyed it.

I typically provide an overview of the social media landscape to give them a sense of how vast it is – not to instil fear into them but to convey just how important it has become to our everyday lives. I then try to tie it to them, bringing it down from the macro level to something they can relate to and perhaps have even experienced themselves. I often ask people what was the last thing they responded to or shared on social media, assuming they are active. Usually, if they reacted to something it was just that – they reacted. Something they saw caused a reaction. An emotional reaction.

Reminding them of that fact can go a long way to getting them on my side because I was able to surface something they remember emotionally. They conclude for themselves just how powerful social media can be. It may still take some time to convince them but progress is already being made because I have them thinking. The goal isn't for me to persuade them but to remind them of evidence from their own experiences that cause them to come to their own conclusion.

Beyond the categories based on the spectrum of knowledge, you will have to design a curriculum based on roles and responsibilities too. You will have training that gets everyone to a baseline familiarity of social media and the goal should be that everyone within the organization, if possible, should go through that training.

People who will be using social media or have social media involved in the work that they do will have a different type of training curriculum that takes them beyond the baseline familiarity into areas such as technology, strategy, measurement, reputation management and community management. Many of these people are the 'doers' when it comes to social media. They may not be pushing send on a tweet, but they are part of the machine that manages the organization's social media presence.

Dell had its own social media university with a curriculum designed as I have been describing here. They had an overview to get everyone familiar with social media and its scope and power. They had training for people who used or had social media involved in their daily work. Finally, they had training for people that were official spokespeople for the organization so the training they received also had an element of media relations incorporated.

You will want people properly trained regarding social media if they have their own social media presence. They need to understand that they are still tied to their employer even if they think their social media presence is their own. There have been too many instances of people saying or doing something on social media that has led to discipline or dismissal by their employer. They are advocates of the corporate brand whether they realize it or not.

When it comes to official spokespeople or what might be considered social media evangelists, training will be critical, especially if the actions of the spokespeople or evangelists could have an impact on the brand, or the stock price if they are publicly traded. They have to understand that anything they say could have an effect on how the company is perceived. That could mean that anything they say has to be reviewed and discussed before being approved for posting. Alternatively, they are sufficiently trained regarding social media and media relations such that confidence is high that they will likely not make any mistakes in terms of what they say or do.

Finally, there will be specific roles and functions within the organization that will need tailored training. This does not mean that everyone will have access to the organization's social accounts but does mean that the curriculum has to provide more context for social media as it relates to these roles. For example, the legal department needs to understand what the social media team is doing on behalf of the organization. They will also need to be sufficiently familiar with social media based on the training they receive in order to be able to contribute to the social media policy discussion and possible links to the corporate code of conduct.

Similarly, the HR department needs to be familiarized with social media to inform the social media policy and code of conduct discussion, support any disciplinary action and learn best practices for using social media for recruitment and building an employer brand. Basically, they need to know more because they may have to respond to situations that arise because of social media activities of employees and/or use social media proactively as part of recruitment and convey corporate culture as part of the employer brand.

I say this with no disrespect intended but not everyone in marketing and communications is familiar with social media. Many students come to work in marketing and communications but want to add to their knowledge and experience because social media has permeated almost every facet of our personal and professional lives to some degree. They need and want to understand it better, potentially use it and, in some cases, know more because they are managing people who are already more familiar. The training needs to reflect these objectives.

There are a lot of stakeholders for whom training has to be tailored. Involving them in the curriculum design will certainly ensure that their requirements are met. They, if you will pardon the phrase, 'don't know what they don't know' so you may have to lead them a bit with questions about their roles and responsibilities to identify where and how social media could be a complement. Be sure to use the results of your assessments to help inform the curriculum development. While they may struggle to articulate what they want to learn or know more about, it is still worth asking stakeholders about the top things they want to know or understand regarding social media. They need to feel safe to ask or admit where they are ignorant without fear of embarrassment. Stakeholder management is more important than many think and training can help.

Delivery

Free or cheap

The bulk of this chapter is devoted to training based on the assumption that the organization is delivering it and/or has a hand in any training delivered by an outside party. Having said that, I don't want to leave out the many free or modestly priced training and certification programs available online. Many of the social media platforms like Facebook, Twitter and LinkedIn provide curricula related to advertising. Social media solutions like Hootsuite provide certification programs regarding their product but also about broader social media topics.

I am not suggesting that you skip developing your own training program, but these available programs may fill some gaps for curriculum required for specific roles. Furthermore, it can help certain employees get up to speed quickly and reduce or eliminate costs while training every participant to the same standard. Look at these options as potential modules to your overall training program rather than being seen as the entire training program itself.

Not to sound self-serving but consider sponsoring training from external sources such as sending someone or some people, even virtually, to participate in courses available from accredited entities like a university or college. This could be part of their professional development plan provided there is a budget for it. This may not suit every situation but for a select few staff members, it may be a potential approach, especially if they want to learn something more specific that isn't or won't be available in the planned training curriculum.

Logistics

We have already discussed the need for a curriculum that meets the different needs of your prospective learners but you might also find yourself facing different needs and wants from your learners when it comes to how you deliver training, if you are delivering some or all of it or if you are going to outsource any of it to someone else. There are a number of things to consider, which we will discuss here.

The different categories of learners, based on their level of social media knowledge, will guide some of what you decide for training delivery, but it doesn't end there. How many learners will you have overall? Are they all in the same location? Are they dispersed in different cities, regions, countries or time zones? Will they be trained in groups live in person, via webinar or a combination of both? Will sessions be recorded for replay and for access later by others? Think of all the logistical issues that have to be addressed.

Will training be developed such that learners can take themselves through it sitting at their desk or in a remote location of their choosing? Will there be lectures, live or recorded? Will training be delivered in workshop or module formats? Organizations are going to make their own decisions but I have found that workshops tend to pump too much information in too short a period of time, which means low retention of what attendees learned.

Breaking the curriculum into modules that are delivered over an extended period of time allows people to implement what they have learned for greater retention. Just think back to how you were taught in school. You weren't taught everything about mathematics in a day. It was broken up into modules that kept building on the modules that preceded them. Unfortunately, organizations sometimes feel that taking the module approach is taking people away from their work more than they would like. You have to weigh the trade-offs and the potential benefits of each approach.

If training is to be delivered live in person, then are there training facilities? If not, how much will it cost to rent some? What is the capacity of the facilities, whether owned or rented? You should also consider what type of limits you want to put on the size of each class if you want to foster interactive participation and discussion. This can even be an issue for online delivery. People may be reluctant to speak up if the size of the group is too large.

Do training resources already exist within the organization and within each city, region or country that is to receive training? If not, is there a budget to send them to conduct live training if that is the preferred delivery method? Given the global pandemic, training-related travel and in-person delivery has obviously been impacted. It may not completely return to the old way of doing things once everyone has been vaccinated.

The digital transformation that the pandemic has brought about has made organizations realize what efficiencies can be gained by leveraging technology. It will be hard to ask for a travel budget in the future when solutions like Zoom make it possible to reach large groups of people in different places and deliver some level of interactive training that can be recorded too, all for considerably lower cost than a flight, a hotel stay and renting training facilities.

Using webinars and video conferencing technology enables scaling training across cities, regions and time zones, but there can only be so much interactivity. Plus, there is a risk that people are not paying complete attention. They could be signed on to the session just to appease their manager and get the confirmation that they attended training. You will not be able to eliminate those issues entirely and key stakeholders need to understand that. Post-module or program assessments can help address that and nurture learning.

In-person training facilitates learning through cross-pollination amongst the participants but with the rise of online training, trainers need to work at making that peer learning possible in an online environment. They need to bring students into the conversation more so that others can learn from what they share about their own experiences. This will also help bring about the cultural change needed for a successful social media program.

From mass to one-to-one

Training to establish a baseline familiarity with social media for the entire organization can take the form of larger-scale webinars, virtual town hall meetings, and lunch and learns. This is about delivering a general overview of the social media landscape to the entire organization in a scalable and repeatable way that also informs all about the social media policy and supports adherence to it.

We have already discussed training to meet the needs of certain roles and functions, but I want to also highlight specific tactical training related to such things as paid campaigns and user training for any technology being used for social media management, brand monitoring, analytics or measurement.

There is a lot of content already available, for free or a modest price, from the likes of Facebook, which explains paid campaigns. Where possible, training should also include specific case examples from the organization's own past paid campaigns to provide real-world examples closer to home. External case studies are helpful but can still lack context specific to the organization.

If certain staff members have requested or made a case for specific external training that is more expensive and/or requires time away from work, hear them out. Can the training be part of their aforementioned professional development plan? There may only be one or a few people in this kind of training requirement situation where sending them to an outside program is an easier route than developing content for such a small group.

Training is available for people in specific roles related to things like social media management, community management or brand monitoring, from the customer success resources from the vendors of those types of solutions. The vendor bears the cost rather than you. They also provide ongoing support and updates regarding their solutions, again alleviating you of any related costs. It is in the vendor's best interest to ensure your success because it means reduced customer churn and potential upsell opportunities.

Tactical training for certain functions or roles like customer service or community management will most certainly include best practices and tips about social media etiquette but curriculum about procedures and protocols will also be necessary. People need to be trained on the communication flow for community management or escalating customer service issues to the appropriate internal resources. They need to be clear about what they can and cannot say to customers. What tone must be maintained? What do they do with confidential customer information? How do they assign tasks or what does it mean when a task is assigned to them? How will their performance be measured?

Disparate stakeholders will need different curriculum in different formats delivered in different ways, all with the intention of meeting their needs. It's a lot to consider and address. It will not be a static thing. It will need to be assessed and revised based on feedback and your own reflection on the process and experience of delivery.

Trainers

As part of the delivery discussion, we need to talk about who will be doing it, not just how it will be done. Do you have internal resources that can deliver training? Can they deliver all of the curriculum or will certain parts of the curriculum require different trainers with expertise in those areas? If so, does the expertise exist internally or will those experts have to be contracted externally? The latter resource situation may mean a hybrid training scenario with internal resources delivering some of the training while external resources deliver other parts of the curriculum. If no internal resources exist, are you prepared to outsource it entirely and is there an available budget? In order to scale, will a 'train-the-trainer' approach be required, regardless of whether an internal or external resource is training the trainers?

If any trainers are being contracted externally then they will need to be properly briefed and provide details about their planned curriculum and delivery to ensure that training objectives are met and the learning needs and preferences of the different stakeholder groups are addressed. This will also apply if they are only doing part of the overall training program. They still need to be aligned with the full curriculum while still meeting stakeholder requirements for the subset of training participants they are training.

Let me say a word of caution about choosing training resources. When it comes to deciding who should deliver the training, regardless of whether they are internal or external resources, it needs to be based on expertise and experience. Some internal resources may be knowledgeable about social media but have never been asked to develop a curriculum based on their knowledge and assess if the participants of the training actually learned what was intended. It may be worth considering involving someone who knows how to develop and deliver training but leverages the expertise of the internal social media resources. As for external training resources, it is easier to determine their expertise by reviewing their curriculum and getting references from others for whom they have delivered training previously.

Sustainability

So you have gone to all the trouble of developing and delivering a comprehensive training program. How do you sustain the skills that you have enabled stakeholders to acquire? How do you ensure that your curriculum remains current? Does your training program address the need to be sustainable for the future?

Let's look at content and delivery first. The overview content that would be used for the baseline training may be sufficiently general that updates are not required as frequently. Role or function-specific training may be more burdensome because social media platforms and related technology are constantly changing and updating, which can have repercussions on day-to-day activities. This change can be happening in between curriculum updates so lean on your vendors and their customer success resources. You can also direct your stakeholders to available third-party content that can fill in the gaps until the curriculum is refreshed.

Consider the frequency of curriculum updates and how to make that as simple as possible. Updating a playbook in PowerPoint or PDF or a training resource document is a lot easier than updating a webinar recording. If things are broken up into modules then not all modules may have to be updated. Maybe only some or portions of some will have to be updated. This is another reason why the modular approach could be the better choice.

If you are using external resources then you may want to build in refreshed content or updates into the contract. Live training is more likely to be based on the latest content and industry information, but once it is a recorded asset for reference later, it becomes material that can expire. It is a hard balance to find between extending the shelf life or usability of curriculum and keeping it relevant and current.

If any external certifications are involved then you will have to consider the requirements for maintaining those certifications, if any. Some certifications require an annual allocation of hours of training or completing refreshers to maintain standing with the governing body. This may only fall to the employers that took certification training, but there could be related costs that the employees pass on to the organization.

As you can see there is a lot to consider when it comes to training the various stakeholders and their disparate needs. There will have to be trade-offs and compromises. Not everyone will be satisfied and there will be moments when training didn't quite hit the mark the first time. Training will be an ongoing process if social media success is the objective. The social media landscape is ever evolving and your training program must adapt accordingly.

06

Analytics and ROI

One thing about social media is that it is data rich. So much so that, if you are not careful, you can get buried in data. In this chapter we will discuss the analytics of social media, what data to focus on, how to answer the questions regarding ROI, how to find the actionable insights and what to do when you find them.

Benchmarking

We've talked about benchmarking before but I want to revisit the topic because it is important, especially when it comes to social media analytics and measuring ROI. You are going to have at least one of, if not both, internal and external benchmarks. If you are setting up your organization's social media presence from scratch then you won't have anything internal to reference so you will be left to compare yourself to external benchmarks such as industry benchmarks and/or peers and competitors.

Internal

Assuming your organization already has an established social media presence then review as much historical data as possible that is available to you. What channels are active? What is the audience size on each? How active are they from a posting and community reaction point of view? Which ones perform the best? Can you determine how the channels have grown audience, engagement and posting volume over time? Were there slow or quiet periods in the past that would explain any drops in metrics?

Beyond organic efforts, review any past paid campaigns. What type of campaigns were they – awareness or conversion? Did the organization run paid campaigns regularly? Did they run awareness and conversion campaigns equally or did they do one more than another? Which ones, if any, did better than others? Were the campaigns considered successful and how did they define success previously? How long were the campaigns and what were the budgets? Did they build on each other based on the performance and learning from the previous campaigns? Did they run them or did an external agency run them? What were the targeting parameters? Did the campaigns reach the intended audience?

By looking at the past, you will be able to see what is possible for the future. You will also get a gauge of what can reasonably be achieved. As you define your objectives, you can determine how aggressive you can be and how audacious your goals can be without being impossible to achieve. If history shows a month-over-month growth rate of 10 per cent then it is reasonable to assume that a stretch goal of 30 per cent growth per month is more likely than 100 per cent. There is being bold and then there is being ridiculous.

Look at the historical contribution of organic and paid to the success of the organization to that point. If paid made a substantial contribution then you will want to make sure that you secure sufficient funding for future paid campaigns to support growth objectives. For certain channels like Facebook, paid is a critical component for achieving success. Paid also helps get new accounts off the ground fast. It can also put a little gas on the fire for content that shows early signs of engagement and is worthy of boosting.

External

Your external benchmark reference points are likely going to fall along a spectrum from very similar to your organization to being in the same industry but apples to your oranges in terms of size and performance. You likely have close competitors with a similar-sized social media footprint, but when you look at industry players to reference as benchmarks then they may be so much bigger in terms of audience size and reach. All of them should be examined but, when it comes to the industry players, take them with a grain of salt. They have likely been at it longer, have bigger budgets and have a more established brand, which gives them some momentum in the marketplace.

Thankfully, there is a lot of social media data available for a vast array of industries. Sources like Rival IQ, Socialbakers, We Are Social, Hootsuite, Hubspot, Sprout Social and more compile industry benchmark data into reports available to everyone. While some of the benchmarks pertain to larger and/or global brands, they are still worth referencing to get a gauge of what more well-known brands can achieve. It is also worth noting that larger brands can see lower engagement rates because of the size of their audiences and their posting volume. Over time the numbers can work against them so keep that in mind when you are reviewing the data.

Similar to internal benchmarking, you should gather external historical data, where possible, about your close competitors and peers, along with the industry players that you want to reference. You can only eyeball historical activity on LinkedIn and see past ad campaigns, but the data will be limited and you will have to compile it manually. While that may be tedious, it is still a worthwhile investment of time and effort, especially if you are a B2B organization and LinkedIn is one of your primary social media marketing channels.

Fortunately, a lot of data is freely available for platforms like Twitter, Facebook and Instagram. You can get a lot of data from the platforms themselves, from free tools and from paid tools. Facebook allows you to track other pages in relation to your own page and their Ad Library allows you to see current and past campaigns from your peers, competitors and industry players.

As I write this, it is still early days for access to TikTok analytics but Rival IQ has already introduced functionality that compiles analytics for the platform. I am sure other solutions will follow. As any new platform emerges, if they make their API available then third-party solutions like Rival IQ can extract data for analytics purposes. Other solutions that help manage and schedule posts also rely on API access. Soon people will be able to schedule posts to TikTok in advance like they do on Facebook, Instagram and Twitter.

While there is a lot of public data available, you won't be able to find out everything. You can learn whether or not your competitors are running paid campaigns on Facebook and what the likely budget range is, but you won't know how successful the campaigns were for raising awareness or how many conversions they achieved. It is still worth knowing so you can determine how often competitors are relying on paid campaigns to achieve their objectives.

How many platforms are your peers and competitors on and how active are they on each of them? Are some abandoned and, as a result, are left as ghost town accounts? What is the posting frequency on each of these platforms? What kind of content are they posting? Are they emphasizing one or more types of content over others? Do they post third-party content? If so, what is the proportion in relation to their own branded or corporate content?

Do they use influencers or evangelists? In what way and can you gauge how impactful they are? Do they currently or have they run contests or campaigns organically or with paid support? What kind of creative do they use for their paid campaigns? Static, animations or video? Can you find any data that suggests how successful their contests or campaigns were? Not all of your competitors and peers are going to be the same when it comes to social media activity. Some may be behind you and some considerably farther ahead. That is what benchmarking is all about. It gives you a sense of where and how you measure up.

Begin with the foundation – the audience. How big is the audience across each social platform for each of your peers and competitors? What kind of growth are they experiencing? Most analytics solutions have certain limits on historical data and, when it comes to audience data, they only begin compiling the data from the moment you configure the analysis. For example, Rival IQ can provide historical data for engagement and posting volume, but it only tracks audience growth data from the moment you configure the landscape for analysis.

It is more of a qualitative analysis type of thing, but it is worth looking at audience composition too, if possible. Solutions like Audiense enable analysis on the followers of Twitter accounts to see demographic, geographic and interest data. Demographic data is harder to find about competitive accounts for Facebook, LinkedIn and Instagram, but you can certainly compile broader demographic data from industry analysis sources.

Moving on to content, how much content are peers and competitors publishing? How often and in what form? Are they emphasizing rich media such as animation or video? Do they have a YouTube channel or a podcast? How often do they release podcast episodes or videos to YouTube? Is any content boosted? What kind of engagement occurs? This is where available data begins to explode. You can determine the top-performing content by channel, type, day, time and format for your competitors and peers. You can compare your efforts and inform your own approach with the insights you gather.

You can get granular insights too. You don't have to stop at just measuring likes. You can see all the different reactions the content generated. You can see how many views and/or clicks the content received and the number of impressions to gauge reach. You start getting a better sense of what you are up against. You can't expect to match or surpass the reach and engagement of your competition's content if you are not posting with the same or greater frequency, if you have a smaller audience and/or you are not putting some paid support behind at least some of the content.

The questions of best time to post and how frequently often come up and these are questions where analytics provide the answers. Fortunately or unfortunately, the analytics may provide answers that were not expected. Industry benchmark data can provide a general consensus of best times to post and frequency, but you will need to compile your own analysis. Your channels, time zones and audiences are not exactly the same as those on which the industry benchmarks were based. What happens for a global brand is likely not the same as what would happen for a lesser-known brand that perhaps only operates in one country.

Frequency and type of content are levers that you can continually push to find the right combination for optimal engagement and reach. For a long time, most said that posting once a day on LinkedIn before the beginning of the workday was sufficient. LinkedIn had provided posting guidance based on the fact that LinkedIn.com saw the highest traffic before the workday began. That meant before 9 am was optimal. After they introduced the iPad app, they discovered a second spike in site traffic in the evening when people were home from work and they were perusing LinkedIn and its content via the iPad app. A new app introduced new user behaviour.

We have also begun experimenting with posting on LinkedIn on weekends to see if visibility is greater on quieter days. Email marketers send emails on Sundays to increase the visibility of their emails in the recipient's inbox because they are foreseeably at or near the top of their inbox and are competing with fewer messages to be seen. By the time you are reading this, this could have already become a best practice.

Some say posting Monday, Wednesday and Friday on Instagram is sufficient while others try to work the algorithm in their favour by posting more frequently, even several times a day. It is going to be different for everyone. Test days and times with your audience. Look at impressions and engagement by day and time to see when your audience is responding to content and how each platform may be different.

Some Facebook pages, for example, can have multiple optimal times in a given day or only a few days during the week when they can really connect with their audience through content. Analysis will help determine days and times and whether or not posting more than once in a given day is worth it. However, analysis is not a 'one and done' type of thing. It has to be an ongoing process. As your audience grows, your reach will grow and engagement will change, possibly downward. Even days and times for optimal performance may change and you have to be prepared for it.

Examine your audience to see if it spans time zones. It may seem odd to schedule posts for when you are asleep but if part of your audience is awake and active then do not miss your window of opportunity to reach them. Be vigilant in reviewing your audience composition to ensure that you are delivering engaging content when they are ready to receive it. Try repeating some content but at different times to see if it gains any traction. I will say it again – 'Test and learn'.

We have been talking a lot about sharing content on particular days at optimal times. That is really about your typical weekly cadence for content but you will have times when campaigns and events warrant more emphasis and, therefore, get posted about more often in a short period of time. There is nothing wrong with that. People need to be reminded about an upcoming webinar or the release of your latest podcast episode. Even replays of webinars, live sessions on LinkedIn, Twitter, Instagram, Facebook or podcasts can drive more frequency of posting. Don't spam your audience. Optimize your efforts to get as much juice out of your content and visibility with your audience.

Analytics

Whether it is part of the overall social media strategy or part of your social media playbook, you will need to establish a standard approach to analytics. What are you analysing, when and for whom? There are a number of common metrics that span all of the social media platforms but each platform has some unique metrics too. You need to specify what metrics you are going to track and confirm with your stakeholders that those are the metrics they want to know.

If you measure too frequently then you can overwhelm yourself with data and end up with too much 'point in time' data rather than trends over time that would indicate progress towards your objectives. Live tweeting an event will generate an anomaly within your metrics for a day or more but should not be seen as indicative of your overall performance for the week or month that you might be measuring.

Conducting analysis for trends over time will hopefully illuminate more predictable behaviour from your audience and possibly new benchmark levels. Campaigns will come and go but is your baseline performance improving over time? Campaigns can help lift the baselines, but you cannot rely on them alone to get the job done. Consistent organic efforts are also required.

Working with one client, we established baseline and target KPIs at the outset of our social media support. We were handling organic social media activities while another agency was doing the paid campaigns. Before we began our support the social media accounts had been left dormant for quite some time. We brought them back to life and saw engagement grow. So much so that we had to revise our KPIs because we were trending ahead of our forecasts. This could happen to you too so be prepared to adjust your metrics and analysis.

In another instance, we had decided to set a channel to a 'maintain' status based on analysis that indicated that applying more effort would not dramatically improve its performance. We cut back on our activity on that channel but after a short time we started seeing signs of improved engagement with content. Now we are reconsidering whether the channel should stay on 'maintain' status or be switched back to a 'growth' channel.

It is not wrong to look at performance on a daily basis, but I would not recommend that you report on a daily basis. For some clients we give weekly highlights, especially for top and underperforming content or anything tied to events or campaigns. However, we typically provide reports on a monthly basis. Monthly reports provide enough information to suggest trends and we can do comparative analysis against the previous month.

In addition to the monthly reports, we often provide milestone reports on a quarterly basis or mid-year point depending on the needs of stakeholders. We also provide annual reports to show trends and impact over time. The longer the period of analysis the less of an impact anomalies such as campaigns and content dry spells have on overall metrics and performance. The holiday period in December or the quiet of summer can negatively impact content performance and audience engagement. Instead of analysing those periods alone, looking at the entire year provides a more valid perspective on what happened and potential changes to strategy.

Try to automate or streamline the process for reporting, especially if you are reporting on the same things every month. You may be asked by stakeholders to produce reports every month by a particular day within the month. Some of our clients want reports for the preceding month within the first 48 hours of the start of the next month. Others are fine with later in the month but they all notice if you miss a deliverable deadline. Standardized reporting can be helpful because stakeholders become accustomed to what is presented and you can delegate reporting to different people depending on capacity and availability.

Many social media management tools like Hootsuite or Sprout Social can provide analysis. No matter the tool, consider your requirements. You will be providing reports on a monthly basis so you want to make sure your chosen solution is up to that task and can help with automating some or all of the process. Additionally, you may need your chosen solution or another to provide ad-hoc analysis. If a stakeholder wants to know what content topic performed best on each channel for a given week or month, can you find that information?

Not all social media tools are created equal. You need to ensure that you can meet your monthly reporting requirements but also be able to identify more targeted insights for continuous learning. Monthly reporting rolls up the metrics for the month but you may also need to drill down within the data to parse it in such a way that you can determine the top-performing content and degree of audience engagement for a particular channel within a specific timeframe.

We hold a monthly metrics meeting with one particular client and over time the discussion is less and less about the previous month, as long as things are trending in a positive direction. Assuming that is the case, the discussion tends to move into more specifics. We get questions that warrant closer examination of certain metrics to satisfy the curiosity of our stakeholders. These questions are often driven by their own internal discussions around content and thought leadership and they want to see how those conversations align with social media results. They want to know where they should be focusing their attention and whether or not they should do more of some things and less of others. Deeper analysis can help inform their decisions.

No matter what metrics you are reporting on or when, make sure that they can be understood by the spectrum of stakeholders that may be receiving them. You are the social media expert and are closer to the data than they will ever be. Everyone is really busy in their workday lives so assume that they do not have a lot of time to review reports. You may not hold regular metrics meetings so reports alone may have to suffice for informing them of what happened. It is critical that the reports speak for themselves. Put a summary of highlights and noteworthy insights at the beginning of the report. That may be the only thing they read. Accept that.

Don't give them a 50-page document or 50- slide PowerPoint presentation. You can put some charts and supporting data in an appendix but assume that that section of the report will be seen as optional. Our monthly reports have only got shorter. In some cases, they are only one page, excluding a cover page. Sometimes the summary is in the email used to send the report as an attachment. The report may not even get read because the summary in the email is sufficient. Just give them the facts. What happened? What changed? What were the underlying causes? Any recommendations for the month ahead or in general? Explain it all in a jargon-free way, especially if you are not going to have the opportunity to review the report with stakeholders.

To recap, make sure you have the tools, team and standardized procedures in place to compile the metrics that you have committed to report on for stakeholders. Identify any gaps in your capabilities and seek additional resources and/or budget, where necessary, to meet your commitments. If you can't get additional budget or resources then inform stakeholders of what you can do with existing resources and capabilities to avoid any future disappointments.

ROI

We have talked a lot about stakeholders. They play a critical role in determining the return on investment (ROI) of social media. It isn't always going to be a black and white kind of thing. The ROI will not always be about how much money the investment of time and effort returned. It may be easier to think of it as a benefit. What kind of benefit did the organization and its stakeholders receive as a result of your social media efforts? As the social media manager, you may have your own thoughts on the ROI of social media but your stakeholders are going to tell you what is important to them. This may include what you prioritize for social media ROI but it can also include or be an entirely different set of priorities.

You may be focused on quantitative metrics such as conversions from social media posts that translate to referral traffic for your website while a stakeholder focused on the organization's brand is focused on awareness and the more qualitative metrics associated with that, such as share of voice and reach.

Your reporting may include qualitative and quantitative metrics to appease disparate stakeholders and interests. Do you need to report on social media ROI to every stakeholder or only to a select group of stake-holders? You will need to work with others within the organization to create a holistic picture of what is happening, not just with social media alone. You will need to know which actions you are taking in social media result in outcomes that are important to the organization. Is social media driving newsletter sign-ups, webinar registrations, content downloads, contact form completions or purchases?

More qualitative metrics such as sentiment or share of voice may not directly align with an outcome such as a purchase, but they are still impor-tant and something that certain stakeholders want to track. They may have committed to their leadership that share of voice would grow and that nega-tive sentiment would decline. Those are still outcomes they are striving to achieve and your social media reporting will provide insights regarding whether or not they are going to succeed. That is going to be their measure of ROI.

When the question of social media ROI comes up, I often respond at some point in the conversation with a few questions about current and historical marketing activities. I typically want to know activities have been tried and what efforts are currently being used. Further to that, I want to know what the results were and how performance is being measured now. Sometimes my questions are met with awkward silences or the responses are provided with caveats and explanations.

If your current marketing strategies are not being properly tracked and measured then it is an unfair burden to put on social media marketing to somehow be the marketing redemption being sought. Social media should complement and extend your current marketing efforts but not become the sole means of reaching your target audience. I only work in social media but would be the first one to say that email marketing, for example, is absolutely necessary as part of your marketing mix. Essentially, everyone has an email address but no single social media platform has the same level of penetra-tion as email.

A couple of my other favourite questions relate to lifetime customer value and cost of acquisition. Do you know or can you find out what a customer is worth to your organization? What does it typically cost to acquire a customer? Is the cost acceptable or is the objective to bring it down and, if that is the case, by how much?

We will get into paid campaigns and costs of acquisition next but don't forget to include the cost of your social media team and management tools to determine whether or not you are delivering value. If the social media team and subscriptions to analytics and management tools constitute thousands of dollars per month then how does that compare to the value being derived from social media every month for the organization?

Many people who oversee social media are doing more than social media so it may be hard to delineate between their other digital marketing activities and other responsibilities versus what is directly tied to social media. If the team is embedded in a broader digital marketing or communications team or department then the lines between activities and associated resource costs can get blurry.

Some organizations see social media as a necessary thing, a cost of doing business. This is exactly the situation when it comes to customer service, which can skew things towards a support cost rather than a profit centre. Measurement in those instances might relate to reduction in calls to your call centre because the support issues were resolved via social media. The public nature of social media means that the support issues of many can potentially be addressed with one tweet rather than one customer getting their concerns addressed in a one-on-one phone call with tech support. As you can see, there are a number of ways to look at the ROI of social media.

Paid

Paid campaigns can be their own unique situation with regards to ROI. They too can drive both qualitative and quantitative ROI. Awareness campaigns that are, as the name suggests, about raising awareness tend to focus on a 'top of the funnel' approach to introduce the organization to a new audience and spark interest before moving them along the customer journey closer to consideration and decision-making stages of their journey.

Look back at the case example of the mining company for whom we ran awareness campaigns using videos for the creative and targeting different audiences. The company had a story to tell and they wanted to tell it to a new audience. Impressions and reach showed awareness objectives being met, while video views and website visits were more by-products of the campaigns but valuable in their own right. Both outcomes correlated to increased online conversations and daily trading volume, stock price and market capitalization increases.

Conversion campaigns are more succinct in their objectives. They want specific and quantifiable outcomes. They want clicks. Clicks that mean something. Ideally, clicks that have a monetizable outcome. Did people click to learn more about something, to register for something or to make a purchase?

Can you show how many clicks the campaign achieved and what the outcome was? Do you have the appropriate campaign pixel in place to accumulate campaign data to leverage for retargeting in subsequent campaigns? Did you use UTM codes to distinguish paid campaigns from organic traffic? You need to be able to close the loop between your campaign efforts and outcomes happening on your website or other designated destinations.

We had a client that sold monthly subscriptions for prepared food. The retail value of the subscription was approximately $50/month or $600/year. We ran regular Facebook campaigns for hundreds of dollars. With even a modest budget for a campaign targeted at postal codes to raise awareness that delivery was now available in those areas, the campaigns were deemed successful. Hundreds of clicks happened through to the landing page to learn more about the subscription offering and only a few had to sign up to have made the campaigns profitable.

When it comes to paid campaigns, we most certainly measure the cost of acquisition like the example I just gave about the food subscription. However, paid campaigns can also acquire other things besides customers. Awareness campaigns about a product or service can indirectly acquire likes or followers. While they may not be customers immediately, they are now part of your audience or community and have expressed their affinity.

If you conduct multiple campaigns with the same or similar objectives then you will also want to track the campaign performance from the perspective of declining costs. You should see the costs per results (CPRs) decline over time if the campaigns are being optimized. Results could be likes, impressions, clicks or views or a combination of those. Ideally, you and your stakeholders previously agreed on which results were the most important and what budget you were prepared to allocate towards achieving those.

Costs for paid campaigns vary from platform to platform and you will have to decide which ones you want to allocate budget towards. A thousand dollar budget might go quite far on one platform while getting used up quickly on another platform. You will likely have to allocate different levels of budget based on each platform's requirements. We have found Facebook on its own or combined with Instagram to be a low-cost platform. Twitter, Snapchat and YouTube tend to come in a bit higher, depending on the type of campaign, while LinkedIn tends to be the most expensive platform. They justify the cost based on the sophisticated targeting they provide.

Emerging and growing platforms like TikTok, Triller or Poparazzi may offer lower-cost advertising opportunities as they establish their presence and business models. Being new means they can't expect the same fees for advertising that the other more established platforms expect. Sometimes trying to be a big fish in a small pond can be worth it if it means lower advertising costs. Having said that, you should vet every platform you are considering to ensure that they have users that are part of your target audience.

The ROI road ahead

You are going to be experimenting with social media, both organic and paid. You will need stakeholders to be patient. You are going to see some early successes and you are going to have some public failures. Some campaigns will knock it out of the park while others will be nothing but a budgetary drain. The pursuit of social media ROI has to be a long-term play.

Some campaigns, whether organic or paid, will be purely to learn what to do and what not to do. To learn which audiences are the most receptive and to what kind of content. All the different combinations and permutations of copy, creative and audience targets produce data from which you can learn. From there you can narrow your efforts to the best performing copy and creative targeted at the most receptive audiences. Rinse and repeat or, here is the broken record again: 'Test, measure and adjust'.

Case studies with permission from Rival IQ

Deloitte Digital

Deloitte Digital is a global, full-service design and digital agency, an arm of Deloitte started in 2011.

CHALLENGE
When Deloitte Digital starts a new project, the first step is to assess the digital landscape. A senior studio manager of technology uses this opportunity to engage executives in the audit and evaluation process for each new project. It's important for senior managers to be able to distil complex digital data, giving clients the most critical information to move forward.

SOLUTION

Deloitte Digital uses Rival IQ to:

- Audit social media performance of clients and competitors.
- Identify social media opportunities.
- Prove value of social media activities to clients.

  Using data to determine where to make social investments removes the guesswork.

  (Senior Studio Manager of Technology)

RESULTS

Deloitte Digital is able to capture the necessary data to prove the value or illustrate where not to invest. The data arms Deloitte Digital with the answers to questions from executives and sets the path for social success.

Stakeholders need insights in order to make informed decisions. Diving into data, sharing insights and helping stakeholders see the strategic value of social media will help to secure their support.

Canadian Olympic Committee

The Canadian Olympic Committee is responsible for all aspects of Canadian involvement in the Olympic Games. The digital team within the Canadian Olympic Committee oversees the fan experience, always ensuring the Team Canada brand is elevated and its athletes' stories are told. They engage Canadians globally, publishing a constant stream of content covering over 500 athletes worldwide.

CHALLENGE

In 2014, the digital team needed to understand their competition. As social media emerged as a critical component of sponsorship proposals, as well as a growing method for engaging Canadian fans, the Committee wanted to benchmark themselves against other sources of information on Olympic athletes.

SOLUTION

The digital team produces content at an impressive rate. The volume of content combined with the need to move quickly means it is critical for them to invest in content that performs well. The team measures itself by the level of fan engagement.

Each month they take time to review reports that show what's worked and what hasn't, comparing performance against large brands, Canadian media outlets and other national Olympic teams.

While the team knows to focus their effort on what's entertaining and exciting, there's more nuance to what they create and share. With Rival IQ the team is able to determine how to engage the maximum number of Canadians inside and outside the Games. But the team doesn't stop with engagement.

The team is able to translate that engagement metric into real ROI by turning social followers into fan club members. The fan club, Canadian Olympic Club, gives fans an even deeper look into the run-up to the Olympics, along with rewards and recognition. Each week top fans rise up the leader board and are recognized.

RESULTS

The digital team has used the insights to place themselves at the top of social media. They lead national Olympic teams globally with the highest engagement per capita. Each year they move the needle significantly on their engagement, most recently increasing Facebook and Twitter engagement rates by over 300 per cent.

07

Employee advocacy
and personal branding

According to LinkedIn, the **employee advocacy definition** is quite simple: it is the promotion of your company by the people who work for it. People **advocate** for their employers on social media all the time.

We have mentioned the idea of employee advocacy previously, but we are going to take a closer look at it here. Increasingly, employers are relying on employees and their social graphs to extend the reach of their brand and leverage their trusted relationships to garner trust for the organization too.

We will look at other benefits, both qualitative and quantitative, that can be derived from an employee advocacy program for an organization and its employees. We will also share statistics that prove the impact of such programs to the bottom line, an organization's brand reputation and employee engagement.

Similar to what we described in Chapter 5, turning employees into advocates will depend greatly on their familiarity with social media and their related sharing habits. Those that grew up not knowing a world without digital will find it quite easy to incorporate advocacy efforts into their workday. Employees who did not grow up digitally but adopted social media and digital technologies over time may need additional training and support but will likely comprise a substantial portion of your advocacy group. Finally, the digital naysayers or resistors to social media may take up more cycles than they are worth.

The first two groups will likely provide enough amplified reach through their respective social networks to help the organization achieve its brand awareness and reach objectives. It could also do wonders for the employer brand and recruiting if people come to learn more about the corporate culture and what a day in the life of an employee feels like.

It's about change

Similar, again, to the chapter on training, advocacy is about change. Some employees will have already identified themselves as natural advocates. Others will have to be convinced, and some will continue to treat their role as putting in a day's work, taking home a salary in return and nothing more.

If you want to roll out an employee advocacy program then you are going to need to build a business case to win over stakeholders. You will also need to support your efforts with training and a clear social media policy if you are going to be encouraging employees to increase their social media activity both during and after office hours. Asking them to speak for you has risks that need to be mitigated and you want to give them confidence that you are looking out for their best interests and to protect them from making missteps too.

According to LinkedIn, the average number of connections per regular user is 400. According to Pew Research,[1] the average number of friends per user on Facebook is approximately 350. Every follower a company has on

FIGURE 7.1 Employee advocacy vs brand page reach

SOURCE Used with permission from Sprout Social

their social accounts is hard won but the relationships people have with brands are quite different to the relationships they have with people. Rarely can brands achieve the kind of reach that surpasses that of a group of its employees and their own personal social connections unless you are a global brand on the level of a brand like Apple or Coca-Cola.

The example from Sprout Social (Figure 7.1) shows how a group of 135 employees and their personal relationships can achieve the same or greater reach than a Facebook page with 1 million fans.

Employee advocacy programs are intent on extracting value from those personal relationships for the benefit of the brand. While that may sound disingenuous, the relationship you have with a brand is more likely through a person rather than the brand itself. Someone in sales or customer service treated you well and made your experience with the brand they represent a positive one. These interactions are more meaningful and therefore more valuable to you.

If employees are to become advocates then they need to feel comfortable and confident in what they are being asked to do and share. It should never feel pushed upon them or that they are being ordered to do something. An employee advocacy program should be an opt-in kind of program and one that they can opt out of if they decide to do so later on. Employees are allowing themselves to be conduits for corporate objectives, and they should not feel like they are being exploited for those purposes.

A lot of concerns about employee advocacy programs and the anticipated changes within the organization can be addressed by preparing a thorough business case and supporting information that explains the benefits of such programs to the organization and to the employees. Err on the side of over-communicating and anticipating potential questions and concerns.

While employees, obviously, are at the core of any employee advocacy program, leveraging their social relationships for extended brand reach is not the sole purpose or benefit of such programs. The programs help to establish the aforementioned employer brand and potentially lower recruiting costs. Marketing distribution costs can decrease as more employees share content to their respective personal networks, thus reducing or eliminating the need for paid campaigns to achieve the same distribution levels. Showing the cost of historical marketing efforts, including content distribution versus potential savings through an employee advocacy program, should be part of your business case.

Some of the more qualitative benefits of an employee advocacy program include increased employee engagement. Think about the employees that already show their affinity for the corporate brand. An advocacy program makes for a logical extension of that affinity. Some employee advocacy solutions go so far as to include gamification features to reward employees for their efforts and expressions of brand affinity. Could your organization benefit from making things a bit more competitive and gamified?

We have already discussed the trusted relationships between employees and their social connections but, beyond seeing employees as conduits for content distribution, what if some of them could become thought leaders in their respective areas of expertise? Then it is not just the organization pushing its position but a collective of thought leaders building trust and authority. Furthermore, employees can speak in a more accessible, albeit human, way than the organization. They can tell specific people why they should look at or read something, because they know first-hand what the relevance of the content is to them. Talk about credibility and trust.

Humanity is a word that is often used to describe the value that social media can provide organizations. However, conveying humanity and being humane requires that humans are the ones doing it. Employees as advocates are participating in human-to-human interactions. Organizations can't replicate those interactions. They have to rely on their employees to represent them and establish trusted relationships based on thought leadership, industry authority and subject matter expertise.

Legal and compliance

If your organization operates in regulated industries and/or is required to have any social media vetted by legal or compliance then your employee advocacy program is going to face some impediments, not insurmountable ones, but impediments just the same. There are a number of different compliance solutions available that enable organizations and their employees to post to social media while still remaining compliant. We are not going to discuss the different solutions by name, but we will explain generally how they work. A list of solutions will be provided in the resources section of the book and online.

Generally, and as described briefly before, compliance solutions act as an intermediary or middle layer between the user wishing to post and the social media platform where the post ends up being published. For example, a financial advisor may wish to share an article about investment tips. If the article has not been approved by compliance and made available within the content library of the compliance solution then, when the advisor goes to click publish, it will be rejected and they will be prompted to seek approval.

Scaling employee advocacy programs in these types of circumstances means that someone or some people are going to have to develop a way to curate and approve content at scale to keep a library of pre-approved content available to employees to draw from for their own social accounts without risking being non-compliant.

Compliance solutions are not free and can vary from modestly priced to very expensive. If your organization is too small or lacks budget then you may want to consider leveraging something like the notification function on LinkedIn company pages that enables you to notify employees once per day about content available to share. This functionality works for organizations that are not constrained by compliance issues, but if you are looking for a way to push approved content to employees then LinkedIn's notification function has you covered.

Personal branding

What does personal branding have to do with employee advocacy? Well, it is actually quite simple. The stronger the personal brand that someone has the stronger and more visible employee advocate they will likely be. People with strong personal brands in the digital sphere will be easy to identify. Helping others elevate their personal brand will be a bit more challenging but still something that is within the realm of possibility.

I worked with numerous sales and marketing teams, financial advisors, mortgage specialists and executives about leveraging social media for their personal brand and to help them achieve their business objectives. I am often brought in by their management to show them where and how they can establish and build their personal brand and make valuable connections.

As part of this chapter and to increase the likelihood of your program's success, I thought it made sense to include a section on personal branding to help you, to help you help your colleagues and to help organizations encourage personal branding among their employees.

This information could also be helpful to anyone from marketing or communications tasked with positioning members of their executive team or other key employees as thought leaders. Organizations are increasingly using their LinkedIn profiles as platforms for key corporate messages and to convey their expertise. Social CEOs help companies build brand trust. Unfortunately, they are busy executives with little time to work on their profiles or share content so they must rely on the support of their marcom teams. I have worked with C-suite executives regarding their LinkedIn profiles and, while we focused on their profiles, they often were going to be relying on marcom teams for the content that would be shared through their profiles.

The following is a series of recommendations and tips that can be applied to LinkedIn and other social media platforms. I am writing this from the perspective of instructing you as an individual but you can share with your colleagues and other stakeholders, including members of your organization's executive team, and even use it as part of your training curriculum if you see fit.

LinkedIn

There is a saying that goes something like this – 'If you are not on LinkedIn then you don't exist.' I have to say that if I look for someone on LinkedIn and I can't find them then I get a little suspicious. Forget the myth that LinkedIn is only valuable if you are looking for a job. There is so much more value to be derived from it if you simply know more about how to make the most of your presence.

PASSIVE

When it comes to LinkedIn, I want you to think about it from two perspectives. First, is the passive perspective. This is how you present yourself to the rest of LinkedIn. What will people see and learn from visiting your personal profile? How can it passively work on your behalf once you have set up your profile properly and with optimization in mind? Let's look at that more closely.

We talked about benchmarking previously and it also has a role to play with your LinkedIn profile. You may not have heard of it but LinkedIn provides a social selling index or SSI score (see www.linkedin.com/sales/ssi). While it has the word 'selling' in its name, I think that that is a bit of a misnomer. It really isn't a measure of how good a salesperson you are but, more importantly, how well you are using LinkedIn.

It measures you on how well you have established your professional brand, find the right people, engage with insights and build relationships. If you have never seen your score before then do not give it too much credence. If your activity on LinkedIn is intermittent at best, then it will be reflected in your SSI score. Don't feel embarrassed or disappointed if your score is low. The objective is to use your score as a starting point or benchmark. The only way to go is up.

Keep in mind that you may have higher scores on one or more of the four key metrics but likely not across all of them. That is okay. Look at where you need to improve and develop a plan of action. You won't have to devote hours to this, but you can't expect to improve your score if you don't take any action at all either.

Establishing your professional brand is the key metric from the SSI score that aligns with your passive approach to personal branding. Let's review the key components of a LinkedIn profile and what you can do to optimize it to support your professional brand. Start thinking about your profile as the most media rich business card you could ever have. Also, while it should match your résumé in terms of roles and timelines, your profile should not just be a copy and paste of your résumé. It has to provide more information and more value to visitors. It will all make sense as you read on.

STARTING AT THE TOP

The first things that people see when they arrive on your LinkedIn profile are the banner image, if there is one, your headshot and your headline. Let's look at each of them and their importance in greater detail.

Most people give little to no consideration to the banner image on their LinkedIn profile. It is a missed opportunity. Putting something there instead of the default image costs nothing but could mean everything. Before writing this book, my banner image was a collection of images showing me on stage speaking to hundreds of people. It made it clear to anyone visiting my profile that I was a thought leader and that I speak at conferences as part of the work that I do. By the time you are reading this, I will have changed the banner image to one that includes an image of the cover of this book, again, to illustrate my thought leadership and my subject matter expertise.

What would you want your banner image to say about you? I worked with one executive that chose an image that conveyed his belief in collaborative and diverse teams. Think about some of your work-related philosophies and beliefs for inspiration. Your employer may suggest some standardized

FIGURE 7.2 SSI score Part I

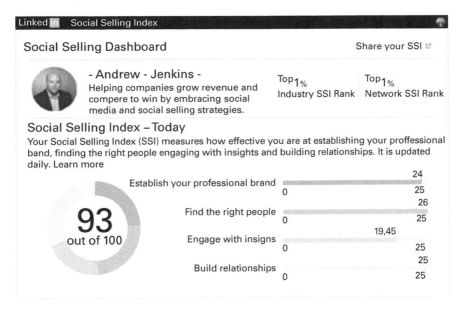

SOURCE Andrew Jenkins

FIGURE 7.3 SSI score Part II

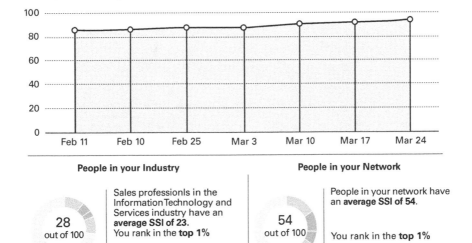

SOURCE Andrew Jenkins

branded images for employee use. Use them if appropriate. It will certainly help convey a unified message.

Working our way down we come to the headshot. There is a lot that can be said here but let me begin by saying that no headshot is never a good idea. LinkedIn shared a blog and supporting video about how to shoot a decent headshot with your smartphone against a neutral background in natural light. Don't be lazy. LinkedIn makes it easy for you.

If you have the opportunity to get a professional headshot done then take it. People check out your profile ahead of meetings and conference calls so make sure your picture is up to date. Avoid using pictures from places outside of work or from events. You might have looked really good at that wedding or holiday party but we can tell where you were and if you have cut other people out of the picture. Avoid pictures where you are too far from the camera to the point where it is difficult to identify that it is you in the picture. This may sound odd but avoid silly pictures or images where you are trying to be funny. This isn't Facebook. I can't tell you the number of headshots of people on vacation or in scuba gear that I have seen. This is about putting your best professional foot forward.

It makes perfect sense to include your job title as your headline but why stop there? Consider adding to it. Think about your areas of expertise. What kind of value proposition can you convey about yourself? When you comment on someone's post on LinkedIn, your headline is visible when people see your comment so why not have a headline that helps you stand out? LinkedIn provides you with 220 characters for your headline so why not make the most of them? You can still include your job title but build on that. Who do you help and how do you help them? What do people know you for in terms of experience and knowledge? You don't have to figure it out right away. Look at other profiles for inspiration and give thought to what you want to say.

These recommendations, and the ones to follow, are not meant to add unnecessary pressure. They are merely recommendations for you to consider and implement if you choose when appropriate. The recommendations do not have to be implemented all at once. Your profile should be seen as a living document that can be changed over time and with regularity. I use the metaphor of building a house when I refer to my LinkedIn profile. I built a house over 15 years ago and I have been adding to the house ever since. I have renovated the interior. I have added additions in key areas. I have landscaped and put a new roof on too. You get the idea.

The key is to build a profile, if you do not have one, or, if you do, then to do some quick and easy improvements to turn it into a profile that can deliver more value to you and your personal brand. Even making just those few changes to your banner, headshot and headline can have tremendous impact. Most people do not even make those changes so think about how much stronger your profile could be with just a few small edits or additions. You just have to get started.

ABOUT SECTION

As we work our way down from the banner image, headshot and headline, we come to the About section. This is the section that will take the most time to work on. I do not say that to scare anyone. It is simply that people find this a particularly challenging section of their profile to work on because most people are uncomfortable talking about themselves. They also find it difficult to figure out what to say because this section is more than a bio section from a résumé.

The About section should be used to provide an overview of work experience, expertise and to stitch together the story of your career. It should emphasize accomplishments rather than responsibilities alone. One important thing to remember is that it should be written in the first person. You are not being introduced by someone else so speak directly to the reader. Think about what you can or should say in the first three lines to attract their attention because that is all the text that LinkedIn displays before the 'see more' link. You need to hook the reader.

Behind the 'see more' link you can expand your story, invite people to connect and list skills, experience and interests that, from a key word perspective, might help you get found via LinkedIn search. You can be more human, perhaps even a bit vulnerable, in your About section. Some people talk about their goals, career philosophies, and who they will and will not connect with on LinkedIn and why.

I like to tell people to imagine their About section going to a networking event on their behalf and to think about what it would say and how it would say it. Your primary goal on LinkedIn is not to get a job but to make valuable connections. That might lead to a job but, as Jon Ferrara of Nimble CRM likes to say, 'Your network is your net worth', so focus on connecting that you can nurture into relationships.

Consider adding media to your About section such as links to videos, podcasts, presentations, etc. This will help make your profile stickier to visitors. Add media to your roles, where appropriate, and without breaching confidentiality. We can tell a lot about ourselves and our work with rich media so take advantage of it and use it to differentiate yourself. If you are involved in your organization's employee advocacy program then provide approved media to employees to add to their profiles, such as corporate presentations and videos, to extend the reach of your corporate content.

HACK YOUR PROFILE

People are more than one thing and often more than one role. LinkedIn limits the number of characters you can use to each role. I hacked my profile by creating a second role for myself at my company. My first role is that of CEO. I added a second role as speaker and panellist. By adding a second role, I was able to list the many conferences where I have spoken or been a panellist. I was also able to add media such as videos, presentations and pictures of me presenting. Visitors to my profile receive content, see social proof of the work that I do and get confirmation that I am a thought leader. What if more people hacked their profiles?

We are more than our résumé, which means, while your LinkedIn profile should match the chronology and facts of your résumé, it can be so much more than that. Be creative and bold. Leverage the features of the platform. Don't just react to content with a like. Share and comment regularly. LinkedIn suggests posting content at least four times a week. Can you handle that?

CONTENT OVER CONNECTION

For a long time, people put emphasis on acquiring connections and actively promoted the number of connections they had achieved. If you have ever heard of the acronym LION then you already know what I am talking about. For those of you who do not know what I am talking about, it stands for LinkedIn Open Networker and people openly displayed the acronym on their profile.

Unfortunately, such behaviour led to people connecting with people randomly and with little to no screening process. They got thousands of connections but no network. These connections were not people they could rely on for anything. They were essentially valueless.

LinkedIn has discouraged being a LION but couldn't really stop it. In an effort to influence a change in behaviour, LinkedIn is emphasizing content and engagement over connections more and more. As part of that effort, they introduced Creator Mode for individual profiles. This mode puts an emphasis on content and encourages people to *follow* you rather than connect with you to see your content more readily. While people can still connect with you, the focus is on following you, assuming you will devote your time and energy to building a following for your content. The goal seems to be higher engagement reflected in comments and following rather than lower quality engagement in the form of likes and reactions.

That means pressure to produce content that engages, informs and educates. It also means producing content with enough volume and frequency that establishes and grows a following. Despite that pressure to produce content, this seems like a logical next stage for LinkedIn to help facilitate personal branding and employee advocacy.

By the time this book is published, Creator Mode will be nearly a year old. It will be interesting to see the level of adoption amongst LinkedIn members. I don't think everyone will become creators but the people who are already sharing content naturally will likely find it to be an easy transition.

This decreasing emphasis on likes and other vanity metrics is not just happening with LinkedIn. Instagram has enabled users to hide likes on posts to remove social pressure. One platform that is emerging at the time of writing this book is Polywork, a hybrid social media platform that seems to be amalgamating the professional elements of LinkedIn with the personal interests of Twitter and other social platforms. They have deliberately chosen not to display likes or followers to avoid repeating the same mistakes as other social media platforms in the past.

After all, if you are focused on likes you are focused on the wrong things. A like takes so little energy or effort to give. It is just a click. Engaging people to the degree that they willingly comment or, if you are so lucky, sharing it with the comments encouraging people to check out your content is what you should be striving for. It's the social proof.

Jay Baer asks 'Is your content so good that people would be willing to pay for it?' Well, is it? If it isn't then what do you need to do to change that? Personal branding and especially your employee advocacy program will be founded on content. You can't expect to succeed if you cut corners or you are inconsistent. It is going to be a daily commitment. Are you or your organization prepared for that kind of commitment?

Planning, delegation and technology can help but only to a point. Break content down into categories such as curated and created and then further subcategories within those that include time bound and evergreen. Give greater emphasis to curated third-party content so you are not always talking about yourself but potentially amplifying the content of others who will reciprocate when it comes to your content.

It will take a bit of effort but leverage trending or timely content that will help establish you or your organization as a trusted source of current news or information. Finally, use evergreen content from your library to avoid the 'one and done' syndrome that so often happens with content. Extend the shelf life of your content and keep it in rotation as long as it is still relevant. You went to the trouble of creating it so squeeze as much out of it as possible.

Podcasting is on the rise and may be part of your content efforts but research from Buzzsumo would suggest that podcasts are not evergreen content and their relevance will expire. Depending on the topic and the guests, you might stretch things a bit but not forever. This means that you have to plan podcasts for the long term. We are talking years, not months. Are you up to it? Look no further than your favourite podcast apps to see all the original podcasts that gave up.

Whether you love him or hate him, Joe Rogan's podcast began over a decade ago as a way for him to hang out and chat with his buddies. No monetization plan. Just conversation. Fast forward to today and he signed a $100 million deal with Spotify. Dax Shepard with his Armchair Expert Podcast has moved to Spotify as well in an exclusive deal. It didn't take a decade but it still took him several years. No shortcuts.

WHAT IS IT GOING TO TAKE?

Social media is not something that you start today and success follows tomorrow. We typically tell clients to expect four to six months before they will see signs of success and impact. That takes patience. Employee advocacy means change and that takes time. Employees have to be convinced and gradually adopt the target behaviour. Training will be required and celebrating early wins amongst peers and colleagues will help build momentum.

In show business they talk about taking decades to become an overnight success. The same can be said of your personal brand. Maybe not decades but not months either. Time, effort, consistency and content will be required. Take your foot off the gas and it will take longer to get to your destination but that does not mean the opposite either where you put the pedal to the floor, and you get there faster.

There is an element of subjectivity that can't be ignored, especially when it comes to content. You are going to be experimenting with content themes and formats to see what resonates with your audience. That can change over time, so you have to ensure you do not become complacent with your content and get into a content rut.

Two of the biggest challenges we have seen when it comes to getting employees to share content is forming the habit because of time constraints and having a steady stream of content. Anything that can be done to remove friction to get content into the hands of employees and make it as simple as possible to share will go a long way to ensuring the success of your employee advocacy program.

Planning that includes a content calendar will help you stay organized as your program rolls out and is managed on an ongoing basis. Populate it with third-party content, evergreen and timely content, leaving some slack for in the moment content too. The goal is to have a library to draw from and distribute amongst employees. They won't ask you for content and only a select few might recommend content so you must do most of the heavy lifting. It isn't particularly complicated but is hard work that takes time. Be patient and persistent and you will start to see signs of progress towards your goal. Rome wasn't built in a day, nor would it have been even if they had Twitter.

Endnote

1   Aaron Smith. What people like and dislike about Facebook, Pew Research Centre, 3 February 2014, www.pewresearch.org/fact-tank/2014/02/03/what-people-like-dislike-about-facebook/ (archived at https://perma.cc/YE8D-MC53)

08

In-house or outsource

Organizations regularly face the dilemma of deciding whether to build social media capabilities in-house or outsource support to an external vendor. In this chapter we will look at the pros and cons of each. There is no single clear choice. The decision an organization makes will depend on their current circumstances, needs and near-term objectives.

We often work with clients who need help with social media in the early stages of their business but over time they build their team and that includes social media resources. Others elect never to staff up and invest in other areas of their business. Neither situation is more correct than the other. It is simply a matter of choosing the right path for them at the time.

Let's start with the pros and cons of building and maintaining social media activities in-house. Considerations will change as an organization grows and matures. We will look at the different stages and the implications for keeping things in-house or outsourcing some or all of social media management.

Considerations

Before you decide what to do, there are a number of considerations that need to be considered. There are good reasons to do things in-house but there are also good reasons to outsource. You need to think about your current situation and your plans for the future. Your needs now are likely different from your needs in the future. That will most certainly have some bearing on your decision.

Situational analysis

CURRENT AND FUTURE

What is the current state of your marketing? Are you at a point of inflection or pivot point? Are things like your brand well established? What kind of marketing are you doing now? What elements will you be adding and in what timeframe? Are you just getting started, at least with social media? What kind of resources do you have in place? What stakeholders do they support?

Starting social media marketing from scratch will require more effort upfront, including paid. This will have implications for resourcing. Are you adding new channels, content types or tactics? Some things may be required on an ongoing basis while others may be needed for a point in time.

How far is your organization from its long-term marketing objectives? What are some near-term milestones being pursued? What has worked thus far? What changes are being made? Is there a clear sense of what success will look like? Has a budget been established? A business case made? If not, are you being tasked with either of those? If either or both exist then are they sufficient?

CAPABILITY

Have you conducted a skills audit of your existing resources? If there is a skills gap, can training be applied to close the gap with existing resources in time to execute? What resources will you need on an ongoing basis versus part-time or for a specific task or project that will end?

Skills can be acquired through training but you can't shortcut experience. How much experience do you have collectively amongst your team? Would you describe any of them, including yourself, as experts? If there is any expertise then what is it? Strategy? Content? Graphic design? Video? Podcasting? Social media listening? Facebook, LinkedIn, Twitter, Instagram, Snapchat, Pinterest, TikTok, YouTube? Some of them or all of them?

It is unlikely that you will find one or more people with subject matter expertise in every aspect of social media marketing. That Swiss Army knife of an expert likely doesn't exist. You are going to have to prioritize what expertise you want to hire or develop internally and what you might want to contract.

How quickly do you need to be executing? Are you conducting an audit and competitive analysis before you get rolling? What kind of ongoing activities such as analysis and reporting do you envision? What kind of content do you need to create? How much and how often?

COST

Later in this chapter we discuss the cost implications of an employee versus a contractor. For now, I want to discuss other cost elements to be considered when it comes to building versus buying social media capabilities.

Social media takes more than just people. No matter whether staff or contractors, they need tools to create and distribute content. They need to be able to monitor for brand mentions and listen for actionable insights stemming from online conversations. They need to be able to schedule posts and analyse the results of their efforts.

Your social media efforts can't scale without tools to help automate some of the time-consuming and repetitive tasks. What kind of tools do you already have in place and what are you being asked to find a budget for? Basically, what does your tech stack look like now compared to what you want to have in the future? Can you afford it? Are you better served buying partial access to some tools through an external vendor who is bearing the entire cost?

Beware the bright new and shiny social media tool. It may be more than you need. You may not be able to make a sufficient case for its use. Perhaps your current or future social media activities are just not at the level to justify the investment in one or more of the tools being considered. You also have to consider whether you are building a toolkit filled with a collection of task-specific tools or trying to find one enterprise solution that covers the majority of your needs. The former can become costly because you are dealing with disparate vendors but you can also negotiate with each vendor independently and potentially drive costs down. Enterprise solutions can be played off of each other to drive costs down, but the mere fact that they are being referred to as enterprise can set pricing at higher levels from the very beginning.

In-house

Why?

BRAND VOICE

Organizations devote a lot of time and effort to establish and build their brand. There is a long-held position that you cannot outsource your brand voice. While this can be argued, organizations are well within their rights to want to manage social media in-house as a means of protecting their brand and eliminating the risk of external vendors getting the tone wrong.

CONTROL

Beyond controlling brand voice and tone, having control over your organization's online presence can be seen as good governance. Numerous organizations have found themselves locked out of their own social accounts because their vendor did not ensure that the client had access to their own accounts. If the client–vendor relationship sours then there is a risk that access can be lost.

Furthermore, control isn't just about access to accounts. You are closer to the strategy and expected outcomes than an external vendor. Accountability is a priority and that can put added pressure on you to ensure your social media efforts are being applied correctly. While external vendors are expected to deliver, they don't always feel accountability to the same degree as you might.

Your accountability will be to the execution of the social media strategy and expected outcomes. Identify what you have and need internally to properly execute the strategy. Determine what you will need on an ongoing basis versus what you may need on an ad hoc basis. You may not always need to be doing paid social media, videos, graphics or blogs so you may consider outsourcing some or all of those things but keep the day-to-day activities within the organization. No sense in having resources idle if you can bring them in on an as-needed basis.

PROPRIETARY INFORMATION

External vendors are not always privy to all of the information that flows within an organization, which means more demands on the client to share information, where applicable, to help the vendor support them. You have to help them help you which means work and would seem counterproductive. You can't help but feel that it would have been easier to have tasked a colleague who already has sufficient familiarity with the organization and its needs and objectives.

Even if a non-disclosure agreement is in place, it does not always mean that the vendor has all the information they need to support you. Often, they are left out of communication threads and this can impact their ability to support you. It can slow things down because there is more back and forth between client and vendor to share information and ensure clarity of expectations.

You also need to make sure that the vendor can manage confidential information properly. They may be privy to confidential information that could affect a company's stock price and/or reputation. What if they do not have proper governance protocols in place? Can you afford to take that reputational or compliance risk?

EFFICIENCY

Beyond the potential impediments related to information flow, outsourcing can also give rise to inefficiencies. Think of the game of telephone where the further a person is from the original message the more likely they are to get it wrong. A vendor is an outsider and is somewhat removed from the day-to-day operations of the organization. They are not exactly another cog in the same machine so they do not have the benefit of being embedded in the process.

You can't yell a question to a vendor down the hall or over the cubicle wall. You can't message them through Slack unless you want to set up a vendor on some of your internal communications channels. Do you want to go so far as to give them a corporate email address? How much do you want them to be like an employee and how do they feel about that? You can see where and how things can get bogged down.

INTEGRATION

Your social media resources may have other responsibilities. Perhaps they will wear many hats. They may be part of marketing, communications or digital marketing. Regardless, they are embedded or integrated into the organization and can collaborate directly with key stakeholders.

This can prove to be advantageous, especially when there are a lot of people involved and lots of moving parts. If a number of people are involved in content creation, including copy and design, and the approval process then having in-house resources can be beneficial to the organization. If changes are required then it can make for a quick turnaround. Vendors may not be able to provide the same turnaround time.

SCALE

Social media should be just one part of your overall marketing strategy and, as such, may not require full-time resources. If you are already actively dealing with digital marketing activities such as SEO/SEM, email, keeping your website up to date and social media then you may find that one or more people with a multitude of digital marketing skills and experience that includes social media will be enough.

If you are just getting started with social media and/or your posting and content production volume isn't too heavy then you may not need dedicated resources for a while. Managing just a few channels with a post or two per day is much easier to manage than producing weekly blogs, podcasts, YouTube videos and all the related promotion. With proper planning and supporting tools, a lot can be accomplished with a little. However, if your social media activity increases then you may have to consider more dedicated resources.

HISTORICAL KNOWLEDGE

If you have invested in training staff and explained the organization's mission, vision and values then, assuming they stay, you do not have to keep onboarding them like you might with resources from an external vendor that can change from time to time and account to account. Your staff are the keepers of the message, which can help keep social media tied properly to the brand.

Vendors can become familiar with your organization but only at a surface level or a bit deeper but likely not to the same degree as staff. They are not embedded to the point of being tied to the culture via osmosis. It is not something that can be replicated with external parties if that is a must for your brand.

COST

You are going to want to talk to finance or accounting to be certain about the implications of employees versus external vendors or contractors. There can be some financial advantages to hiring rather than contracting.

Contractors can charge you a premium because you are not paying them like an employee with benefits. Furthermore, they may have other costs being incurred to service your needs so they may embed those costs and pass them along to you.

Employees can potentially be a bit cheaper on paper excluding benefits, training and supporting resources like computers and software. Be sure to confer with finance or accounting to make an informed decision and build the proper business case depending on the direction you take.

Outsource

Why?

BRAND VOICE

Worrying about an external agency getting your brand voice is a legitimate concern but it isn't insurmountable. Agencies work with companies all the time to build and extend their brand. The key is to communicate. Provide extensive briefs and err on the side of over communicating by providing lots of feedback and input. Ironically, external agencies are often the ones who write the brand guidelines and briefs for internal stakeholders and external partners.

While you may still feel that external partners will never know your brand to the same degree as you, they should know it well enough to devise a social media strategy under your oversight that will be sufficiently on brand. After all, they have done it with other clients, assuming this isn't their first engagement.

CONTROL

Assuming you have instituted proper governance then you shouldn't have any real concerns about control. An external agency can have access to your social media accounts but should not have a level of control where they could deny you access to your own accounts. Ensure login credentials are kept in a centralized location so that more than one internal resource has access to them.

In the case of LinkedIn and Facebook, ensure that no one from the agency has administrative privileges that supersede anyone else's from your organization. Ideally, you want their admin rights to be subordinate to your organization, but there may be times when they will have to be on par with yours. The key is to make sure that you have at least a couple of representatives from your organization listed as administrators.

EXPERTISE

You might very well be an expert when it comes to social media but you are likely involved in a number of areas and, even if you are solely focused on social media, you can't do it alone. You likely need help. Getting external expertise, especially in areas where you may be lacking in knowledge or experience, will certainly prove helpful.

External agencies pride themselves on staying abreast of the changing social media landscape and maintaining subject matter expertise. They make it their job to stay on top of things while you may not have the time or inclination to do so. In some cases, they have direct relationships with the major platforms and can leverage those relationships to ensure your social media strategy is based on the latest best practices and recommendations.

I speak with Facebook regularly and review different client campaigns to ensure they are designed optimally and make any necessary adjustments. I also bring the learnings and insights back to clients so they see the value begin delivered and our expertise being validated.

We focus solely on social media, for good reason. There is enough to worry about just with social media. There are new apps, changes and updates to existing ones, platform updates and changes regarding advertising. It is hard for us to stay on top of it all and this is what we do for a living.

Expertise just isn't about the social platforms and related strategies. Now you have to be an expert on Facebook's ad manager, how to use Canva for graphic design and be versed in Boolean queries for your social media listening. It is hard to find all of that in one person, which is where external agencies can play a role with their team of experts.

Agencies like us invest heavily in tools and technology to serve customers and they keep up to date with the latest capabilities of those tools. A number of our vendors have customer success representatives who work with us to make sure we are getting the most from their solution. This makes us more productive and more loyal.

EFFICIENCY

As mentioned previously, you are busy and have to manage multiple tasks and stakeholders. Being able to delegate to both internal and external resources makes things more efficient. Ultimately, it all rolls up to you but that does not mean you have to be involved in the 'doing'. You most certainly will oversee the development of the social media strategy and its execution but you won't necessarily be tasked with building the ad within Facebook's ad manager.

You will want to define a workflow between internal and external resources and make sure everyone knows who is responsible for what. For example, who will be responsible for presenting performance metrics to key stakeholders? Will the agency provide the information and brief you in order for you to present? Will they present instead? Maybe it will be a hybrid where you present and agency representatives join you as backup and to provide colour to the information being presented.

INTEGRATION

If you have a solution already in place like Slack, Microsoft Teams, Trello, Basecamp or Asana then consider providing limited access for your external agency to help with communications, tasks, deliverables and due dates. Make it an integrated or collaborative relationship. It will go a long way towards your mutual success.

With some of our clients, we even have our own corporate emails so that we are on the same calendar and can better communicate with internal stakeholders. You may not feel the need to go that far but it is worth consideration because you may run into issues where your IT policies make it difficult to do certain things involving external agencies.

Some clients have created generic emails specific to social media activities and we access the accounts that way or via password managers like Lastpass or Dashlane to maintain good governance. These are all things you may want to consider or have in place before you engage an external agency.

Typically, external agencies are just that – external. However, there may be situations where one or more resources may work directly with you on site. If that is the case then how often might that occur and are there any implications related to such things as facility access and security?

We assume that you would already have the basics like a non-disclosure agreement in place but if you are going to have an external agency or consulting resources working with you or other internal resources at your location then what will be required to make that work?

When I consulted with one of Canada's largest banks, I had to have a thorough background check beforehand. I worked on site with a security pass to access the building, a corporate email, a corporate-issued computer and a corporate-issued phone. That is how embedded I was within the organization. That may be taking things to an extreme, but you will need to consider what will work best and what will be required to succeed without incurring unnecessary costs.

SCALE

Typically, external agencies are better suited to scale social media management. In fact, they are built for it. They already manage multiple stakeholders, platforms and tools with scalability in mind. They help manage the day-to-day while still being able to respond to ad-hoc requests in a timely manner. They are configured to manage resources and capacity while taking advantage of economies of scale.

They typically are using purpose-built tools and technologies that no single client would invest in nor could likely justify. In most cases, these solutions are more than any one client would need but that the agency can use to provide value distributed across multiple clients.

We, like many other agencies, invest heavily in tools and technologies. To a certain degree, it provides a bit of a competitive advantage. We can provide a lot of value quickly without the need for a large team. You may not need everything we are capable of providing on a daily basis, but we can provide analysis and reporting as needed while continually compiling data over time. This is core to our value proposition and not something clients can or wish to invest as extensively in.

At the time that I am writing this, we are managing approximately 250 social media accounts and publishing over 1500 social posts per month. In order to do that, we built a process and used the required tools to research content, create content, submit it to clients for review and approval, schedule it and provide reporting on a monthly basis.

At any given time, we have resources researching, creating and scheduling content. We have copywriters and designers working simultaneously to put together engaging content such as animated gifs, carousels and graphic quotes. We are reviewing brand monitors to ensure we are getting relevant mentions. We produce analytics and brand monitor reports on a monthly basis but sometimes are tasked to do ad-hoc analysis regarding competitors or to seek deeper insights for clients.

We research and write blogs on a monthly basis for disparate clients in various industries. We create videos and other rich media as audience tastes change regarding engaging content. We devise and execute paid social media campaigns across Facebook, Twitter, LinkedIn, Instagram and Snapchat with budgets ranging from hundreds to thousands of dollars.

You are likely not dealing with that kind of volume of activity but it should give you a sense that an agency may be better suited to do certain things related to your social media efforts. As previously mentioned, identify your strengths, weaknesses and preferences and defer to the agency for where they can best deliver value.

INSIGHTS

You are the keeper of the historical knowledge contained in your organization. The external agency is focused on providing the information and insights to inform your strategy and to help you garner support with key stakeholders.

Agencies have access to vast amounts of information and insights. They can tell you the best time to post on various social platforms and what type of content to post and in what format. They stay abreast of the latest specifications for image sizes and other aspects of content for each platform.

Do you know what blog topics for your industry are trending upward? Which topics are showing fatigue? Who are the top sources for content related to your topic and/or industry? What is the optimal length of a blog for engagement? Well, your agency can likely tell you because that is what they focus on every day.

You may have an idea of who is influential in your industry from a social media perspective but your agency can likely tell you how real their influence is and how much of an audience and reach they have.

While you may have experience doing paid advertising, you likely have not been involved in the number of campaigns that your agency has. Leverage their cumulative knowledge to ensure a greater likelihood of success for your campaigns.

Your agency is accustomed to conducting brand monitoring and social listening. Furthermore, they are well versed in constructing Boolean search queries to find the conversations happening online that are relevant to your brand. They also know how to refine the queries to ensure they are as comprehensive as possible, making sure every combination and permutation of how something is expressed is included.

COST

Your toolkit is likely to consist of tools necessary to get the job done but come up short in terms of robust data and insights unless you make a substantial investment. There are free and low-cost solutions available, but they may not be sufficient. What is required for daily, weekly, monthly, quarterly and on-demand social media activities? Once you have determined that then you can determine what tools and solutions to put in place for your own use and what you can leverage through your agency.

You might be handling the day-to-day management of your social media channels and related post scheduling while your agency provides complementary services such as brand monitoring and analytics. For example, we have some clients who chose to manage their own social media accounts. We provide them with third party content that we have researched and analytics so they know when to post on which platforms. We also provide performance analytics so they know what content is performing best on what platforms.

Generally, clients outsource the majority of their social media efforts. That may mean that the agency is using the client's social media toolkit but the agency is still responsible for the ongoing management. For others, we provide the tools and do the managing too.

Agencies have been doing their thing for a while so they have acquired tools and methods over time that you may not be very familiar with nor have the time to acquire. In our case, we have some solutions that we have been using for over a decade. Furthermore, those long-standing vendor relationships can translate into favourable pricing, which we are able to pass onto our clients.

Agencies might have chosen one or more enterprise-grade solutions. Maybe they chose a kind of Swiss Army knife of a social media solution that can do a lot or all of what they need done. Others, like us, may have chosen to compile a collection of tools that have specific capabilities and benefits without any trade-offs that can come with selecting an all-in-one solution.

It is worth noting that an agency has the familiarity and expertise to review and select the most appropriate solutions to meet their needs and those of their clients. They use these solutions every day so they know what questions to ask and can quickly identify strengths and weaknesses. They can also often play one vendor off of another to get the best price.

Your organization may not need some of the agency's tools every day so let them incur that cost and you can tap them for access on an as-needed basis. For example, you may not be running paid campaigns that often so don't incur costs if you don't have to. If your agency is on a monthly retainer then be clear about what they are to provide each month within the scope of the engagement and where additional costs will arise for anything else.

Even though I own an agency it will surprise you to hear me say that I have seen agencies try to find revenue opportunities beyond their retainer so watch out for those situations but, by the same token, do not try to expand the scope of the engagement without being prepared to incur additional costs. Either scenario does not foster a good working relationship.

There are tools and solutions for graphic design, copywriting, content research, hashtag research, video and animation creation, video editing, content spinning (i.e. creating multiple social posts from a single piece of original content), analytics, competitive analysis and brand monitoring to name a few.

We, like many other agencies, have built a robust tech stack that no single client would acquire themselves. It simply wouldn't be cost-effective. We spend more per month on technology than some pay for a salary but we spread the cost across multiple clients so they can all benefit without incurring the entire cost on their own.

Clients don't necessarily need all of our tools or they don't need them all the time but we certainly do. As mentioned above, we are researching, creating and scheduling content every day. We are running analytics every single day so that we can provide robust reports every month and as needed. Increasingly, we are being tasked to make more content from what already exists so we are doing a lot more spinning. We know how to do that at scale so our clients benefit without having to develop that capability themselves.

The right tech stack matched with the right talent means agencies can do a lot with a little and provide a cost-effective service to clients where they couldn't replicate it themselves at the same price. There lies one of the key reasons for considering outsourcing to an agency.

Your choice

You are not alone in choosing between keeping social media management in-house or outsourcing to an external agency. There are also other stakeholders you will want and need to involve. They will have questions, concerns and possibly even a wish list of things they will task you to fulfil.

Seek input from others in similar positions or that have gone through the same situation recently or in the past. Consider joining groups of other social media practitioners on Facebook or LinkedIn where you can seek advice from peers. Consider joining socialmedia.org, which is an organization that exists for just that purpose. I gain nothing from recommending them but think you should consider joining. I can't because I would be considered a vendor.

External agencies will want your business and they will try to get it. They may even have your best interest in mind. You mustn't rush your decision. Put the onus on the various agencies pitching for your business to illustrate their value proposition and where they expect to show impact in pursuit of your objectives. Remember that you are going to be working closely with these people for an extended period of time. You will not be basing your decision solely on price so be sure to think about what collaborating with them will be like. They will be more like colleagues than simply a supplier.

Consider what you can and wish to keep in-house. There is nothing to stop you from going it alone for a while until you face some challenges. Then consider outsourcing to address those challenges. Outsourcing can be a gradual process rather than an all or nothing scenario. You are in the driver's seat. Don't let the situation overwhelm you.

As I mentioned at the beginning of this chapter, there is no right or wrong approach. You will need to assess your own situation and make the best decision based on available information and resources, your objectives and budget. What you decide now may change in the future because your circumstances may have changed and that is okay. Do what you need to do now but be open to change in the future. Social media is a very dynamic environment and you may need to be just as dynamic.

09

Beware bright shiny syndrome

Bebo, Orkut, Google Wave, Vine, Path, Google+, Ning and Myspace. What do they all have in common? Well, at one point in time they were the hot new social network. The one that everyone just had to be on. The bright new shiny social platform. Through acquisition or simply outright failure, they are all essentially gone.

In this chapter we will discuss emerging platforms and how to evaluate them in relation to your business and objectives. How do you decide whether to invest time and energy into them? Which ones should you pass on and which ones should you at least keep an eye on to see how things progress?

You're merely a tenant

You may have already heard the expression 'You do not own social media and you are merely a tenant' or at least something along those lines. The point is that, with the exception of LinkedIn, you are not paying for your social media accounts. They're owned by the platforms and you get to use them in exchange for allowing them to advertise.

Being a tenant means you have no say in the direction the platforms choose or the features and functions they decide to add or take away. We are still holding our breath for the dislike button but will have to settle for either the sad, shocked or angry reactions that Facebook has so 'graciously' made available to us.

Don't get fooled again

When NESTA had me research all of the predominant social networking sites at the time, which happened to be 2008, I joined every one of them.

From Classmates, Friendster, Orkut, Myspace and Second Life to Bebo and Twitter, I spent time on all of them.

Myspace came, went and came back, only to subsist as an also-ran. Bebo launched in 2005 and was acquired in 2008 by AOL for $850 million. The founders bought Bebo back in 2013 for $1 million. They pivoted the platform into streaming and gaming events that led to being acquired again by Twitch, Amazon's gaming network, for a reported $25 million.[1]

Not every social network has the same ups, downs and financial outcomes as Bebo. Many of the top social networks from 2008 are gone. Some were acquired or merged while others simply petered out. Facebook, LinkedIn and Twitter were still relatively new but Facebook and LinkedIn had managed to get into the top 10 while Twitter had only managed to crack the top 20 by that point.

How many on the list in Table 9.1 do you remember? How many did you use? Just think about how many of them are gone and that Snapchat, Instagram and WhatsApp hadn't even been thought of yet. No one could have predicted which ones would stand the test of time and which ones would fall by the wayside.

TABLE 9.1

	Website	Monthly visitors	Monthly visits	Change in total visits from Feb 2007
1	myspace.com	65,744,241	955,057,928	−1%
2	Facebook.com	28,563,983	326,418,930	77%
3	Classmates.com	11,978,068	22,488,912	11%
4	myyearbook.com	3,019,762	20,022,490	284%
5	bebo.com	3,540,465	19,282,335	3%
6	blackplanet.com	2,109,069	13,746,246	9%
7	hi5.com	2,424,699	11,828,458	1%
8	linkedin.com	3,828,407	11,155,614	729%
9	tagged.com	2,376,671	10,599,014	11%
10	reunion.com	6,741,879	10,109,933	28%
11	firendster.com	1,867,423	6,625,522	25%
12	orkut.com	469,664	7,093,888	74%
13	flixster.com	3,311,187	6,752,495	118%
14	fubar.com	1,667,262	6,610,080	3272217%

(continued)

TABLE 9.1 (Continued)

	Website	Monthly visitors	Monthly visits	Change in total visits from Feb 2007
15	tickle.com	2,105,741	6,320,987	61%
16	cafemom.com	1,572,890	6,009,659	495%
17	xanga.com	1,897,345	5,939,039	–66%
18	yuku.com	921,186	5,483,587	1400%
19	twitter.com	629,531	4,166,086	4368%
20	ning.com	1,181,109	3,816,990	4803%

SOURCE Compete.com

We have to resist the urge to jump on every new platform or latch onto the latest social media app or solution. We should be watching and listening for what is emerging but with an eye to where and how it applies to your business and objectives, if at all. We also need to be mindful of how the new players onboard users, scale under the weight of growth and, finally, deal with issues of privacy and transparency.

You only get one chance to make a first impression

A new platform announces that it is coming. They capture emails from those early adopters who are willing to join their beta program or at least get early access. They formally launch and, to build hype, they will limit the number of users who can join. They continue to build hype and flame the FOMO fires by trickling out invitations and special access codes via the early adopters. Suddenly, invites for an essentially unknown social network become the hottest, most sought-after commodity.

You secure an invitation and excitedly set up your profile. If you are lucky, the onboarding experience goes well. If you have to install and authenticate yourself on an app then hopefully that all goes smoothly. If it doesn't, many users can be lost never to return again. Attention spans and patience run very short these days, and users can be very unforgiving.

Increasingly, focus has moved to user experience. The goal is to onboard users as seamlessly as possible and enable them to become active almost immediately. Some platforms have leveraged pre-existing relationships from other platforms to help users establish and build personal networks on the new ones.

The key is to understand just how much authority is given to the new platform when it comes to accessing your contacts, personal data and other information. As a rule, I do not use 'login using Facebook' to new services because it is not always apparent how much information gets exchanged between them and Facebook. You can always find out what information gets shared but sometimes it can be too late.

Privacy and transparency

Most social media platforms are based on sharing information. People used to joke about Foursquare, referring to it as 'Come Rob My House' because its whole purpose was to share where you were and what you were doing when you weren't home. However, you had a choice to use it or not. You had a choice about what information you shared. That hasn't always been the case with other platforms.

Klout wasn't so much a social networking site as it was a solution for measuring social influence. It launched in 2008, using 1 to 100 as a scale to measure influence. The higher your Klout score then the higher your supposed influence was. High Klout scores resulted in Klout perks from brand partners of Klout.

At that time, I had a Klout score of 69, which suggested that I was influential. I even managed to win a Klout perk and was given a Cadillac for a weekend test drive. Most of what drove my Klout score was my activity and followers on Twitter. Klout leveraged Twitter's API and all the data that it made available. Other platforms weren't so forthcoming with data, which made people grow increasingly suspicious of Klout and its approach to measurement.

Tying so much to Twitter meant that it could potentially be gamed, especially if people bought followers. Barack Obama was president at the time and his Klout score was lower than some bloggers. This, obviously, made people grow suspicious of Klout's credibility as a measure of influence.

2008 was still early days for social media. None of the dominant social platforms had even existed for a decade. They were still figuring things out and that included how they addressed privacy. Klout was not exempt. They were criticized for violating the privacy of minors and the UK's Data Protection Act of 1998.[2]

They were also criticized for their lack of transparency regarding the criteria and approach to determining someone's Klout score. Resentment also began to grow because of fears for the societal effects that would result from people striving to become more influential and drive up their Klout scores in the process.

In 2010, a new mobile social network called Path launched. Initially, it deliberately limited the number of friends you could have to 50 so as to foster greater engagement and interactivity. Later they raised the limit to 150 and then eventually removed the limit altogether.

As Path grew in popularity, it faced similar challenges to Klout with regards to the way it handled user data, especially underage users. In 2012, Path was criticized for accessing and storing user phone contacts without knowledge or permission and, in 2013, was actually fined $800,000 by the FTC for storing data from underaged users.[3]

With the fallout from Facebook's Cambridge Analytica scandal, any new social network must make privacy and transparency top priorities or run the risk of being doomed from the start. In most cases, user trust is theirs to lose but, once lost or called into question, it is rarely restored.

What if we built a social network and nobody came?

In 2009 Google announced Google Wave at one of their developer conferences. It essentially came and went within six months. They did the FOMO-type launch with limited users and distributed invites to control user onboarding.

Unfortunately, early impressions showed that it was designed more for developer collaboration than as a social network. There wasn't a social feed to see what your connections were up to. You had to prearrange with other people when you were going to meet up on the platform. Basically, you were hosting a party and had to ensure that people showed up otherwise you were left to talk to yourself.

Google Wave never caught on. It was just a brief flash. It was missing many of the attributes that make social networks attractive and sticky. Eventually, it was renamed to Apache Wave when the project was adopted by the Apache Software Foundation as an incubator project in 2010 but was eventually discontinued in 2018.

Orkut was a social network that began as a side project of a Google engineer who named the network after himself. It gained early popularity in Brazil and India but never really hit the mainstream globally and was shut down in 2014.

Google's most successful attempt at a social network was Google+. It was launched in 2011 and, initially, showed promise based on its early growth. Sadly, growth slowed and design flaws were disclosed that risked making personal data accessible. Google+ was shut down for business and personal use in 2019.

In later years before shutting down, Google played down Google+ as a social networking site and tried to spin it as 'connective tissue' between all of your Google-related accounts like Gmail. At least that was the way it was described to me by a Google employee.

Ironically, one of the most vibrant social media discussion groups that I was a part of was Google+. In further irony, it was a discussion group composed of LinkedIn experts who convened there to discuss all things LinkedIn. We didn't even gather on LinkedIn, the very platform on which we were experts. With the demise of Google+, we moved the discussion group to Facebook, ignoring LinkedIn yet again.

What have you tweeted for me lately?

We often hope that the latest social network will improve upon that past, avoiding past mistakes and offering sought-after features and functions. Some will point out their differences as strengths, suggesting they have listened to past complaints about other platforms and made sure to solve those issues. Sometimes this can be promising but, if they do not gain sufficient traction early on, all may be for not.

Twitter Blue

Twitter introduced Twitter Blue, which finally makes it possible to undo a tweet rather than deleting it and starting over. Even though I subscribe to Twitter Blue for other features and out of curiosity as someone who specializes in social media, I have to say that I have yet to use the undo feature. Furthermore, I have tended to be pretty focused on what I am writing before posting and even if I have made mistakes I haven't got that hung up about it. Twitter Blue has only been rolled out to a few countries at the time of this writing, but I suspect it will either roll out globally as a subscription service as it is now or its features will be rolled into the free version of Twitter. We will just have to wait and see.

TikTok

TikTok is the first social platform not owned by Facebook to reach 3 billion downloads.[4] It's growth rate and level of user engagement suggests that it is here to stay. The COVID-19 pandemic had a tremendous impact on its growth as people took to it to help cope. It is a network of content creators sharing truth, vulnerability and humour. The #momsoftiktok community has driven 2.4 billion video views. Moms found a community where they could support each other, especially with humour.

TikTok's secret sauce is its algorithm, enabling one of the most engaging user experiences and entertaining content feeds referred to as the 'For You Page'. They have even gone so far as to make their algorithm available to others.[5] Content creators can establish and build an audience and influence faster and organically than they could on other platforms.

The old adage of being a big fish in a little pond has given way to many big fish emerging as the pond gets bigger. Every day sees new faces joining the community and creators reaching new follower milestones. Many of the most influential people on TikTok became famous and influential on TikTok. They were not famous or influential before or elsewhere.

TikTok has shown what Twitter's Vine could have been if it had been allowed to live. It gave us the right content format, video, in the right amount of time, a minute or less. They have since increased the length that videos can be to three minutes, allowing creators to tell their stories in a single video rather than multiple parts.

It is an empowering platform where anyone can find their voice and audience. People are sharing laughs, tears, DIY tips and life hacks. The phrase 'I learned it from TikTok' is becoming commonplace. People can ask a question and others can respond by riffing off of the question or 'stitching' their answer as it is called on the platform. Content begets content. Can you tell how I feel about TikTok?

TikTok, like Facebook and Instagram before it, attracted young people first. Facebook and Instagram saw their user base gradually skew older as the younger users who had come first seek out a new platform to call their own. TikTok still has a strong youth component but older users have shown up to see what all the fuss is about and have gradually found their own flourishing communities.

Clubhouse

As podcasts and social audio has grown in popularity, now comes Clubhouse. Imagine a social app where you host live audio-only discussions in virtual rooms and you have Clubhouse. 2021 was the year it exploded onto the social stage. It has strong backing with Andreessen Horowitz as one of its venture capital investors. The Andreessen in Andreessen Horowitz is Marc Andreessen, founder of Netscape.

If imitation is the highest form of flattery then Clubhouse must be very flattered. Twitter already has a Clubhouse-like live audio feature called Twitter Spaces. Additionally, LinkedIn and Facebook are both slated to introduce competing offerings. Other competitors will likely pop up too to grab their piece of the social audio pie. Who will win the day remains to be seen but social audio is gaining momentum. Will new upstarts dominate the space or will the old guard outlast them? Watch this space or better yet *listen*.

Polywork

I am writing about Polywork when it has really only been on people's radar for a few weeks. Its goal is to be the social network that shows us who we really are. What I mean by that is that we are more than our résumé. We have interests and hobbies outside of work. Our work is more diverse and complex than a few bullet points on our LinkedIn profile.

I won't go so far as to say that it is a LinkedIn killer but early indications suggest that they are onto something. When you set up your profile you add badges that speak to what you do and have done as well as incorporating humour and humanity, something not seen on LinkedIn. Nothing against LinkedIn but Polywork is trying to be less stuffy yet still professional with an added dash of creativity.

Its mobile app is still in beta and every social network worth its salt has to have a mobile app to remain viable and competitive. Coincidentally, LinkedIn introduces many features and functions on the mobile platform first, which speaks to the mobile-centric nature of social media in our everyday lives. We can anticipate that it will be the same with Polywork once they get out of the beta phase.

These are just a few examples of social platforms that have emerged or are emerging recently. By the time this book is published, there could very well be an entirely new crop of social networks and apps. Deciding where to put your time and energy will remain a challenge. Hopefully, the following will help you navigate the ever-changing landscape.

But it's so shiny

With every new social network or app that emerges, you need to ask yourself a series of questions and consider a number of before deciding whether you should devote any time to them. We are all time-starved. We are busy enough just trying to deal with what we already have on our plate. Who needs or wants to have to deal with a new and unproven social network that your boss' daughter says is the next big thing?

Is my audience there?

So often, a client or prospective client will say that they are too old for social media or they simply are not interested, but they recognize its power and importance regarding the audience they want to reach.

Assuming you are clear on who your audience is and where they congregate online, you need to determine whether or not the new social network is or will be of interest to them. Are there any early signs that your audience is already there and, if so, in sufficient numbers to warrant your attention?

A broad range of demographics are represented by each social network but each of them tend to have higher proportions of certain ages, genders and political and religious affiliations. If any of those aspects are important to you then you need to examine each social network, new or old, with those in mind.

LinkedIn is seen as the white-collar professional network. Facebook used to be for the kids but now skews 40+ in terms of age and right-wing in terms of political leanings. Twitter skews college educated and left-wing. Snapchat is for the young and Instagram is where the millennials gather. Pinterest skews 40+ females with interests in fashion, decor and crafting. Those are just anecdotal details so you need to do further research, but it gives you an idea that you can't focus your efforts on a single social network and expect to reach your business objectives.

As much as Clubhouse is experiencing media attention in 2021, it remains a platform that demands a great deal of time and energy. It is similar to hosting a webinar where you have to promote upcoming Clubhouse events, gather guests of interest to your audience and have resources in place to help you moderate the discussion. One shortcoming has been the inability to record Clubhouse chats so a number of people have found a hack or workaround to record their Clubhouse chats and turn them into podcasts for later consumption. Hopefully, Clubhouse will have addressed this by the time this book is published because it will affect adoption if users can't make the most out of the content they create on the platform.

How much work will it be?

There is an entire ecosystem of tools and services to manage and analyse our presence on the established social platforms like Facebook and Twitter. It took a while but thankfully we can now schedule and publish Instagram posts from our desktop. That comes as a huge relief to social media managers everywhere.

New platforms do not have that ecosystem so more time is required to learn about them, learn how they work and what you have to do to establish and build your presence. Many have little to no analytics capabilities to inform your strategy. They also tend to require rich media, predominantly video, as their foundational content. They do not come with functionality, directly or indirectly, to schedule and publish posts from your desktop. That means if you are an enterprise using TikTok, for example, you are managing your account from one person's phone. That doesn't give people a lot of comfort from a governance point of view.

You have to devote time to research new platforms and technologies to learn about the best practices, etiquette and how users are innovating. You can't determine fit for your brand without a thorough understanding.

The live audio nature of a platform like Clubhouse might make people in highly regulated industries nervous about what might be said. This means a greater need for media training and clear social media policies about what can and cannot be shared. Anyone who has represented an organization properly at in-person conferences and is accustomed to speaking to the media while remaining compliant should not have a problem. If you are producing the content then you just need to make sure you have people familiar with compliant disclosure of information.

Video, animations, gifs and audiograms are increasingly the types of content in demand. If you or members of your team are not skilled or staffed to deliver content like that then you are going to find it very difficult to keep up with the demands of the new platforms. The audience wants to be engaged and entertained. Your blog is likely no longer enough to do it. You will need to complement it with things like an animation or graphic to draw attention to the blog. Every content idea that is part of your overall plan will likely need a variety of content assets. Yes, you will be working harder but you will also be working smarter, squeezing more value out of every piece of content instead of moving onto the next piece of content to be created.

Look at what inhouse capabilities you have, where training could be applied and what you will need to outsource in order to meet the demands of creating rich media content on a regular basis. Consider how many people will have to be involved in the ideation, creation and approval process. I have been through a ridiculous number of approval steps for a single post that, in the end, was extremely costly to the organization and, frankly, not worth the effort for the end result.

Hopefully, you will find yourself in a situation where speed is prioritized over quality. I am not suggesting that you publish inferior quality content. If the COVID-19 pandemic and platforms like TikTok have taught us anything, it is the fact that lower production value content can outperform highly produced content by a wide margin. The audience wants immediacy and reality. If it takes you days or more to identify an emerging trend, conceive of content that is aligned with that trend, create that content, get it approved and then publish it then you are doing it wrong.

I recognize that not every organization is configured to quickly turn around content, including the approval process. Over time, strive to design a workflow and approval process, if applicable, that removes as much friction as possible. Some of the most engaging content is content that is in the moment, leveraging what is trending and current for your audience.

Do you remember the now infamous Oreo tweet from the Super Bowl in 2013?[6] Oreo and their agency managed to capture lightning in a bottle. There was a blackout and during the blackout they published a tweet that said: 'Power out? No problem. You can still dunk in the dark.'

Well, the tweet went viral and, in the days that followed, the media spoke of what an example of 'in the moment' marketing it was. If you read the history leading up to that fateful day, you will come to understand that a lot went into being prepared for that moment. Being responsive meant being prepared.[7]

They were already versed with real-time marketing so, to some degree, this was just more of the same, except for the part about how much media attention that the Super Bowl gets. They also had already developed the war room idea, bringing together all of the necessary parties, literally and virtually, that would be required to execute quickly. They were prepared to take the creative in a number of directions depending on how things played out. Pardon the 'play' pun.

After this viral event, lots of brands wanted their Oreo moment but it is hard to catch lightning in a bottle twice. You can't schedule serendipity but you can be prepared for luck and opportunity to collide by having the right resources in place to coordinate their efforts.

Most of you won't have the luxury of having an agency at your disposal or deep creative bench strength. That is not the important part. Social media moves really fast and while planning, like we have discussed elsewhere in this book, is helpful, you still need to have slack in the system for agile responses to emerging and trending themes. Easily said yet challenging to do but with potential for huge engagement dividends.

Tools like Lately or Headliner can help you simplify some of the production requirements in order to create short, captioned video clips and/or audiograms. No disrespect to specialists in video or audio production but new tools are being introduced almost every day that empower social media teams to produce cheap and cheerful content very quickly. People are budget constrained and sometimes it can be cost prohibitive to engage a specialist. They can still rely on the specialists for the important content but handle the smaller stuff themselves.

Competition

I already mentioned earlier in this chapter that the likes of Clubhouse face competition from existing social platforms like Twitter, Facebook and LinkedIn. The obstacle that Clubhouse has to overcome is to convince people to install yet another app and adopt the associated behaviour in order to derive value from the experience. What is going to make them do that when they can have a similar audio experience from an app that they already have installed and are already familiar with?

The answer is not as clear cut as you might think. Snapchat has had numerous features copied by competitors like Instagram only to watch Instagram continue to grow in audience size and engagement. On the other hand, Instagram introduced Reels as a supposed response to TikTok, but Instagram has not captured the competitive edge it was hoping for. TikTok continues to grow rapidly and their engagement levels are to be envied.

Sure, when incumbents introduce features and functions to compete with upstarts, we need to pay attention. We can't always assume who the clear winner will be. The established players are often slow to innovate or produce inferior offerings in response to their competitors. Sometimes the new entrants are arrogant and ignore their competitors, to their peril. This can be a lot for social media professionals to deal with but it is necessary to remain relevant and competitive.

Your competition may decide that they want to establish a beachhead on an emerging platform to be ahead of the competition. Maybe they have deep pockets and can afford to make the investment. Maybe they want to real-locate spend to emerging areas where they can still benefit from organic growth and paid campaigns at a lower cost. You should be thinking about the same things. Where should you allocate your time and money?

Dilution risk

You have likely experienced the growing challenge of organic growth on the established platforms. As they matured and the audience did too, it has become increasingly challenging to reach your existing audience and reaching a new audience is essentially impossible without running paid campaigns.

If you are looking at adding a new platform to your marketing mix, what does that mean for the ones that you are already on? For each, consider which ones are intended for growth, to be maintained or to no longer receive support. You may think that you can continue to allocate equal amounts of resources to all of them but not all of them will provide the same return on investment.

Your metrics are going to continually inform you about which platforms are delivering on your efforts and which ones are experiencing diminishing returns. Adding a new platform does not immediately mean that you will be offsetting the diminishing returns. You may start to see early signs of success in terms of engagement and audience growth but likely not enough to replace your more established channel(s). That can change over time but investment will have to be made.

You have to rationalize how many channels you can manage and how many you need to be on in order to reach your cumulative audience. You need to have a multi-pronged, multi-platform strategy but you can't be a mile wide and a foot deep. You will need to prioritize which channels are essential for achieving your goals. There is no shortage of channels that have been built and abandoned. Yes, oftentimes you have to experiment. Social media is a test and learning environment. The key is to experiment based on an informed perspective stemming from research.

As mentioned earlier, not every platform is going to deliver equally. That does not mean you abandon all but the top performer. You need more than one outlet to ensure you are reaching everyone within your audience, but avoid spreading your efforts so thin that you dilute your brand and risk turning your audience off with lacklustre content.

There is no perfect or ideal mix of platforms or channels. You will have to determine that for yourself depending on the type of audience you are trying to reach and your type of company. You might experience tremendous success with two while others find success with four. Maybe your entire audience is only spread across two social platforms where another's audience is found in pockets on nearly all of them. Where your audience can be found and which platforms you can reasonably manage in terms of content production and distribution will likely be the determining factors for how many channels you will be on.

How we define success is subjective. Instagram, for example, is invaluable to fashion and beauty brands because of its engagement levels and dominance with influencers. It is just not a great referrer of website traffic. It most certainly has a role to play, especially related to brand awareness. You just have to accept that that is the role that it plays and look to other platforms to deliver in other ways towards your objectives. No single platform is going to get you across the finish line.

Endnotes

1   M Brian. Twitch buys Bebo to build out its sports platform, *engadget*, 19 June 2019, www.engadget.com/2019-06-19-twitch-bebo-esports-tournaments.html (archived at https://perma.cc/46JU-H3L2)
2   Wikipedia. Klout, 22 September 2021, en.wikipedia.org/wiki/Klout (archived at https://perma.cc/7KHQ-BQYQ)
3   Wikipedia. Path (social network), 2 January 2021, en.wikipedia.org/wiki/Path_(social_network) (archived at https://perma.cc/R8MH-V8YS)
4   R Hodge. TikTok hits 3 billion downloads, *cnet*, 14 July 2021, www.cnet.com/tech/services-and-software/tiktok-hits-3-billion-downloads/ (archived at https://perma.cc/N38G-DQ6J)
5   K Gupta. TikTok's algorithm no longer a secret, available to firms: thing to know, *Business Standard*, 5 July 2021, www.business-standard.com/podcast/companies/tiktok-s-algorithm-no-longer-a-secret-available-to-firms-things-to-know-121070500883_1.html (archived at https://perma.cc/S7BJ-ABN3)

6 Oreo Cookie tweet, 4 February 2013, twitter.com/Oreo/status/ 298246571718483968/photo/1?ref_src=twsrc%5Etfw%7Ctwcamp%5Etweete mbed%7Ctwterm%5E298246571718483968%7Ctwgr%5E%7Ctwcon%5Es1 _&ref_url=https%3A%2F%2Fdigiday.com%2Fmarketing%2Foral-history- oreo-tweet%2F (archived at https://perma.cc/NY6F-6LT2)

7 digiday.com/marketing/oral-history-oreo-tweet/ (archived at https://perma.cc/ BNL6-KJQR)

10

Your social media operating model

Imagine, if you will, an organization with different departments, units or teams, a multitude of social media accounts, uncoordinated content efforts and varying degrees of engagement. Frankly, you should not have to imagine such a company because they are quite common.

Many organizations start small with social media and then different teams or business areas branch out by establishing their own social media accounts and before you know it you have a social media hodgepodge with no cohesive strategy.

Nobody seemed to be asking questions along the way regarding whether the organization (or the subunits) needed all of those social media accounts. Where was the rationalization? Every channel opened requires resources and content and that is where so many companies fail.

Without a defined approach and governance, people can go rogue and lead the organization down a path that gets them into a situation where they have a collection of social accounts lacking in brand consistency and coordination.

The following considerations are for firms who find themselves in that situation. Hopefully, they will also help those just getting started avoid the situation altogether. So let's begin the process of turning chaos into well-oiled operations.

Analysis

Resources and tools

Begin by examining the current situation to understand what currently exists. Survey stakeholders to understand who does what and the points of demarcation between teams and different areas of the organization. Those same stakeholders will be able to provide a wealth of information. They will be able to tell you what is working, what isn't, where improvements could be made and what their wish list would include in terms of resourcing and support. They know first-hand because they are living it every day.

Conduct an audit of how resources are distributed and what tools they use. Map the structure including workflow and reporting paths. If possible, audit skills and experience and populate a skills matrix to understand current capabilities and gaps. Are they managing social media activities well or are they overwhelmed? What is the organization's receptiveness to change in these areas?

Assess the current tool set, reporting capabilities and related expenses. Are you overspending in some places? Are you getting full value from every tool or is more training needed? Many suppliers have customer success reps in place to ensure you are getting the most out of their offering and reduce customer churn. Make use of them. They can be really helpful.

Accounts and content

Compile a list of all of the existing social media accounts, who manages them, how many people have access to them and where and how are administrative rights, permissions and login credentials being managed and by whom. Which ones are active and which ones, if any, are not? Some may have been abandoned, forgotten or used only for a specific purpose or period of time with no intention for long-term activity.

Analyse the currently active social media accounts to see how they have been performing and how they stack up to other accounts within the organization and to the competition. Which channels are strong and which channels are under-performing or not performing at all? Where is the opportunity or opportunities for the organization to improve or even surpass its competitors?

What kind of content has the organization specialized in in terms of format and subject matter? Are there any signs that the audience is experiencing content fatigue? Are certain formats performing better than others? What might that mean to your current resourcing and tool situation? Who produces the content? Is it only internal resources or is some of it outsourced? Are there long gaps between pieces of content being produced and distributed? Are there any areas where content production has died off?

Content production is relentless. It requires planning and organization. Does a content calendar exist and is it up to date? How far in advance is content production planned? What is the status of production? Beyond a calendar, what is the workflow for content planning, production and approval? If you are in a regulated industry, who needs to be involved to address compliance? Is there an opportunity to remove friction from the process and collapse the number of people and time it takes for approvals? Could you get to the point where you and your team are trusted implicitly such that you no longer have to get content approved? Maybe that is a pipe dream but it doesn't hurt to ask.

A lot of the discussion surrounding content pertains to content authored or created by the organization. There is always a reluctance to incorporate third-party content because it does not feel like it is aligned with the organization's objectives. In time people come to realize that engaging content, regardless of where it came from, serves the organization's objectives. It keeps the social accounts active and vibrant, tuning the algorithms so that, when you distribute your content, it has a greater likelihood of being seen. This isn't obvious in the beginning but can be proven over time with supporting analytics.

If you want to be certain that third-party content is aligned with your objectives then research content that matches the topics and themes you have planned on your content calendar. We have clients who tell us the content themes for the coming month and beyond. We research complementary content for their review and approval. Once approved, we begin spinning the articles to create multiple pieces of copy and extract as much value as possible out of every piece of third-party content.

Marrying authored and curated content and then spinning every piece to get multiple posts with different copy will make your content go farther, lessen the burden on everyone to come up with more content and make the entire content development process more efficient.

Rationale

Once you have your list of social accounts and have a sense of the activity across all of them, the organization needs to rationalize what channels to keep and which ones to divest. Be warned. The rationalization process could be filled with friction as some groups may be unwilling to relinquish their accounts for divestiture or hear criticism even though they are under-performing.

When I was working with a client that had quite a number of brand sponsorships, I originally suggested social accounts for each sponsorship. As I worked more closely with each brand manager, it became evident that none of them had the wherewithal to manage the accounts and provide supporting content that would ensure success.

After further consideration, I suggested consolidating the social accounts by brand category such as sports and the arts, thus reducing the number of channels to be resources and the burden for content across each of the brand managers. Now they only had to come up with a smaller percentage of content to keep fewer channels populated. Sadly, even this proved to be challenging for them, but it was still better than the alternative.

Look for those opportunities where efficiencies can be gained. It is natural to want to hold onto what you have invested time and energy in, but sometimes you have to cut your losses and allocate resources elsewhere. It isn't necessarily your fault. Audiences evolve and so do their interests. Your content and the channels that distribute it have to evolve too.

Rationalizing your social media channels is not a one-time thing. You should be running analysis on your social media channels on a regular basis so it won't be hard to see which channels are performing and which ones are not. Consider reviewing them every quarter when you are conducting your regular quarterly review of your social media metrics. You won't necessarily need to divest a channel but at least you can flag any channel that is causing concern and investigate the root cause. Maybe it can be salvaged and divestiture avoided. This is only possible if you review performance metrics regularly.

Implementation

Let me clarify something here. The intent is not to rationalize which social media accounts to keep and which ones to divest, only to go back to the old habits of ad-hoc posting and uncoordinated activities. There has to be a new way of doing things and the approach worth considering has to do with infrastructure and the associated operations.

The organization already has resources managing disparate accounts with varying degrees of success, but what they are often missing is the ability to scale content curation across all channels while minimizing the impact on existing resources. Often the existing resources are challenged to produce and/or curate the necessary amount of content every channel requires. That is where most organizations fail.

As mentioned previously, every opened channel requires content and resourcing. While an organization can stretch some resources across multiple channels, it's hard to stretch content across channels without proper planning and a coordinated strategy. That is where an enterprise oversight approach can help.

Leveraging social media analytics, it is important to determine which channels need content, how much content is needed and in what format. Then leverage the learning from the content audit and identify what existing content can be used to populate the content calendar with proper planning. Additionally, how much of the existing and previously used content be repurposed or updated?

So many organizations create content that gets used once and then they move on to the next piece of content. Frankly, that is a travesty. If organizations actually calculated how much that one tweet for that one blog cost, they would never allow it to happen again yet we see it happen again and again. Perhaps greater accountability should be part of your operating model.

Once you have a sense of the posting cadence happening across all of your channels, compare that to your content calendar and start building placeholders for your content on the calendar. Think about how many times a single piece of content can be placed on the calendar if the creative assets and/or copy are varied. Challenge yourself to create three to five distinct pieces of content for every blog, video or podcast you created or curated. That is a more manageable challenge than having to come up with distinct pieces of content for every channel every day.

Consider using AI-based tools to help you with content spinning, copywriting and content excerpts. Do not be afraid. AI-based social media tools are not going to replace human beings. They are just going to make humans more productive. An editorial eye will still be required and, again, this is about scaling content production with limited resources.

You can use free tools like Google Alerts or paid tools like Buzzsumo, UpContent, Feedly or Anders Pink to help with your content discovery and curation. I am a heavy user of Flipboard combined with Pocket to bookmark content. I also use Pocket to bookmark content within my browser or from Twitter. I am always on the lookout for content. Consider forming the same habit for yourself. It isn't hard and you can automate it to a degree.

Many of these tools can be configured to find the latest content based on the criteria you define and/or the sources and RSS feeds you prefer. Once you have them configured, you can save your settings and you will get fresh content delivered to your inbox on a regular basis. Let them do the heavy lifting and you can focus on your editorial efforts, getting stakeholder approval and creating multiple social posts for distribution.

Social media management solutions and command centres

SMMS

A social media management solution (SMMS) is part of the aforementioned infrastructure needed to ensure proper implementation of your social media strategy and ongoing operations. There are many to choose from and at varying price points. I can't recommend one specific solution because everyone's needs and budgets are different. Furthermore, some choose to go with a single solution with as many features and functionalities as possible while others compile a tech stack composed of purpose-built solutions. Neither is more right than the other. It comes down to preference.

One solution means one vendor that is accountable and one vendor that is tasked with supporting you. A collection of vendors can bring unnecessary complexities, especially if a number of the solutions do not talk to each other. It can be a missed opportunity to become more efficient. Furthermore, it puts more demand on the social media team to be well versed in disparate solutions. You really have to believe that the tech stack from multiple vendors is superior to a single solution from one vendor.

There will be trade-offs but a single solution with the majority of your technical requirements integrated may be the route to go, especially if you do not have the time or capability to train every member of your team. Having multiple people trained means you have backup and can more easily delegate tasks.

Regardless of single or multi-tool solutions, you need to start with confirming your needs, the resources that need and will use the tools and what outcomes you are expecting. A B2B organization may not have to deal with as many social media inquiries as a B2C organization. Therefore, a social inbox to capture inquiries may be less important than integration with third-party content curation tools to support their thought leadership goals.

Needs will vary depending on the type of organization. There are solutions best suited for B2B and others best suited for B2C. B2B tends to be lower volume in terms of posting and puts greater emphasis on content marketing and thought leadership. B2C definitely has higher posting volumes and demands engaging content, especially rich media, to attract the attention of fickle consumers with limited attention spans.

These disparate audiences with disparate needs will often require different social media solutions to serve them. Work with your vendors to ensure you are getting the most from every tool and service. Make them work for your business. They know that the social media technology landscape is filled with competitors anxious to scoop you as a client. Pit them against each other to get the best price and solution to meet your requirements.

Many vendors offer discounted pricing if you pay for an entire year upfront. Trial a solution or service for free whenever possible to confirm it meets your needs as well as the needs of other stakeholders within your organization. If you are not going to be the primary user then make sure you get input from the people who will be using it every day. You do not want to buy something that they do not want to use.

Work with your stakeholders to compose a use case that includes a list of the features and functions they need/want, aligns with the operating model you envision for the future, can handle the current volume of activity but can scale as you grow and is within budget.

Consider going with month-to-month pricing if you are not prepared to make a long-term commitment. Sometimes vendors are putting their best foot forward to woo you, but once you settle into business as usual the picture changes, support diminishes and you discover their solution does not work as promised. You would be challenged to get out of that situation and switch to another vendor if you had signed on for a year or more.

Some of the key features that are typically sought from SMMSs are the ability to delegate tasks within your team, a centralized inbox so everyone is aware of any inquiry or comment that comes in via social media, analytics and reporting, scheduling and a calendar, social listening, a content library, integrations with other solutions such as content curation tools or RSS feeds, being able to save posts as drafts and the ability to present drafts for approvals from stakeholders.

Maybe you do not need most of those features or you can't afford some of the enterprise-grade solutions that offer them. Start with the most critical things you need and find the most cost-effective solution but one that can potentially grow as you scale. You want to avoid having to switch solutions every time you reach a new growth milestone. You can accomplish a lot with Google Alerts and Tweetdeck, which are both free. Also, if posting volume is manageable, you can leverage the scheduling and native posting functionality of Tweetdeck and Facebook.

Bootstrap where you can. Allocate budget to things like paid campaigns that may have greater impact, especially if you are just getting started and want to grow your audience quickly. Having the most expensive SMMS will not solve your audience growth challenges by itself. You may want to go with cheaper or free solutions and hold back the budget to apply else where.

Command centres

Enterprises that have a SMMS in place may have set it up within their social media command centre. Generally, this is a room with a number of monitors, a social media management solution up and running that either has listening capabilities or is integrated with a third-party listening solution and is staffed to respond to any situation or crisis that arises.

It isn't about the tools or technology. It is about their reason for being. Not every enterprise needs a command centre but organizations like the Red Cross do. They are deployed when humanitarian crises arise. They need to monitor what is happening, distribute the latest information and route inquiries to the appropriate parties. They need to be a conduit between online and offline because they are dealing with life and death in real time.

If your business is not mission critical or you do not have stakeholders that need 24/7 support then maybe you do not need a command centre. However, you can have a situation where you have an event like the Super Bowl that is for a limited period of time but it has a level of heightened intensity and awareness. That doesn't mean you have to have a permanent command centre set up. Maybe a temporary one will suffice.

The command centre for the Super Bowl was built just a few weeks before the game and is there to serve the public before, during and after the game. There are a lot of events that happen in the host city in the days leading up to the game so the command centre acts as concierge and customer service, addressing inquiries and sharing information.

A few monitors, computers, social media tools and the right people can be your virtual command centre for the time you need it. You may not be putting on an event on the scale of the Super Bowl but you can still take the concept of a command centre and put together what you need to support your event.

Sure it would be nice to have the budget that some command centres have but it is not about the equipment. It is about serving your stakeholders and if a command centre is necessary to do that then make the case for it.

CENTRE OF EXCELLENCE

Social media activities are often happening in different pockets within an organization, happening without coordination. An operating model or structure may need to be established at an enterprise level that spans across the entire organization and incorporates the activities happening in those different pockets.

If there is reluctance by parties in those different pockets to defer to the enterprise centre of excellence (ECE), then there is a possible compromise. The ECE can operate behind the scenes as a middleman or operational infrastructure. If the ECE focuses on augmenting the content creation and curation efforts along with the distribution across all the various channels, then the different business units can remain as the voices of their part of organization, engaging stakeholders on the front line.

The ECE can scale content and distribution without overstepping the roles and responsibilities of the different social media primes. It's about helping and collaborating rather than politics, silos and turf wars. It is easy to say that here but we have all seen some units within a company lord their power over others even though they are not reflecting best practices.

The ECE can be a conduit between different social teams, sharing learnings from one part of the organization to another, exemplifying best practices and potentially leading a social media steering committee that brings together representatives from across the organization. The focus of the steering committee would be to ensure alignment and coordination related to the organization's overall social media goals and the tactics being implemented by each social media team to achieve those goals.

Newsrooms

You may not be familiar with the term newsrooms in the context of social media. It typically comes up with larger organizations who have social accounts associated with different divisions, geographies or some other defining attribute that separates them from the main accounts.

In order to make it easier for stakeholders to find the accounts, organizations will create a section on their website where all of the accounts are listed. Some go so far as to include a section showing the latest posts from key channels. Scania provides a good example of incorporating their social newsroom within the News & Events section of their website, all media in one place.

A social media newsroom will be overkill for an organization with a single location and a small employee base. It is best suited for situations where you have multiple divisions, departments and regional offices, all with associated social media accounts.

For the smaller organizations with few social accounts, you can get by with displaying your social icons with associated links on the header or footer of your website. Sadly, I continue to be amazed by how many organizations do not have their social accounts displayed on their websites or have broken or outdated links.

Which model is best?

We have talked about quite a few things that have to be considered in this chapter, but they all roll up to the overall operating model. The SMMS you choose, the command centre, centre of excellence and/or newsroom that you set up are all part of your overall social media operating model.

When I was brought into the Royal Bank of Canada to be their Head of Social Media, part of my mandate was to establish and grow their social media operations. There were resources in place but there really wasn't a coordinated strategy across different lines of business and there was next to no collaboration.

Lots of meetings were held with stakeholders. Some wanted to be involved while others simply wanted to know that social media was being taken care of, but they would have input when need be. We sat within the Enterprise Communications Team with a purview across the entire organization. We are talking about an organization with over 80,000 employees spread across an entire country with multiple offices and branches. Your organization may not be that large or that distributed but, hopefully, what I am about to share about our approach will still prove helpful to your own situation.

This was in 2011 and most of the social platforms were not even a decade old yet. It was still relatively new territory with a lot of learning as you went. As I came to understand the organization, its current structure and could juxtapose it with the social media landscape then, I conducted research to see if there were any insights or resources available to help guide the recommendations I would ultimately have to make.

Thankfully, I found the Altimeter Group and their framework describing five ways for organizing a social business. We will look at each of the five ways in greater detail and, hopefully, you will be able to determine if one of them makes sense and is suitable for your organization. It is okay if it doesn't. These are provided as options for you to consider if you find yourself unclear of how to configure your social media operating model. Despite more than a decade passing, this framework has stood the test of time and I have yet to find a worthy alternative.

Organic

This is the situation I found when I arrived at the bank. Resources focused on social media were distributed across the organization, but most were operating independently. Coordination was limited and there was no overarching consensus regarding strategy. That was part of the reason I was brought in by the Chief Brand Officer. He wanted a strategy defined at the enterprise level that took into account the different lines of business and teams.

Centralized

This most closely resembles the typical organizational chart that you see. Teams report to departments. Departments report to business heads. Business heads report to senior management and so on and so on. The front-line social media resources and their activities ultimately roll up to centralized oversight. Does this sound like your organization? Would this be the most applicable approach?

Coordinated

This is typically when the social media team or department supports different teams, departments or business units. Think of it as the organization having their own internal agency focused on social media. That does not mean that resources being supported cannot be executing their own social media strategy. It is simply that they may be drawing upon the additional internal bench strength because they have the subject matter expertise.

Multiple hub and spoke (aka 'Dandelion')

This is often the approach seen with organizations that span geographies and business units while still being under one brand. The approach may need to be tailored for geographies and differing audiences for various business units. There should still be coordination to ensure brand alignment but autonomy can exist in different regions and lines of business. This was the approach that I recommended to the bank. It addressed both the regional and line of business requirements, allowed for autonomy, while still tying things together at an enterprise level.

Holistic 'honeycomb'

This may be more of a 'dream state' where every employee is socially enabled to be in customer service and be a brand ambassador for the organization. This is predicated on a robust training program like Dell's and a comprehensive social media policy. This could be possible with a smaller organization. Larger enterprises could find this a challenge but may still want to pursue it, even philosophically (i.e. socially enabling as many employees as possible), but it will depend on the readiness of the internal culture.

Do not fall into the trap of trying to fit your square peg of an organization into the round hole of an operating model. These five examples are provided to inspire you and to draw from. None of them might apply to your situation 100 per cent. Take what might work and ignore the rest. These came about from social media research within enterprises over a decade ago. Use them as reference points. Talk to other practitioners. Research best practices. Reach out to your network and beyond. Do not be afraid to contact someone in a similar role that you do not know and see if they would give you 15 minutes of their time to share their approach. You might find a kindred spirit and an ally.

Keep in mind that the approach you take now may evolve over time. We have already mentioned how fast and often social media changes. That will most certainly impact the operating model you establish in the beginning

FIGURE 10.1   Altimeter Group social media organization

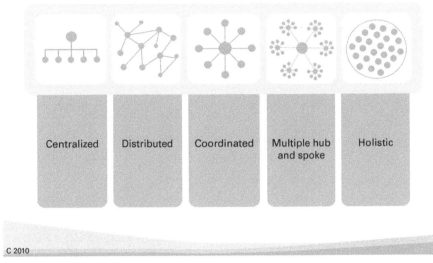

Companies organize for social in five ways

Centralized	Distributed	Coordinated	Multiple hub and spoke	Holistic

C 2010

SOURCE Reproduced with kind permission, from the Altimeter Group, 2010 (https://web-strategist. com/blog/2010/04/15/framework-and-matrix-the-five-ways-companies-organize-for-social-business/)

and how it morphs as your requirements and strategies change. For example, if you outsource some things and then bring them in-house as your organization matures and scales then you will most certainly have to adjust your operating model. You might find yourself shifting your content focus from blogs to videos or podcasts which will require different resources and workflow. You won't be able to establish an operating model to address every need or scenario, foreseen or unforeseen, so there is no point in trying. Deal with the known but be prepared to address the unknown as best you can.

Change is hard

I want to make sure that I speak to the issue of change when it comes to establishing a social media operating model. Earlier in this chapter I mentioned defining the workflow and the resources involved. Once you have done that, you want to minimize resistance by mapping your operating model as best as you can to the existing workflow and resourcing in place. It may mean taking a phased approach with your operating model where you implement certain elements in the beginning and introduce other elements over time. Bend social media to the needs of the organization rather than bending the organization to needs of social media. The latter will be met with resistance and impede your efforts.

This is not to suggest that the organization will never evolve its social media operations. It is just that you can't steamroll social media over the organization and expect everyone to accept it with a smile. Your long-term goal may be to dramatically change the current operation model but your near-term goal should be to make incremental changes that are more easily accepted by the organization.

Start with one change to process or the introduction of a new solution that will make their work easier. You want to be able to show early signs of progress such that they experience it themselves and feel the momentum building towards the organization's objectives. Roll out change gradually to make adoption and acceptance easier. You will get to your operating model with more stakeholders on side than had you forced change upon them too quickly.

I have made some suggestions for your social media operations that are by no means easy (nor crushingly difficult) to implement. It cannot be over emphasized that change management is one of the biggest and most overlooked aspects of doing anything related to social media within an organization. Respecting the process, the stakeholders and their reluctance to change will help move the organization from chaos to a well-oiled social operation with broader reach and content curation at scale.

11

Giving up control

When the topic of social media comes up with companies I am speaking with, I often hear them say that they are not active on social media or if they are they want to have more control over what is said about them, by whom and how they are perceived. When it comes to the former, you are active on social media whether you know it or not. Companies are being talked about online whether they are there to participate in the conversation or not. As for the latter, you can't control what is said about you so don't bother trying. You can only influence it. But you have to be an active participant in order to do that.

So if companies have to accept that they can't control the message, as difficult as that can be for some, then where should they focus their energy when it comes to reputation management? What kind, if any, of social listening or brand monitoring are they doing? If they are not doing any then they need to set that up because they can't participate in online conversations without listening first to see where and how they can insert themselves into the discussion.

Before going any further, we should distinguish between brand monitoring and social listening. While both involve listening, they differ based on the resulting actions. Brand monitoring involves listening for mentions of the company name, the names of any company spokespeople, the company website, social handles, company content and branded hashtags. Social listening dives deeper into the data captured through brand monitoring efforts to capture insights and trends.

Social listening can also happen independent of brand monitoring because listening goes beyond or ignores references to the brand entirely and seeks to identify relevant conversations, influencers, tangential conversations and sentiment. This kind of listening is important because it can inform your approach to your content and messaging. You can learn what topics are dominating the conversation and how the participants feel about them.

Social listening tools have evolved over the years such that they can capture mentions spanning Twitter, online news, websites, Reddit and comments on Facebook, Instagram and YouTube. Platforms like LinkedIn, Facebook, Instagram and forums are partially or completely closed to listening tools. Having said that, a lot of the online conversation that is monitored is driven by Twitter. It serves as somewhat of a proxy. While valuable insights can be derived, it should not be seen as being 100 per cent representative of a brand's community of stakeholders and their feelings. In the absence of an alternative, we continue to leverage Twitter.

Ironically, a lot of content that drives engagement on platforms like Instagram and TikTok came from Twitter. Meme and influencer accounts repurpose humorous content from Twitter and reach users who have either moved on from Twitter or never bothered to sign up for it. Regardless, Twitter still holds a place as the social platform where news breaks and trends emerge.

Brand monitoring

Brand monitoring means monitoring things in case the status quo changes. If it does then we can act. Hopefully, a company never has to worry about becoming the centre of a brand reputation situation. The saying goes that every day on Twitter someone is 'it' and you just need to hope and pray that it is never you. I'd like to add that becoming famous can be a goal, being infamous shouldn't be.

Most of the time brand monitoring is focused on such things as customer service, tech support, tracking competitors and capturing relevant mentions. It is about making sure that customers who need assistance get it in a timely manner. If people are evaluating your product or service and reach out during their consideration phase then how and when you respond will impact their purchase decision.

Tracking mentions of competitors can help determine share of voice, how their customers are engaging with them and competitors are responding. I once sat in on a presentation by someone from Salesforce Marketing Cloud, formerly Radian6. In this presentation they talked about how they monitored mentions of their competitors and routed any product-related comments to their product group to inform their product roadmap and flag what the customers of competitors liked and disliked.

We conduct ongoing brand monitoring for a number of clients. We typically watch for mentions of their spokespeople in conjunction with the company name, Twitter handle and website. We look for spikes in mentions and try to determine the cause. Was this a news release? An interview that sparked conversation? Whenever there is an anomaly while monitoring, there is usually an underlying reason that just has to be investigated.

The longer a company conducts monitoring the more data that is compiled and a company can start to see trends over time. This may also be part of a company's social media objectives if they are tracking customer services issues, comments or share of voice. For example, companies will track customer service issues but also track their ability to resolve those issues and how long it takes. They may publicly state a timeframe of 24 hours for responding but, internally, they are committed to responding within several hours. The goal being to under promise and over deliver.

If a company has stated 'share of voice' to be one of their social media objectives then that will mean that they have to actively participate in the conversation. They will need to produce content to share and that will hopefully spark conversation. They will have to identify influencers and conversations that are active and current to join. However, they cannot barge into those conversations and online relationships. They have to be invited or earn the right to participate. They can't be overly promotional. Constantly pitching will not be well received. Being helpful and informative will be. Adding to the conversation rather than dominating it should be the objective. Amplifying the contributions of others first will likely be rewarded with reciprocity.

Social listening

Insights from brand monitoring and social listening can prove very valuable and it is worth noting that a variety of stakeholders within an organization can benefit. They include the aforementioned customer service and support but, depending on the type of company, we can add product development, HR, finance, sales, marketing, communications, investor relations, customer experience and the C-suite.

For example, HR would benefit from knowing what, if any, comments there are related to the company from an employer brand point of view. Some social listening tools can pick up comments on job rating sites as well as social channels. HR would want to know what is being said, by whom and what kind of impact is having. Are there people that are acting as advocates for the company, whether current employees, alumni or otherwise? Are there detractors and, if so, who are they, what are they saying, is there any truth to what they are saying and what needs to be done to address it?

I remember speaking with a friend who worked for a social media management and listening solution provider and he talked about how listening led to them winning a utility company as a customer. The company had social accounts for broadcasting information but did not have a management solution in place to deal with customer inquiries or comments. During a hurricane, customers went to social media for help and information. The company had to step up to serve their customers and proactively disseminate information regarding the status of power and in what areas. Now they are a source of information and not just related to power, during times of crisis.

Life insurance

We have conducted listening projects for a variety of industries, all with the intent of compiling data and deriving actionable insights. In one instance we were tasked with investigating online conversations regarding life insurance. Here is an example of a situation where the social listening strategy will not be very successful if it is literal. There is a greater likelihood of success if an indirect approach is taken. Let me explain.

People rarely discuss life insurance or its related purchase in social media. What they tend to do is mention life events and things that could be conversation triggers that would be relevant to insurance companies. What I mean by that is people share about births, deaths, job changes, job promotions, home purchases, moving and other life events that might correlate with the need for life insurance or a change to an existing policy.

The key is to listen for these life events and conversation triggers, but it can be challenging to capture everything. Just the topic of birth can take the form of a multitude of expressions. How many different ways can someone say they are having a baby? I am or we are expecting. The family is growing. We are having a baby. We were two and now we are three. There is a bun in the oven. The pitter patter of little feet. You get the idea.

It can be challenging to think of all of the combinations and permutations of how something gets expressed and be able to properly configure a query to capture it. We often find ourselves spending more time tuning a query to eliminate irrelevant mentions than the time it took to construct the original query. There is a bit of art of science to it and the longer a company listens and refines its queries the better and more valuable the insights will be that they derive.

Cough drops

Laurie Dillon-Schalk specializes in social media listening and she was working with a cough drop brand. They were having a discussion about the customer journey and the brand management was adamant that the customer's purchase decision was based on them having a cough. Laurie refuted this belief by telling them that the customer bought their product when they had a tickle, which is an earlier stage in their journey than the brand management would have considered. It was through social media listening that Laurie and her team were able to derive this insight and inform the brand. Think about how many assumptions are made that can either be confirmed or refuted through social media listening.

Healthcare association

My team and I were approached by an agency working with an association in healthcare to conduct social media listening and audience analysis. The agency had developed a number of personas to describe members of the association and wanted to know if they were correct in their assumptions about those personas and whether or not members of the association's social media community reflected any attributes of the personas they had defined.

The followers of the association were examined to determine key attributes such as brand affinities, social, economic, demographics, age, gender, education, geography, interests, spare time activities, news sources and other influences, and household incomes. We were able to confirm for the agency that the personas they had defined were, in fact, accurate. This helped inform the communications and content strategy that was to be implemented.

Mining, batteries and EVs

A mining client approached us with a new initiative they wanted to promote. While they were well known to traditional mining audiences, they had developed a patent-pending for the battery and electric vehicle industries through a joint venture involving one of their subsidiaries. Given the new technology and related audience, we needed new audience insights to guide our targeting because their traditional mining audience was not going to be the main focus. They wanted to raise awareness about this new story with existing investment audiences as well as potential investment audiences interested in battery and electric vehicle technology. With client input, we focused on the following: responsible investing, corporate social responsibility, green and clean tech, batteries and electric vehicles.

The client is publicly traded and not accustomed to doing paid campaigns – this was new for them. We acknowledged that we couldn't draw a straight line between the campaign and stocks being purchased. Spelling out the ROI of awareness-based campaigns can be a challenge. However, the struggle is twofold when you're expected to produce results with an audience you have limited first-hand experience with.

We conducted listening and audience analysis based on topics and influencers to compile target audience segments. We took the most appropriate segments and used them to guide paid campaigns promoting videos and an article explaining the patent-pending technology. While the campaigns were running online chatter grew that correlated with increases in the daily trading volume, in their stock price and their market cap.

Below are some key figures that highlight the success of the campaign(s) over the course of 90 days:

- The combined campaigns garnered 3.5+ million impressions and 2.8+ million total views.
- The client saw a rise in conversation volume related to their brand and new patent-pending technology (both from new sources and audiences).
- The client experienced a boost in website referral traffic, including 7000 new visitors from the promoted article and press release about their new technology.
- The campaigns coincided with a 5× rise in daily trading volume, increasing shares from the hundreds of thousands to the millions.
- The client saw a 3× rise in their share price, leading to a 3× market capitalization increase of several hundred million dollars.

While we could not claim full attribution for the boost in trading volume, share price or market capitalization, these increases coincided with increased website traffic, video views, brand awareness and conversation volume stemming from the campaign. In fact, the results of the campaign(s) were so positive, the client decided to move forward and ramp up more.

The primary objective was to raise awareness for the new initiative based on the patent-pending technology. That objective was achieved and the added bonus of increased share price and trading volume led to the client having several subsequent campaigns with a dramatically increased budget.

Needless to say, investor relations, the executive team and the board were very pleased and it all started with listening and audience insights.

Autism Awareness Month

For Autism Awareness Month, we conducted social media listening to examine Facebook's topic data. The Geneva Centre for Autism could see the volume of conversations happening around autism and strategize the best ways to consistently engage. On a macro level, we aggregated and presented the data in visual and interactive charts and graphs that made it easy to interpret, make sense of and use the data. On a micro level, the data could be narrowed by keywords, gender, age, language and geographic locations.

Health and wellness

We had a client that was a software company in the health and wellness space. They'd given us five competitors to monitor to determine share of voice. But two of the competitors they'd given us had common names. And the hashtags were commonly used by others. It took us a bit of time to refine the alerts to make sure we found only relevant mentions. With time, we've introduced some tweaks and managed to eliminate most of the noise.

What I like about social listening is some of the interesting and noteworthy insights that surface as a result. From the ongoing share of voice analysis we did for the software company, we noticed that two of their competitors have released branded research. Our competitor research used to focus on how often the competitors get mentioned by name. But we started to see how much volume of conversation specific to those competitors was about their research. It was creating an additional augmented amount of discussion around them because they had distributed branded content.

There was already some planning underway by the client to conduct some research. As a result of our efforts, they were more encouraged to see it through because they recognized they were not spoken about at the same volume as their competitors.[1]

McDonald's – Your Questions Our Answers

A few years ago, I had the good fortune to hear a marketing executive from McDonald's Canada speak about a campaign they did called Your Questions Our Answers. He provided some backstory and context to explain why the campaign was so important and what it meant to them as a company.

They had been conducting brand monitoring and social listening and, while they heard customer complaints about their products and service, more importantly they discovered just how much misinformation was being disseminated about their products, their ingredients and their processes.

People had misperceptions about them, and it was reflected in their likelihood to recommend their food and in their sentiment towards McDonald's. They wanted to meet the issue of misinformation head on and turn sentiment around such that people would have a higher propensity to recommend their food.

They devised a bold response. Their campaign was designed to solicit questions from their customers. No question was off limits, and they would answer everyone. They even went further and used video to respond to questions so that more people could be reached and that the right information they wanted to convey gained visibility. Talk about transparency.

For example, someone asked why their hamburgers look so enticing on TV or in their print ads but the burgers they get in the restaurants look so much less appetizing. One of their marketing staff used video to show them ordering a hamburger in a restaurant and then, without cutting, they got in a van and drove to a studio where a photoshoot was being conducted for a print ad for one of their hamburgers.

It took one minute for the hamburger to be ordered and received in the restaurant, but the photoshoot was scheduled for four hours to get everything just right. Why would it take so long? Well, every facet of the burger is meticulously dressed for the camera. They do not cook the meat completely. They only sear the edges of a frozen patty so that it stays thicker. Condiments are placed with extreme care so that every one of them is visible through the camera. A butter knife was heated so that when it touched the corners of the cheese slice they would gently droop over the edge of the burger. Talk about mouth-watering.

I worked on a McDonald's commercial and my experience was similar to the photo shoot. The company flew a representative from Montreal to Toronto to cook hamburgers that ended up covering a couple of tables.

Like the photo shoot, every hamburger was dressed meticulously so that all the condiments, cheese and bun were perfectly positioned for the camera.

My job was to give a fresh burger to the cast member eating on camera after every take. I would step in with the spit bucket so they could spit out the cold bit they just bit off and then hand them the new burger. Their job was to spend the entire day biting into cold hamburgers and make it look delicious every time. Well, at least we could say that we were in 'show business'.

Those are some examples that explain why the hamburger in an ad looks so different than the one in the restaurant. It's supposed to be that way and the video from McDonald's explained it thoroughly for all to see. Such efforts were well received with sentiment and propensity to recommend improving.

They also learned just how much interest there was in vegetarian options and, because of the campaign, they were considering the introduction of vegetarian products, all because they listened and learned.

Sentiment

Some companies can get caught up with the topic of sentiment and how people are expressing their feelings about the company. While tracking and measuring sentiment is important, seeking the underlying reason driving the sentiment being expressed is more important. For example, are customers having difficulty getting through to customer service directly? If they are having trouble, then it is no surprise that they would take their frustration to social media and complain publicly in hopes that publicly shaming a company would lead to a speedy resolution to their problem.

I once had a client who was running a paid acquisition campaign, but they were causing an increased volume of negative comments about the company, wait times at their call centres and delays in setting up new customers. The pandemic had caused unexpected customer growth and the company was trying to catch up to the demands of the new customers, but they weren't quite there yet. The longer the campaigns ran the more negative comments appeared. To add insult to injury, some of the comments weren't even from customers. There were people piling on to troll our client and/or to promote a competitor with whom they had supposedly had a better experience.

The negative comments were persisting, and Mondays were especially bad because the comments would accumulate over the weekend without anyone to respond to them. Executives were informed daily about the issue.

Thankfully, our client was able to add staff to their customer service area and wait times as well as set-up delays were reduced. This correlated with a decline in negative comments even while acquisition campaigns continued.

During this period, we were tracking sentiment. Typically, sentiment falls into three categories – negative, neutral and positive. While the percentage for each category can vary, neutral is usually the largest and most consistent proportion. Negative sentiment did grow during this period when the paid campaigns were inviting complaints, but it never outgrew neutral sentiment. It is rare that negative sentiment would be larger than neutral or positive.

Sentiment was an important key performance indicator (KPI) for this particular client but once the customer complaints decreased, we told them that neutral sentiment would be the predominant portion for the foreseeable future with variations only occurring in the size of the proportions. However, we would be watching for anomalies causing any sudden changes in sentiment. Only something catastrophic could cause negative sentiment to surpass the other two categories and, given that the client is a financial services company, only a recession or a depression could have such an effect but, even then, it would not be a certainty.

I remember speaking with someone from the Red Cross about sentiment and they told me that they ignored it. Not because it was not important but because the situations in which they are usually involved (i.e. crises, natural disasters, war/conflict, health issues) are always correlated with negative sentiment. It's a given so they focus on monitoring the situation, looking for those who need assistance and disseminating information.

It is important to note that many of the social media listening solutions currently available, while very powerful applications leveraging AI and algorithms, are not perfect and can often get things wrong. Thankfully, many of them can be taught. We can identify where they captured a mention and incorrectly classified it in a particular sentiment category. For example, one of our clients was mentioned in a post as being a 'best kept secret' but the use of the word 'secret' meant that the post was classified as having negative sentiment. However, the post was actually positive.

These examples of language being misinterpreted mean we must still scrutinize the mentions that we capture and ensure that they are correctly classified. Even we can be our own worst enemies. A client recently shared their perspective on some financial market trends. They expressed some criticisms and some of the things they said were not always positive. We usually exclude comments from a client when we are conducting ongoing monitoring. We want to capture comments about them rather than from them. However, in this case, others shared their comments, and their negative comments caused a spike in the overall negative sentiment. The client initially expressed concern until I was able to explain the root cause that their thought leadership and commentary about the market trends were incorrectly classified. Again, this highlights the art and science that is social listening.

Crisis? What crisis?

No company wants to find themselves in the midst of a crisis related to their reputation, especially if it involves social media. I do not purport to be a public relations expert but there are some key things that a company can do, from a social media perspective, that can help mitigate risk to their reputation and, if a crisis exists, help resolve it.

I once saw a marketing executive from the Four Seasons hotel chain presenting about their use of social media. He shared an approach for dealing with irate customers that I still share because it is so appropriate. He said that when you have an irate customer in the lobby of the hotel the first priority is to get them out of the lobby.

Using that example, if a bank has an irate customer expressing their frustrations in social media, the priority should be to get them off of social media and onto the phone where they can exchange private customer information and, hopefully, quickly resolve the customer's issue. One potential added benefit is the prospect of the customer coming back onto social media once their issue has been resolved to praise the bank for their assistance. I know that most companies don't want customers to complain, especially in public, but one of the silver linings about social media is that, while customers can complain publicly, they can also praise publicly. This signals to other customers, prospective and otherwise, that the company resolves customer issues and is focused on customer satisfaction.

When a company is experiencing a social media issue that might impact their reputation, there are several considerations, steps to be taken and decisions to be made in order to successfully navigate and resolve the issue. I describe it as a triage process. Let's go through them in greater detail.

Like the patient intake process at a hospital, we have to ask a series of questions and collect key pieces of information about the situation. What

FIGURE 11.1 David Armano's decision tree, reproduced with kind permission

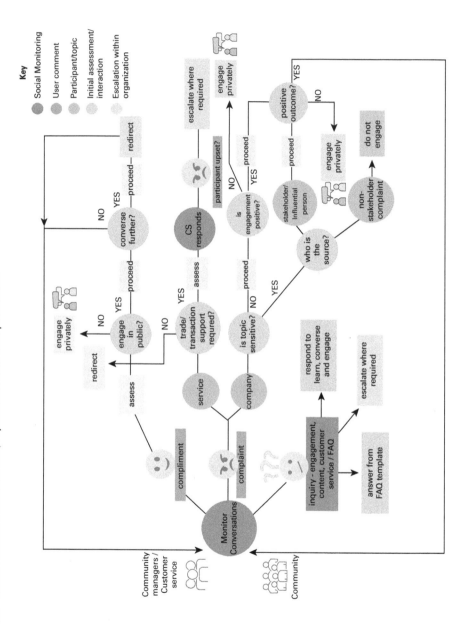

exactly is happening? On what channels? How long ago did it appear? Is it showing signs of dying down or is it growing in intensity? Who needs to be made aware and/or consulted and what should be reported? Is an escalation warranted? What, if any, preliminary actions have been or should be taken?

Let's use a real-world example to explain the triage process. We were working with a pet food company once and out of nowhere someone posted on the company's Facebook page a claim that the pet food they had purchased from the company had killed their dog. Needless to say, the fact that this accusation was made publicly on their Facebook page caused immediate panic within the company and the issue was raised all the way to the CEO overseas.

They came to me and asked what to do. I sat down with the CEO to discuss options and to learn more about the source of the complaint from what the CEO had heard from the staff. It turned out that the person had complained before and appeared to still be mourning. I walked the CEO through some of the things that were helpful to the situation. First of all, Facebook's algorithm meant that the complaint was not necessarily visible to every single person who followed the page. The more actively someone engaged with the page the more likely they were going to see this person's post. Furthermore, Facebook's feed would naturally push the post down as more recent content replaced it in people's feeds.

While those Facebook attributes were going to help, they did not address the core issue of how to deal with the customer. In situations like this, companies have to ask themselves, is what the complainant saying true? Are they influential? Does their online behaviour suggest that this is unusual or typical behaviour for them (i.e. are they a troll or likely someone with a legitimate complaint)? Does the company bear any responsibility?

In this situation, the company was not going to accept responsibility for the death of the person's dog nor should they. Their dog had died a couple of years before, yet the customer was bringing it up again. After conferring with the CEO, we devised a plan to have the communications team respond to the complaint. In most cases, the key to responding to any complaint is to simply acknowledge it. People just want to know they have been heard and it can go a long way to diffusing the situation.

Companies do not need to claim responsibility, admit to anything or be compelled to act in a way that is not warranted. All they have to do is tell the complainant that they understand that there is an issue that has been raised. They can then offer to discuss the matter further 'thus getting the customer out of the lobby' without promising the complainant prematurely.

The communications team reached out to the customer, acknowledged the complaint and invited them to call to discuss the matter further. The customer never called and the situation dissipated. As mentioned previously, sometimes people just want to scream into the void. They are venting their frustrations with no expectation of a resolution.

We have seen people pile onto client social accounts to make a comment about the industry in which our client operates without being critical towards our client. They were just using them as a platform for their complaint. Even though the comments were not necessarily directed at our client, we have to be careful regarding how we deal with them. We typically hide the comments if we can so that they are not aware nor come back to find their comments deleted, which can cause the situation to go from bad to worse.

Most companies never have to deal with a social media crisis so they don't have a social media playbook to reference or procedures defined to deal with those kinds of situations. As companies become more active in social media, the need for a social media policy, governance and procedures for handling a variety of social media related situations will become increasingly apparent. No company can anticipate every scenario but having a clearly defined social media policy and procedures laid out in a playbook can help employees navigate various situations as they arise.

Depending on what a company has planned or has to address, it may be wise to conduct some scenario planning to ensure the company is prepared as possible to deal with social media events. For example, a friend of mine was leading the social media team for an online only bank that was loved by its customers because it was not like the other older and more traditional (read stuffy) banks. Well, wouldn't you know it? This much-loved bank ended up being acquired by one of the old guard banks.

Before the acquisition was announced, the social media and communications teams created virtual war rooms to run their scenario-planning efforts. Their goal was to determine the kinds of comments, complaints, questions and issues that could arise once news got out. Having compiled a list of what they thought they could expect, they developed responses and key messages to address concerns pre-emptively and highlight the positives of what it would mean to customers.

Were their complaints? Absolutely there were but the social media and communications teams were able to mitigate the risks and maintain a degree of control over the situation. Things never got out of hand because of planning and preparedness. Is your company planning or dealing with anything where scenario planning could help?

Even debriefing after a customer service issue can prove helpful to deal with future customer service issues or complaints. In hindsight, what could have been done differently or better? Do new policies or procedures need to be documented and put into place? If so, who needs to be involved? Ask yourself and others in the company if there is a collective agreement for dealing with customer service issues or complaints? Who is on the front line? What are they empowered to do to help resolve the situation? What is the escalation path in terms of who is to be made aware and/or consulted within the company and how often is the customer to be updated regarding their issue? Who has decision-making authority? What time frame, if any, has been defined for resolving issues? Is the time to resolve the issue different for what is told to the customer than what has been defined within the company (e.g. 24 hours or next business day for the customer but internally it could be 3 hours)? How many people are involved and who has direct contact with the customer? Does someone from the social media team hand off to someone and, if so, to whom? Will the social media team be involved again before the issue is ultimately resolved?

That's a lot of questions but many of them only have to be asked once. The defining of policies and procedures will answer many of those questions once and for all. While it won't eliminate the risk of a social media crisis entirely, it will give people the proper resources to deal with a crisis and expedite a resolution that hopefully meets the needs of the various stake-holders involved.

Endnote

1   A Jenkins, How Volterra finds audiences and conducts competitor research with Awario, 2021, awario.com/case-studies%2Fvolterra/ (archived at https://perma. cc/S5ZM-37XG)

12

Paid social media

Visibility for your organization and its content on social media grows more challenging by the day. Some platforms like TikTok are still enabling rapid organic growth but, for more mature platforms like Facebook, it is nearly impossible to get traction organically, especially if you are just starting out. This has resulted in a growing reliance on paid social media.

This chapter is going to discuss paid social media strategies and best practices but it won't focus so much on specific ad formats because the various platforms are continuously introducing new ones and I cannot predict what will be available to you by the time you are reading this. With that in mind, we are going to stick to fundamentals that really haven't changed that much.

PESO model

For those of you in public relations or communications, you are familiar with the PESO model. For those who are reading about it for the first time, it stands for paid, earned, shared and owned media. We will focus on the paid aspect here but the other elements have been discussed directly or indirectly elsewhere.

As noted above, sometimes you have no choice but to incorporate paid campaigns into your marketing efforts. You can also combine paid with other aspects of PESO. For example, if members of your community create user-generated content or provide testimonials, perhaps you can put paid in place to promote them for more visibility.

Several years ago we shared a client with Pointman News Creation, a PR & Communications company in Toronto. Pointman had arranged an interview with a morning business news show. The client purchased a recording of the interview and we used it as a creative asset for a Facebook campaign.

With a modest budget in the hundreds of dollars, we were able to generate over 80,000 views of the video and in the days following the interview and our campaign, the client generated thousands of dollars in sales. Don't think paid is a standalone activity. It can complement other parts of the PESO model and drive desirable outcomes.

Where to start

As with any new marketing initiative, you need to define your objectives. What is the purpose of the campaign or campaigns that you are going to run? Are you promoting a new product or service? Increase brand awareness? Do you want to survey or poll existing or potential customers? Generate revenue or drive conversions? Promote an upcoming event?

You will likely be doing one or more of these at any given time. You might be targeting the same audience with different offers, different audiences with the same offer or different audiences with different offers. Regardless of who you are targeting and with what, you need to be clear about the who and the why to ensure success.

No matter whether you are a B2C, B2B, non-profit or government organization, you are going to conduct different types of paid campaigns depending on your objectives and what stage your target audience is at in relation to those objectives. At each stage you will want to be able to capture relevant information to inform your strategy but you will need to confirm that that capability exists. You need to ensure that the right tools and capabilities are in place to track, measure and report on progress and outcomes.

Landing pages, lead forms and more

We will discuss metrics more later in this chapter but when it comes to responding to calls to actions (CTAs), people are typically clicking on an ad and being redirected to another destination. This can be your website's homepage, a specific landing page on your website or e-commerce site. It could be another destination link such as a webinar registration page or your Amazon page for your book. You might use a lead form that keeps your target on the particular social platform where you are running the campaign but drives a conversion from the ad and conducts a lead capture.

Don't start a campaign until you have mapped out the flow from ad placement through to lead capture, making sure that there isn't a step missing or a potential break in the flow when it comes to accumulating data related to the leads or the transaction. You are putting so much effort into the campaigns. You do not want to miss anything that could affect the performance or outcomes of your campaigns.

I should highlight the potential implications of a campaign that incorporates a lead form compared to one using a landing page. If the lead form is on the social platform, then you can anticipate higher-quality leads. You are being more specific about your objectives from your conversion campaign because of what is being asked of your target audience. If you are capturing personal information then they see enough value and/or have an interest in what you are offering. Higher quality means higher costs so be prepared to pay a higher cost per result.

Sending people to a landing page resident on your website or elsewhere tends to be part of a traffic or awareness campaign, which gives you more latitude in terms of budget and ad sets. While you are able to reach a broader audience, there can be a negative impact on the quality of your leads. You are reaching more people at a lower cost per result, but you need to reach a lot more people to get the math to work in your favour and get the quality leads.

You may want to consider running two campaigns, one after the other, where you use the landing page in the first campaign to experiment at a lower cost per result followed by another campaign using the lead form. Assuming success on the first campaign, run the second campaign using the lead form because now you can justify the budget based on the fact that your first campaign proved its viability.

Broad versus one-to-one

When we think about advertising we tend to think that is something that is visible to many. I am not here to suggest anything different. Many of our paid campaigns are designed with visibility in mind. That is not going to change any time soon nor should it for you.

You will likely devote most of your time, effort and budget to paid campaigns that are one-to-many, especially if you are trying to raise awareness on a budget. There is nothing wrong with this approach and should be considered a best practice. Furthermore, it will most certainly have some bearing on your cost per result.

Having said that, you may wish or need to reach people in a one-to-one context. They may be existing customers that you want to solicit for feedback. They may be qualified leads or people with whom you have communicated previously such that you can send them a direct message.

This one-to-one communication can drive tremendous value and results but there is a degree of intimacy and privacy that can't be ignored. You do not want to blow your chances to make a good first impression. You want to be welcomed into their inbox rather than marked as a spammer.

Platforms like LinkedIn empower users to manage the ads they see and from whom. You do not want to end up in LinkedIn jail because your campaign was deemed inappropriate. The goal with sponsored DM campaigns is to be targeted, personal and deliver value.

People are time starved so do not send them a lengthy message. Get to the point and use the WIIFM (aka What is in it for me?) concept where the 'me' in this case is them, the DM recipient. If you do not deliver value to their inbox you won't be allowed back in again.

Ad options

Depending on your objectives and the platform(s) you are considering, one or more of the following ad options could drive success. Some ads ask little of the audience and are designed to raise awareness, drive reach for the brand and its content or garner website traffic.

Other ads begin to ask more of the audience, seeking to have them engage with content such as video views, convince users to install an app or sign up for a trial in order to have ongoing interaction with the brand and its solutions and, hopefully, convert to become paying customers.

Finally, there are ads that are meant to drive conversions or transactions, exchanges of value. Prospects could be asked for contact information in exchange for access to valuable content, book a demo or have a representative contact them as part of a lead generation initiative. E-commerce companies leverage ads to acquire store traffic and subsequent catalogue sales.

Pixels

Conversions or transactions are key objectives and you will want to ensure that wherever possible that you incorporate conversion trackers (aka pixels) into your website. Most social media platforms have them. They accumulate anonymous visitor data from your website and tie it back to your paid campaigns. This is especially important for retargeting ad campaigns that market to your target audience as they move down the marketing funnel. Let's take a look at each stage of that funnel to understand more and where pixels can play a role.

The marketing funnel

Awareness (top-of-the-funnel or TOFU)

I know that I am stating the obvious when I say that you can't reach your sales and marketing objectives if nobody knows you exist. You must raise your awareness for your organization, your products or your services.

You might start very simply with promoting your social accounts to establish and build an initial audience. Establish a beachhead from which to build. While you may have used paid social media to do it, your newly established audience will also respond to the organic content you share and potentially share it, thus amplifying your brand and raising awareness indirectly for you.

FIGURE 12.1   Marketing funnel

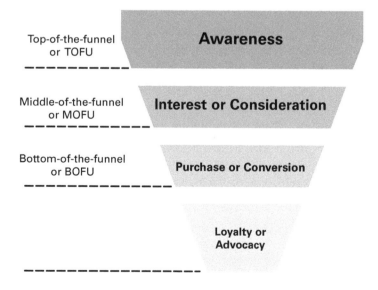

If you are a new organization and/or have a new product or service being launched then raising awareness is critical. We worked with a new app company that ultimately wanted to drive installs but ran campaigns to introduce themselves first. It was very difficult to drive installs when they were an unknown entity. The lack of awareness also correlated with a high cost per install (CPI). As awareness grew, the CPI began to drop.

People buy from whom they know, like and trust. Moving from unknown to trusted takes time and effort. The Rule of Seven applied to marketing suggests that someone has to see an ad seven times before they buy. Think about what that means to your paid campaign efforts in terms of budget and duration to ensure ad recall.

Interest or consideration (middle-of-the-funnel or MOFU)

Now that awareness has been established, you need to move your audience down the funnel and start to build interest in what you have to offer as they begin to consider what you have in relation to others. This is where messaging and content gets more specific, perhaps addressing a specific pain point or need while potentially differentiating from competitors.

People who responded to your awareness campaign can be retargeted with new creative and/or you can create a lookalike audience with similar attributes and target them too. Every stage of the funnel provides new behavioural data based on ad response that can be used to continually refine your approach for existing and future campaigns.

Purchase or conversion (bottom-of-the-funnel or BOFU)

Running ads for awareness and to increase consideration is a necessary step in the process but the ultimate goal is a transaction or conversion of some kind. To achieve this you need to have a strong CTA. Buy now! Learn more! Register now! Click to install! Get it now! Click to download! Sign up for our newsletter! You get the idea. Maybe you back it up with a limited time offer, something that creates a sense of urgency. Lifetime licence! Limited time offer! X days or X hours remaining! Respondents can also be retargeted when you have something new to offer. The conversion tracking data strikes again!

Loyalty or advocacy

So now they are a customer. You don't want to harass them but you do want to leverage their belief in your product or service. Offer them incentives to refer others. Giffgaff, a mobile virtual network operator (MVNO) offers incentives such as credits to their customers for referrals and if they provide support to each other. This lessens the customer service and tech support burden on Giffgaff and delivers value to their customers, building loyalty and advocacy in the process.

If you do not have something new to offer, you can still use paid to reach your customer base for testimonials, reviews, surveys/polls and other forms of advocacy that you can reward with discounts, gift cards, swag or some other form or recognition. Look for people praising your products or services, especially on social media and acknowledge and reward them. Anyone going out of their way to mention your product or service in a positive way should not be overlooked or ignored.

When you do have something new to offer or something to add to what they have already purchased then you can use a combination of paid and organic promotion to reach them and remind them periodically. The added metrics for these efforts could include share of wallet, account penetration or upsell rate with existing customers or sales to net new customers compared to existing ones.

Metrics

A lot of metrics for paid campaigns are common across the various social media platforms. They include things like click-through rate (CTR), conversion rate, cost per click (CPC) or cost per impression (CPM).

If you are using video as one or more of your creative assets, you will want to focus on the video views and the percentage of the video being watched. This will give you a sense of whether or not people are abandoning the video early or watching it through to the end. Facebook, for example, shares through plays, three-second views and different percentage views of videos. You will also want to determine repeat views versus unique views. Repeat views would indicate heightened interest and that your creative is working well.

You will also want to track reach, impressions and clicks, unique and otherwise. These metrics will provide a sense of how your awareness and conversion objectives are being met. In the case of clicks, you will want to differentiate between repeat visitors and net new ones, similar to repeat versus net video viewers.

Campaigns and ad sets

The various platforms will provide an aggregated view of your campaign performance, which will give a sense of how things are going overall but you will want to drill down a bit to see if your ad sets are performing equally or if one or more ad sets are outperforming the rest. If you find that to be the case then you can look deeper to determine if the creative, copy or audience targeting have any bearing on the results you are seeing.

We have run numerous campaigns where we have used a static image or graphic, an animated gif and a video as the creative assets. Consistently, the ad set with the static image or graphic performs the worst with the gif doing better and the video performing best.

That has been our experience but we continue to experiment with our campaigns because things can vary from campaign to campaign, especially if objectives and audience targeting parameters are different.

We ran an awareness campaign using a corporate video (i.e. no talking heads but footage of operations, etc.) and a video of the CEO giving an update. The corporate video ad set performed best but, regardless of video, the cost per result was high compared to what we had typically seen.

We ran a subsequent campaign with video views as the objective, which is the only change that was made. The CEO video became the top-performing video and the cost per result dropped down considerably, reaching the costs we were used to seeing with previous campaigns.

Recommended best practices from the platforms suggest multiple ad sets with multiple creative assets in various formats. This approach allows for experimentation and for the platforms to optimize delivery on your behalf, even if you turn some ad sets off based on poor performance.

Objectives and measurement

If you are introducing a new product or service then you will want to focus on things such as sales, pre-orders, expressions of interest and the aforementioned upsells. Can you build anticipation and excitement with organic and paid strategies? Think of the ways new apps and social networks introduce themselves but limit access to their beta versions or by restricting invites.

Paid strategies can have follow-on effects that include mentions in social and online media so track how far your reach ends up being, who is talking about you, your product or service and in what way (i.e. sentiment). Did some campaigns reach farther than others? If so, what do you think influenced those outcomes? Do you have any historical campaign data that could prove helpful for comparison? With subsequent campaigns, did your reach expand and was that driven by any changes in targeting, budget or both? Are the people or entities talking about you influential? Did their mentions drive any complementary outcomes – icing on your cake?

A lot of time and energy goes into creating and distributing content. Different types of content come into play at the various stages of the marketing funnel. Distributing content organically should be the default approach but then it should be augmented with paid when and where it makes strategic sense. Again, what are you trying to accomplish and how does content serve that objective? Where should paid strategies be applied to help?

Not every piece of content needs to have paid behind it. Wait to see if a particular piece of content gets some initial traction and then throw some gas (i.e. paid budget) on the fire. Allocate budget for milestone or substantive pieces of content such as e-books, research reports or case studies. If you are going to gate the content and ask for contact information in exchange for access then you want to make sure that the content has sufficient value to the prospective customer.

Blogs, long-form videos and podcasts can be lengthy pieces of content and not necessarily conducive to immediate engagement or consumption. Consider promoting excerpts to tease and excite your target audience, and then redirect them to the full versions. Track things like views, downloads, engagements, page visits and bounce rates. Getting people to visit your blog only to quickly click away is not the kind of outcome you want. Having them linger to read and, ideally, share your content is the goal.

During the pandemic we all saw the increase in webinars, virtual conferences, panels and one-on-one interviews. Paid can help get virtual bums in virtual seats and, when the world opens back up again, actual bums in actual seats at your event. You are combining raising awareness about events with driving registrations or ticket sales. If you have content from past events that can be repurposed to show prospective attendees what they can expect in terms of experience then do it and support it with paid. Get your guest speakers to promote their involvement to their own personal networks for organic amplification.

Be mindful if you are using a third-party site for registrations and/or for hosting your virtual event. You will need to ensure that they can capture and share the number of visitors, registrants and attendees. You are going to know how many people you drove to their landing page but you won't have any visibility into what happened after that unless they provide you with that data. Don't assume they can provide it. Confirm it.

Do not think that when your event is over that the promotional opportunities have ended. Many people register for webinars to gain access to the recording to watch at their convenience later. Operate with that assumption in mind and promote the recording to them as well as to those who missed the opportunity to attend.

Consider promoting excerpts and keep the original content gated. You do not want to diminish the value of your content by giving access to everyone if you had made the original registrants feel like they were gaining access to exclusive content.

Kate Chernis of Lately.ai refers to this as 'after the fact marketing', and they have seen a 98 per cent increase in engagement with their webinar content. At first glance, this would seem counterintuitive. Why bother having a webinar if you are anticipating most of the engagement to happen afterward? Don't look at it that way. It doesn't mean you should abandon webinars altogether. Look at it as a phased approach with your content that extends the life of every piece of content related to the webinar – squeezing more juice out of the lemon.

First, you use content supported with paid to drive awareness and registrations for the event. Second, you hold the event for the attendees as promised. Finally, you take the resulting piece of content (i.e. the recording) and parse it into excerpts to distribute for promotional purposes. Use these teasers or snackable pieces of content to create follow on awareness and interest in the webinar content. Incorporate paid to increase visibility and engagement. Don't be surprised if you see greater performance afterward than with the original content promoting the webinar but focus on the cumulative impact.

Paid resources

Go direct

If you have the opportunity to work with representatives from the platforms then take advantage of it. They can provide a wealth of information based on all of the learnings they have from the millions of campaigns that have been run on their platform.

Groups

Join groups related to paid social media on LinkedIn and/or Facebook to share and learn. I have learned a tremendous amount from the groups that I am a part of. They also provide hacks and insights that even representatives from the platforms are not necessarily aware of.

Corporate sites

The corporate blogs for each platform are great sources of information, especially for news about changes to the platform, new ad formats and policy changes. They also have tons of resources and self-directed courses that are very helpful and some provide industry recognized certifications.

Third-party sites

Look to third-party sites, especially social media management solution providers like Hootsuite, Buffer and Sprout Social who have a relationship with the different social media platforms, for resources for paid campaigns. They are valuable sources of information because of the volume of posts and campaigns that are run through their platforms and they are sometimes privy to information that agencies and individuals are not.

Audiences

You may be very clear about your target audience but translating that into one or more targeted paid campaigns is more involved. With LinkedIn, you are most likely targeting job titles, locations and company size to name a few audience attributes. In the case of Facebook, you could be targeting interests, location and pages the audience has liked whether similar or competitive to your own. Audiences on Twitter might be targeted based on key words in their bio, location and/or if they follow certain accounts. Different platforms mean different nuances related to audiences.

Having pixels in place can prove very helpful. They can help establish your initial audience and help refine your targeting over time as the audience grows and responds to your campaigns and creative assets.

Persona-based audiences

I am defining persona-based audiences as audiences that have been built based on what an organization defines from their existing customer base (e.g. job title, location, company size, industry), pre-defined personas (e.g. demographics, gender, marital status, life stage, interests, etc.), competitive insights (e.g. like or following competing accounts) or a combination thereof.

Lookalike audiences

According to Wikipedia, a lookalike audience is a group of social network members who are determined by the characteristics they share with another group of members. If you have a defined audience, perhaps one of the persona-based ones mentioned above, then you may want to use it to define a lookalike audience, especially if you have already run campaigns.

If members of your persona-based audience responded to your campaign(s) then a lookalike audience that shares similar characteristics would have a high likelihood of responding to your campaign(s) too. This approach can prove valuable for awareness campaigns when you are trying to reach new people.

Custom audiences

You can create custom audiences based on people who have responded to your previous campaigns such as clicks, video views, website visits and more responses. The key here is that this audience is composed of people who have responded in some way to your previous campaigns. Get in front of them again if they visited your site but stalled there or went so far as to begin shopping only to abandon their shopping cart. If they are retargeted with new campaigns with new offers, new creative and/or new copy then you should see high conversion rates given that the audience has shown positive responses in the past.

Putting them all together

Assuming you are conducting your first or initial paid campaign and have the opportunity to run more than one campaign and do so consecutively, consider starting with a persona-based audience leveraging information already known.

You can choose to incorporate a lookalike audience then or wait until you see how the audience responds to your campaign and then determine whether a lookalike audience would be helpful to your objectives. Furthermore, if you wait to accumulate campaign performance data then your pixels can provide additional information of value.

Once you have some initial campaign performance data, you can set up a custom audience to retarget based on past ad campaign responses. You retarget them with the same campaigns but risk ad fatigue or you can retarget them with new ads with new creative and/or copy and see how they respond to your subsequent campaigns.

Imaging each audience aligned with the stages of the marketing funnel. The persona-based audience is broad and helps if you are casting a wide net to reach as many people as possible. Lookalike and custom audiences are constructed based on insights captured as respondents move down the funnel. The more that is learned, the better the targeting becomes and the greater the likelihood of the campaign objectives being achieved.

13

Hashtags

FIGURE 13.1 Chris Messina tweet, reproduced with kind permission

With that one question the hashtag that we now know and love was born. It is now an integral part of any given social media strategy. It denotes trending topics and perpetuates memes. Used correctly, it can augment your strategy and aid discovery. Used incorrectly, it can generate a backlash and negatively impact your brand's reputation.

Chris Messina's original suggestion for the hashtag was to help organize groups on Twitter. It evolved into helping organize content by topic, trending news, online chats, campaigns and more. It is used now on almost every social platform but not always in the same way or with the same objective. In this chapter we will look at the different ways that hashtags can be used, how to research them and how to avoid missteps.

Brand hashtags

If you are a new or not widely known organization, don't think that a brand hashtag doesn't apply to you. It is worth establishing or 'seeding' a brand hashtag and using it repeatedly. Over time it will become known in association with your brand.

It will take time to see it being used by others. Frequency and consistency are required, especially if the hashtag is tied to your brand but not your brand name. For example, in 2019 the Toronto Raptors won the NBA Championship. #Raptors is most certainly a brand hashtag but so is #WeTheNorth. The latter came about as a result of a campaign developed by the Raptors' advertising agency and is now ubiquitous.

You can find #WeTheNorth all over social media, offline and emblazoned on Raptors merchandise. That is a peak brand hashtag! That doesn't happen in every instance but it speaks to how much a brand hashtag can permeate the social media conversation and even our everyday lives.

Brand hashtags can extend to products and services. #Nike is an obvious example but, when you think about the different type of shoes that Nike offers, other hashtags such as #airjordan, #nikeairmax or #nikefootball come into the mix.

Brand hashtags are meant to last so give them proper consideration. You do not want to have too many brand hashtags, but you do not necessarily have to stop at one depending on your organization and its areas of focus. You may want to start simply with a main or foundational brand hashtag and add to it over time, if appropriate.

Campaign hashtags

The definition of a campaign can vary depending on the organization and what is being promoted. Promoting a webinar, a particular piece of content, a contest or a special offer would all qualify as campaigns.

#HalfPrice is a hashtag but it is not a branded campaign hashtag. It is just a promotional offer. Your campaign hashtag should have an obvious connection to your brand. Dove has a history of powerful campaigns. With #PasstheCrown, they wanted to end race-based hair discrimination in the US so they teamed up with the National Urban League, Color of Change and Western Centre. Dove learned that 70 per cent of women didn't feel represented in media and advertising. The campaign was driven by Dove's belief that everyone should be able to embrace their natural hair without judgment.[1]

A campaign hashtag can also support a cause or a movement. Bell, Canada's largest telecom company, has chosen mental health as a cause to support. As a result, #BellLetsTalk is used to promote support for mental health and reduce the stigma related to talking about mental health issues.

The hashtag denotes Bell Let's Talk Day that happens every January but is not isolated to just that day. It is tied to the company's support for mental health and can be seen on social media throughout the year. Influencers and even competitors show their support because mental health issues touch almost everyone.

Your campaign may not be repeated every year. Campaign hashtags are typically for the short term. You want to make a splash and establish a strong association with your brand while raising awareness for the campaign. You may have to incorporate paid support with your campaign and/or involve influencers to help get your campaign off the ground.

Trending

Twitter is probably the best example of trending hashtags. It tends to be where news breaks. As I write this, the world is coming to terms with the Taliban taking power in Afghanistan. As a result #Afghanistan became a trending hashtag.

Sometimes you can take advantage of trending hashtags. This is not one of those times. You should avoid using the hashtag unless you are raising awareness about what is happening in relation to it.

Some brands such as Kenneth Cole or American Apparel thought it appropriate to take advantage of a trending hashtag and turn it into a marketing campaign. The latter thought that when #HurricaneSandy was hitting the Northeast and Mid-Atlantic regions of the US in 2012 it would be the perfect time to promote their #SandySale.

Needless to say the tone-deaf promotion was met with a backlash that was rightfully justified. Brands like American Apparel or Kenneth Cole may believe that any publicity is good publicity, but the risk may be too high. What if you go so far as to never recover?

Call it drafting behind a trending hashtag or newsjacking but whatever you call it, be careful about how you hitch your wagon to it. If you look to be marketing at the expense of someone experiencing something bad like a hurricane or earthquake then you deserve the response you get.

You are probably better off not to seek a marketing opportunity at all surrounding trending hashtags. It may be more of an opportunity to build your reputation as a trusted source of information or show your support and try to improve the situation in some way and in the future, having earned the right to market, you can be more promotional.

Another reason to be mindful of trending hashtags, and news for that matter, is to ensure that you do not have social posts previously scheduled that could make you look insensitive or tone-deaf. It was never your intention to draw negative attention to yourself. Numerous organizations have found themselves dealing with the fallout of pre-scheduled posts when juxtaposed with trending news that resulted in them looking foolish and insensitive.

Community

I don't know how many of you have participated in a Twitter chat but, on any given day on Twitter, people congregate at a specific time to join a discussion around a particular topic. For example, every Tuesday evening at 8 pm EST is #LinkedInChat. There are lots of regularly scheduled chats and others can happen on an ad-hoc basis, perhaps tied to an event like a conference or presentation.

If you can't attend live, you can follow the hashtag to follow the discussion. Moderators sometimes push questions out to those that show up. Other times, they have a guest who responds to prepared questions and others pile on with their thoughts. It can feel a little frenetic but it fosters connection and community.

Beyond chat-related communities, hashtags can link people together as groups. In the early days of Twitter in Toronto, where I live, someone established the hashtag #geeklunch and would tweet out that they were going to a particular restaurant for lunch. If you wanted to join them then all you had to do was reply with the hashtag. I met a lot of people in the digital space in Toronto through that hashtag and others, connecting with more people as a result.

Hashtags like #liberal, #conservative, #democrat, #christian, #muslim, #atheist or #catholic are examples that denote groups, communities, values and beliefs. Hashtags do not always carry that much weight but you can see how powerful and polarizing hashtags can be, especially when connected to the political or religious climate of the present day.

Community hashtags do not have to be labels. They can be movements. Think about #MAGA, #BLM, #METOO or #justiceforgeorgefloyd. They are not labels for members of those communities. They identify those movements that have communities of supporters. Supporters that can be local or from anywhere because community hashtags like these can foster momentum globally.

As with trending hashtags, community hashtags related to causes or movements should not be seen as opportunities to promote your own agenda. Unless you are supporting the movement, do not even think about doing something promotional. The backlash you could incur would be like nothing you have ever seen before.

There are a lot of people online who have what has been described as 'keyboard courage' where they feel that they can say whatever they want without fear of repercussions. You do not want to poke that bear and draw unnecessary attention to yourself and bring their vitriol down upon you, your organization or your brand.

Related

When I am talking about related hashtags I am talking about hashtags that could relate to your industry, your location, your job, events and more. These are not necessarily campaign hashtags but could be used in conjunction with them. For example, every year the Canadian Imperial Bank of Commerce (CIBC) holds its Run for the Cure to raise awareness for breast cancer and to raise funds to help fund finding a cure. You will see #runforthecure related to the event but, because it happens in cities across Canada, you will see additional hashtags identifying the city where the poster is running.

Every month there are awareness days, national and international something day and possibly something about this day in history that could be an opportunity to develop content, show support or engage a relevant community. It is worth researching and putting placeholders in your calendar where applicable. However, heed my previous warnings. Don't use the hashtag or the opportunity if it is not a fit for your brand and you risk looking disingenuous.

Content

Hashtags related to content topics are probably one of the most common types. LinkedIn used to organize content into channels based on the topic such as leadership. Now topics are organized by a related hashtag and you can choose to follow #leadership to see content being shared by others on the platform. They have included the hashtag to denote that the content being shared relates to leadership.

You can research hashtags on LinkedIn within the search field to see which relevant hashtags have the most followers if you are trying to ensure visibility for your content. When we research hashtags on Twitter we look at volume and frequency to gauge a hashtag's usefulness. For Instagram it is similar to LinkedIn in that popularity of hashtags plays a role. You won't see how many people follow a hashtag but you will see how many times a particular hashtag was used so you can use the popularity rank to determine which hashtag and hashtag combinations are the best to use.

Be sure to research how many different variations of hashtags there might be related to a topic. For example, artificial intelligence (AI) is often accompanied by #artificialintelligence and/or #ai. Sometimes you will see it in combination with #machinelearning. Look at the combinations of hashtags being used because it is rare that a hashtag is being used in isolation.

CTAs

Calls to action hashtags are less likely to be something that people are tracking and more likely to just be something you use in the body of your post to get someone to take action. #BuyNow, #booknow, #reservenow, #registernow, #limitedtime, #todayonly or #whilesupplieslast are just a few examples.

You can have fun with them because it is not about making them trend on social media. It is about grabbing the attention of those following your social feeds. Try humour. Try puns. Anything to spark interest.

Sometimes you can combine a CTA hashtag with a campaign. Coke prompted people to #ShareACoke as part of one of their campaigns. The Bell Let's Talk initiative might use #TalkAboutMentalHealth to prompt action and to reduce or remove the stigma related to talk about mental health issues.

Popular vs long tail

LinkedIn ranks topic hashtags based on followers and Instagram ranks them based on usage. Depending on your hashtag research methods and tools, you can find out the frequency and volume of various hashtags on Twitter and use the results to inform your approach.

Regardless, you are going to be choosing your hashtags on a variety of criteria. Most likely, you will default to popularity to maximize the visibility of your posts. However, including long-tail or niche hashtags may give you unique visibility with specific groups. You may find niche communities and discussions happening online when conducting your research. If those communities and conversations are relevant to your organization then you may be wise to put more of your energy into nurturing them rather than a potentially scattershot approach to larger and more disparate groups.

It is not that one is more right than the other. Your hashtag strategy may change depending on the marketing phase you are in. If you are just starting out and your community is nascent at best then popular hashtags may be the ones to use. If you have a well-established community but growth is an ongoing objective then branching out into niche communities with long-tail hashtags may be appropriate. Don't go so niche or long tail that your chosen hashtag or hashtags have never been used. That would be counterproductive. Also, there is nothing to stop you from using both types of hashtags in combination to cover all the bases. Always be on the lookout because new popular and long-tail hashtags can appear often for you to make use of. Like I have said a number of times already in this book, test, measure and adjust.

Best practices

Beyond what I have already shared about hashtags, I wanted to share some additional best practices for you to consider and perhaps adopt for your ongoing social media strategy. They are not carved in stone because we have already talked about how much change is always taking place within social media. These are for consideration and you can elect to use them or dismiss them as you see fit.

Keep checking the optimal number of hashtags for posts across each channel. Channels like Instagram tend to require more hashtags while other platforms less so. Sources like Hubspot, Hootsuite and Sprout Social stay up to date on the optimal number of hashtags.

- Organize combinations of hashtags and save them if they are going to be used regularly in conjunction with certain content and/or campaigns. Some social media management solutions allow you to save hashtag groups to save you time and effort when composing posts.

- Be mindful of hashtag placement. You can hide hashtags in the caption or first comment on Instagram if you want to give emphasis to the rest of your copy without sacrificing discoverability. LinkedIn is now tracking hashtags in comments to keep that in mind too.

- Use hashtags within the body of your copy if you are dealing with character count limits like on Twitter.

- Use humour and create hashtags that are meant solely for that purpose. They may have never been used before until you used it to bring a little humour and humanity to your community. For example, if you are having a rough day and want to find some common ground, use #dontwanttoadulttoday. It's a hashtag for no other purpose than bringing a smile to someone's face. If someone within your community shared that they are having a rough day then perhaps send a humorous gif and a relevant hashtag to show you understand. Be human and foster community. Don't pitch.

Fails

We have talked about hashtag research for identifying hashtags to use but now I want to talk about doing hashtag research to identify hashtags you should avoid as well as to find out if the hashtags you have in mind related to your brand or campaign have already been used and to learn in what way. The more you know and learn the better you can avoid any missteps.

We were contracted to conduct some social media listening for another agency that had a client, an association in the healthcare industry. One of the hashtags that the association was using in their social media posts was #MAID to denote 'medical assistance in dying', which was a topic of debate at the time.

Little did they know that #maid was also a popular hashtag within the pornography industry and if you were following that hashtag you were at risk of having your social feed filled with objectionable content related to women in French maid outfits and other maid-related content. It took us a while to purge that type of content from the mentions our social listening efforts were pulling in. It just goes to show that you should research a hashtag or hashtags before putting them into use to protect your reputation.

You can have more innocent situations but still situations where your chosen hashtag is being used already and in a different way than you intended. I was involved with a charity that funded educational field trips for children. Every year we held a gala to raise money for the charity and the event was being shared and discussed on Twitter and Instagram. During the gala, a trivia contest would run and each table would compete to win the highly coveted trophy.

The trivia contest was called Battle of the Brains. I conducted research to see if #BOTB could be a likely hashtag. Unfortunately, it was already being used by what seemed to be every radio station in the world running Battle of the Bands contests. Given the volume of their usage, there was no way that our charity would have any visibility so we opted to just use the charity's name as the hashtag. Have a plan B for your hashtags.

Researching a hashtag is no guarantee that you won't still make a mistake with your hashtag strategy. Run your hashtags by a few people to see if they make sense. Do they have any potential to be misinterpreted? Do they have any alternative meanings that you may not be aware of, even if it is in another language? We once had a client whose name included Abra and they wanted to use #abra but abra is Spanish for open so it is a very common word that would drown out our client's intended hashtag.

Take the singer Susan Boyle who had a new album to promote. It is not clear who exactly suggested the hashtag, but #susanalbumparty now lives in infamy. As people began reacting to it and Susan's team realized how their chosen hashtag could be misinterpreted, they quickly changed it to #SusanBoylesAlbumParty. It may have fixed things then but this example of hashtag misstep still gets referenced nearly a decade later.[2]

Just search hashtag fails and you will see the hall of fame hashtag fails where brands innocently thought their chosen hashtag was appropriate only to learn that it meant something entirely different in the urban dictionary or to the intended audience who were happy to oblige by telling them what it really meant.

So you research your hashtags. You get others to take a look at your hashtags and tell you if they see any issues with them. However, you can still run into a hashtag fail. This seems to happen most often when an organization uses a hashtag to solicit commentary from their community.

On the service the hope is that it will result in positive stories where people express their gratitude and affinity to the organization asking for their comments. Unfortunately, what often happens is that more people who have an issue with the organization respond and drown out the original positive responses that were being sought.

If you are a company that has a reputation for poor customer service and you try to connect with your customers through a hashtag, you are playing with dynamite. Your customers will take this opportunity to tell you how they really feel. You might have been looking for thank yous and praise, but you are going to end up with social feeds filled with complaints tied to your hijacked hashtag.

Much of the social customer service movement began because of the now famous video that went viral of a Comcast technician falling asleep on a customer's couch while on hold with Comcast's customer service line.[3] The original video may have been taken down but others seem to be keeping it alive on YouTube some 15 years later.

Frank Eliason, author of *At Your Service*, became the head of social customer service for Comcast and incorporated some of his experiences there into his book and later went on to a similar role at Citibank. Organizations were increasingly becoming aware of the need for social customer service, often stemming from these hashtag debacles that were so embarrassing.

It can really take on a life of its own if you are not careful. Your intentions may be good but the intended audience may respond with their own ideas or agenda. Like the Comcast video, when customers respond with evidence of the image or video kind in response to your hashtag things can really go viral but not in the way you would have hoped.

When the New York City Police Department asked their Twitter followers to post pictures of themselves with cops, things took a turn for the worse. Accounts such as @OccupyWallStNYC took the opportunity to show cops beating protesters with batons in the streets. Over 70,000 tweets depicting police brutality were shared resulting in the campaign being shut down.[4]

The Massachusetts' Bay Transit Authority asked audiences to post 'What they love about it' and use the hashtag #Nextstoptheworld. Users relished the opportunity to use irony to troll the MBTA with numerous examples of customer service failures on the MBTA. You have to realize that if you are asking for someone's thoughts or feelings about something then you need to be prepared to hear an answer you may not like or expect.[5]

Lastly, McDonald's wanted to engage their customers and hear their stories about experiences they had had at their restaurants. The objective was to hear positive and heart-warming stories. The result was the complete opposite. Using #McDStories, people overwhelmed the hashtag with stories of nasty experiences and claims of questionable things, like fingernails, being found in their food. That is definitely not what McDonald's had in mind in the beginning.[6]

What to do

I know that I have probably cast a lot of fear and doubt into your mind. So much so that maybe you are thinking about avoiding using hashtags altogether to eliminate any reputational risk. My apologies if that is the case. It was not my intention. I simply wanted you to be aware of what could happen and what has happened to others who didn't thoroughly consider their plans and potential outcomes for their hashtags.

Having said that, nobody can prepare for every possible scenario but if you conduct thorough research, test your hashtags out with people to get their initial impression and feedback, and check for potential alternate meanings or uses then you should be able to mitigate most of the risk.

Hashtag fails get a lot of media attention, but it is not something that is happening necessarily on a daily basis. As I mentioned, a lot of the fails stem from soliciting responses from customers. Regardless of whether you are a global brand or a relatively small organization, if you treat your customers and stakeholders well then you should not have anything to worry about. If customers are happy then they will tell you so in social if you ask them. The goal is to make sure they are happy.

Hashtags are intended to help get content discovered, make it easier for people interested in certain topics to find others with similar interests, raise brand awareness and drive momentum for campaigns. Some people may react unexpectedly or negatively to your hashtags and you cannot eliminate that possibility entirely. If you focus on the bigger picture and your objectives then you should, for the most part, come out unscathed.

Endnotes

1 B Peters, 7 of the best social media marketing examples in 2021, Meltwater, 30 June 2021, www.meltwater.com/en/blog/best-social-media-marketing-examples (archived at https://perma.cc/PL75-KBPB)

2 H Waldrum, #Susanalbumparty: top five Twitter hashtag PR disasters, *The Guardian*, 22 November 2012, www.theguardian.com/technology/shortcuts/2012/nov/22/twitter-susan-boyle-susanalbumparty (archived at https://perma.cc/B8NN-WN6M)

3 H Waldrum, #Susanalbumparty: top five Twitter hashtag PR disasters, *The Guardian*, 22 November 2012, www.theguardian.com/technology/shortcuts/2012/nov/22/twitter-susan-boyle-susanalbumparty (archived at https://perma.cc/CES2-4XWE)

4 Track my hashtag, www.trackmyhashtag.com/blog/hilarious-hashtag-fails/ (archived at https://perma.cc/FX4W-48MV)

5 B Appleton, 10 Social media fails to avoid in 2021, blog.hubspot.com/marketing/avoid-social-media-fails (archived at https://perma.cc/B4PU-V3H9)

6 H Waldrum, #Susanalbumparty: top five Twitter hashtag PR disasters, *The Guardian*, 22 November 2012, www.theguardian.com/technology/shortcuts/2012/nov/22/twitter-susan-boyle-susanalbumparty (archived at https://perma.cc/8YQ9-TNJE)

14

Humanity

There has been a lot of talk about humanizing brands and being more human with your social media efforts. Being human has been fundamental to social media from its inception. You can't be 'social' without being human. Sadly, many brands have lost touch with that fact over the years as the demand for marketing and sales results outweighed allowing for time to be more human and to truly build a socially engaged community.

In this chapter, I am going to talk about ways to put humanity back into your social media. I am also going to share some examples of brands being more human from my own experience and from others. I am also going to talk about how brands showing humanity offline can spill onto social media.

Finally, I want to make sure that one of the key takeaways from this chapter for you is the word 'delight'. The more brands show their humanity by delighting their customers the stronger the affinity those customers will have for them. There will be increased word-of-mouth marketing, a higher propensity to recommend their products or services.

Some of the examples of humanity by brands are based on their desire to delight people. The earned media attention and overall halo effect for their brand could not have been predicted or quantified. How do you measure the value of a smile or the feeling of joy? While that may not be possible, you can certainly quantify the follow-on effects such as engagement and sentiment. We will talk about all that and more in this chapter.

Transparency and authenticity

While I would like to think that being human should come naturally to most people and brands, that is not always the case. For some it has to be learned and developed before it becomes second nature. It's like developing a new muscle or reflex.

As part of that effort, brands need to be willing, and prepared if need be, to operate with greater transparency and authenticity than they may have been accustomed to in the past. People can be lightning fast with their keyboards, fact checking you and finding examples from your past that may contradict your current stance on something.

You can't gaslight anyone nor can you try to rewrite history. Just because you deleted that tweet doesn't mean it never happened. There is always a screenshot. You are going to have to own your past, present and future.

If you can admit when you are wrong and speak to what you are going to do to do and be better in the future then your community will respond positively. What they will not respond positively to is being misdirected or ignored while you continue to behave in a way that contradicts your supposed brand values.

We live in an era where you can be cancelled in a heartbeat. What you do offline can be pulled into the online conversation and vice versa. While that may be anxiety-inducing, it is simply today's reality that we have to deal with. Cell phones are everywhere and they are enabling truth and situations taken out of context to spread rapidly with little to no ability to get ahead of it.

People increasingly want and expect brands to be authentic and transparent because they are part of their core values and not something that they are doing just for the optics. They can see through that quite easily and you also run the risk of being called out for it which defeats the purpose in the first place.

Brussels sprouts and Boeing

Brussel sprouts

While it may seem somewhat trite, adhering to the Golden Rule of treating others like you would like to be treated makes complete sense in relation to being more human. So often brands forget about the Golden Rule when it comes to dealing with people, and they inevitably pay a price for it.

I am sharing an experience by my Facebook Friend, Mark Schaefer, with his permission. Mark was out for dinner at a local restaurant. When it came time to order his meal he asked to substitute Brussels sprouts for the side vegetable that was coming with his entrée. His server said that they didn't do substitutions.

What makes this situation even more dumbfounding is that the original side vegetable and the Brussels sprouts were the same price on the à la carte menu so there was nothing being gained or lost by Mark's request.

The server held firm and reiterated the restaurant's policy of no substitutions. What the server and the restaurant did not know is that Mark Schaefer is well known in the social media world. He has thousands of followers on Twitter, Facebook and LinkedIn. He has authored a number of books and spoken at numerous conferences. He truly is a social media influencer.

Now I will be the first one to say that there are some social media influencers who give that title a bad name. They can be self-involved and expect better treatment than others because of their influence. That's not Mark. In this instance, he wasn't asking for something more or better, just different and of the same value, but the restaurant and the server weren't having it.

Mark shared this experience on his Facebook account and even named the restaurant. He and I live in different cities in different countries, but I am still aware of this restaurant and how they treated Mark because of social media. I have used his experience in numerous presentations to illustrate actions taken offline having unexpected repercussions online.

I am not trying to destroy the restaurant's reputation. I am not even naming them or sharing their location. I am not trying to make Mark seem entitled either. I am simply trying to illustrate that had the server been empowered to make the substitution of an item that cost a few dollars at most, we wouldn't even be talking about it in this book or my presentations and Mark would have had the meal he wanted.

Boeing

I was at a conference and one of the speakers shared a story about his young son, Harry, who liked to draw aircraft. Harry loved aircraft and hoped to make them some day. He had drawn a picture of a plane and decided to send it to Boeing.

Rather than acknowledge receipt of the image and thank Harry for his submission, Boeing responded with a corporate-sounding rejection letter stating 'We do not accept unsolicited ideas.' It was a standardized response intended to protect Boeing without really giving any thought to what the submission was all about and who it was from.

What Boeing didn't know was that Harry's father was John Winsor, founder of Victors & Spoils, a marketing agency. John decided to blog about what had happened and that is when things started happening.

FIGURE 14.1 Harry Winsor's Boeing

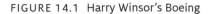

SOURCE Used with permission of John Winsor

The media caught wind of it, and the story received coverage in the press and on television. Eventually, Boeing learned of it too. They initially responded with 'We're expert at airplanes but novices in social media. We're learning as we go.'

Boeing ramped up their efforts to turn things around. They invited Harry and his family to come out to Boeing, visit their Museum of Flight and get unprecedented access. John shared their experiences on the same blog that started it all. What began with a bumpy start became a heart-warming story of brand redemption. Boeing committed to doing better when it came to dealing with children and their love of aircraft.

The solution to these brand missteps is often inexpensive. It can be as simple as letting a front-line worker have the decision-making power to delight a customer without fear of reprisal. Everyone can agree that your brand reputation is worth a lot more than a plate of Brussels sprouts.

Dragons and kangaroos

We have talked mostly about Twitter, LinkedIn, Facebook and Instagram in this book. Reddit is well known but not as mainstream as the others.

Ironically, something that goes viral in mainstream social media typically got started on Reddit and got voted up in popularity and then spilled over to other social media platforms.

A Reddit user posted the exchange he had had with Samsung Canada on their Facebook page. He tried to charm his way into receiving a free Samsung Galaxy phone by including a picture of a dragon to ingratiate himself with the company. Samsung Canada politely declined the request but responded in kind with their own picture of a kangaroo on a unicycle. The exchange got up-voted to Reddit's front page.

But wait, the story didn't stop there. Three months later, Samsung Canada sent the user a brand-new phone with a custom case emblazoned with, you guessed it, his dragon drawing. It was their way of saying thank you for all of the positive Reddit exposure.[1]

These opportunities to delight someone happen all the time. They don't cost much but can pay huge dividends. This particular one cost a phone, shipping and their time but paid off huge! Imagine what could happen if brands were always on the outlook for these opportunities, ready to turn a brand conversation into an earned media and word-of-mouth opportunity.

Exclusivity

Exclusivity can foster stronger connection with your community. This could be access to exclusive content, early access to something or elevating members of the community by giving them exclusive profiles.

In the latter case, one of Canada's oldest and best-known newspapers had an online community tied to the digital version of the paper. They had chosen to move the community from their old community platform to a new one. They were concerned that there was a risk of diminished engagement on the new platform once the migration was complete. What could they do to mitigate that risk?

Working with the vendor of the new platform, they identified key members of the community who often initiated conversations on the platform. They approached them and asked them to become ambassadors on the new platform. They weren't going to be paid for it, but they would be recognized within the community for their role. Their profile avatar or image would denote that they were a community ambassador, elevated in relation to the rest of the community.

Simply being recognized for their contribution and treating them as ambassadors was enough to make for a seamless transition and while still maintaining engagement. What kind of recognition could you give key members of your community who are unpaid advocates and ambassadors? Nobody asked them to show their affinity for your brand but yet they have. Isn't that worth something? Show your gratitude.

Storytelling

Storytelling is an overused word. It is the latest marketing buzzword but it still has meaning. By telling your story and that of your brand, your audience will hopefully see themselves in your story and connect with it.

Don't be afraid to be vulnerable. Entrepreneurs and founders often share their stories and include truths about the challenges they faced and overcame, even disclosing how close they were to quitting or shutting down. Ultimately, it is your call regarding what to share and how much but people most definitely respond to stories familiar to them.

It's going to come down to what you are comfortable sharing. I'm not talking about sharing confidential information but sharing what you went through, what you learned and how you have been changed by the experience. Being vulnerable is scary but it can be rewarding.

Emotions and empathy

When you think about the content you engaged with over the course of the last month, did it spark emotions? How did it make you feel? Most of the content we engage with and go on to react to, comment on or share sparked some sort of emotion.

So many people have been impacted by the pandemic. Social media has been a place to find an outlet for emotions and solace from what is causing us anxiety. If you can find a way to genuinely engage with your audience with content that provides an escape, makes them smile, causes them to laugh or makes them feel that they are not alone then you are on the right track.

That kind of thinking may seem out of place for your organization, especially if your organization is B2B, but social media has proven that we engage with brands that make us feel something. They show that they have solutions for us because they know us. Everyone tends to buy from people who know them and like them.

Let me add that it's not always about the transaction. People will remember how you made them feel. A lot of brands sent disingenuous emails to people during the pandemic saying that 'they had your back'. It felt hollow. However, brands that stepped up and showed their empathy for what people were going through did better as a result.

The pandemic will dissipate, possibly by the time this book is published, but that does not mean that brands should revert to their old ways. Showing empathy has changed the dynamics of the relationship they have with their customers and should not be taken lightly. Everyone has been irrevocably changed by the pandemic and brands will need to recognize that.

Start a conversation

Organizations are so accustomed to adhering to their agenda on social media that it leaves little room for humanity. I like to ask people if it would be permissible to say something like 'good morning' or 'TGIF' on their social accounts. Most times there is a bit of an awkward pause. They are not used to showing signs of humanity on those channels.

What I can't understand is that the kinds of exchanges we have online when we arrive at the office, jump on Zoom or enter a business are not the kind of exchanges that seem to happen or be allowed on social media. People say 'good morning'. They ask 'How are you?' We are human with each other offline but it seems to be challenging to be that way online.

I can't believe that saying 'good morning' might be pushing the limits for your organization. Rarely do transactions occur without some rapport and trust being established beforehand. Furthermore, starting a conversation on social media shows that there are humans behind the logo.

I have spoken about using tools and automation to scale your social media efforts but let me say that that does not apply here. You can automate conversation and relationship building with your community. You need to show up and let them know you are there regularly to help and support them.

Starting a conversation can begin with something as simple as a typical greeting or something more specific to them. By making it about them and not about you, your product or service, you will earn the right to do that over time but the focus should be on your community members.

Aroma Espresso

Several years ago, my son was taking a class on Saturdays and I would find a Starbucks nearby where I could read or do some work while he was in class. Each Saturday, I would drop him off and upon arriving at Starbucks I would check in on Foursquare.

For those of you who may not remember or have heard of Foursquare, it was a social platform where you checked in at various locations and the notification was sent out over Twitter. The more you checked in at a particular place, the more likely you were to become the Foursquare mayor of that place. It combined social and competition. You could also leave tips and hints for others about the restaurant, store or whatever. Foursquare still exists but has moved away from that form of usage.

Anyway, one week I checked in and a friend saw the notification on Twitter and suggested that I check out the new Aroma Espresso across the street next time. Fast forward to the following week and I checked in at Aroma Espresso saying that I was there to check them out for the first time.

They responded and there began a conversation with exchanges happening every week. One particular week, I checked in and asked if they had missed me. I didn't get my usual speedy response but hours later they replied and apologized for the delay explaining that they had been on a plane and couldn't respond earlier.

At one point they sent me a private message asking for my address. That led to them sending me a $20 gift card. Now $20 isn't much. It wasn't very costly to them and it didn't exactly make me rich either. What it did do was make me a loyal customer and an advocate for them.

Starbucks has never engaged me in conversation on social media. They have never sent me a gift card. They have rewarded me with loyalty points but I had to earn those by spending a lot of money first. I will concede that they will give me a free coffee on my birthday that still does not change the way I feel about Aroma Espresso. When given the choice between Starbucks on one street corner and Aroma Espresso on the other, Aroma wins every time.

I have shared my experience with Aroma Espresso in a number of my keynote presentations, with my classes every semester and now here with you in this book. I have shared the story with thousands. That $20 investment on the part of Aroma Espresso was definitely worth it for them, don't you think?

Hot sauce love triangle

A TikTok user recorded herself talking about her visit to a restaurant on her vacation where she asked for some Tabasco to spice up her meal. The restaurant gave her a mini bottle of Tabasco and she loved it so much that she talked about it on her video.

Tabasco was listening too and sent her a box of mini bottles. Tabasco's competitor, Frank's RedHot sauce, caught wind of it and began doing their best to woo her. They sent her a box of corporate swag that included custom labelled bottles that included the user's name stating that it was her favourite hot sauce. They then invited her to their headquarters and gave her even more swag, including a giant bottle statue that barely fit in the cargo area of her SUV.

During the wooing, the user described it as being similar to the movie *Twilight* and having to choose between Edward and Jacob. Frank's RedHot sauce ran with that idea and did a photo shoot that was Twilight-themed with their bottle at the centre of it all.

Just when you thought Tabasco was out of the picture, they came back and invited her to a Tabasco party along with 10 of her friends. They sent more sauce and swag before the party and filled the party with even more swag and sauce.

The amount of attention this brand lovefest received was phenomenal. It came about because they were listening and sparked up a conversation. If only more brands paid attention to people talking about their brand and expressing their strong affections, there is so much brand love that can be developed with only the investment of time and a bit of their swag budget.

Other emerging brands have since deemed the TikToker a hot sauce influencer, sending her samples to try and talk about the experience. She was game because she believes in supporting small businesses. It is amazing to see the impact and the number of people and businesses that can be touched with humanity from a brand.

Ask questions

When I suggest that you ask questions, I am not suggesting that you ask questions that relate to your product, your service or some other aspect of your business. I am suggesting something more fundamental. Ask questions to learn, to help, to engage or to start a conversation. Don't be afraid to ask questions completely unrelated to you, your product or service.

Lately, the content AI company I have mentioned elsewhere in the book has taken to asking questions purely for fun. These questions are short and simple. They are intended to provoke debate and conversation but not in a polarizing way. It is meant to be good, harmless fun.

They ask questions like 'Bruno Mars or Eminem?' to learn something about your musical preferences. It has nothing to do with them as a company or the product they offer. Their questions span music, the arts, food, fashion and more. In one tweet they asked, 'Sweet or savoury?' In another, 'Would you rather have to wear stilettos to sleep or have to wear slippers everywhere you go?'

In one particular exchange that involved me they asked, 'Would you rather never use social media again or never watch another movie ever again?' I replied 'As someone with a film production degree who runs a social media marketing agency, this has to be one of the toughest "would you rather" questions.' They responded with an OMG gif to round out the conversation.

It's these types of exchanges that foster rapport and trust. I am a bit biased because I know some of the Lately team. I love their product too. However, the exchanges I have been having with them over Twitter are with others within the company and we are just having fun.

These questions as distractions are interspersed throughout their Twitter feed as a break from their regular programming. What if you considered something similar? Maybe you aren't ready to infuse your social feed with pop culture references but you could ask people what kind of hacks they are doing to stay productive at home.

Ask them to show their work-from-home set-up. Are they using a stand-up desk? What is their favourite thing to do to take a break from Zoom? You get the idea. These are not questions that relate to you. They relate to them and illustrate that you understand the situation they are currently dealing with.

Similar to your approach to content planning, can you spark conversation and engagement over the course of our work week? Can you motivate people on Monday? Can you offer value with a #tuesdaytip that is a lifehack for them for their work or at home? What can you say or ask to help to get them over hump day Wednesday? What can you leave them with on Friday to send them feeling good and excited about the weekend? I will leave that with you to think about but there is definitely an opportunity for you there with your community.

Emojis, gifs and memes

Emojis, gifs and memes are now part of our everyday lives, whether it is with social media or text with our family and friends. A picture speaks a thousand words and an emoji, gif or meme can often make for a better form of message than just text.

Incorporating these forms of content into your copy and communications can bring humour to your conversations. It can show empathy. It can say a lot with a little. One well-chosen gif can turn someone's day around. It can summarize what is being thought or felt with one succinct image or graphic. It might even cause them to share what you shared and spark conversations with others.

In another exchange with Lately, they asked 'Angelina Jolie's lips or with Jennifer Aniston's hair?' I replied with 'Do you mean "The Rachel" from Friends era or her hair now? Either way, I am not sure I could carry it off.' That led to a series of gif-based responses and a number of my Twitter followers jumping into the conversation and inserting an embarrassing photoshopped image of me with 'The Rachel' hairstyle added to my follicly challenged head. The exchange was the highlight of their day and mine. It was a lot of fun but be thankful I am not including the photoshopped image here. You can't unsee it.

It can help you stay current and relevant but be careful. You do not want to try too hard and risk looking foolish and embarrass yourself. Not every meme is suitable for use by a brand and it can actually backfire. I am not saying not to try because you should. People will respond positively. You just need to choose emojis, gifs or memes that fit the moment while still avoiding them detracting from your brand.

Humour

A lot of the things that have gone viral, not that that should be your goal, do so because they made people laugh, and they wanted to pass along that good feeling to others. This is not about you or your organization becoming comedians. It's about finding common ground with your community and finding the humour in your work and everyday lives.

This could take the form of gifs, emojis or memes as described above or sharing a video from YouTube or TikTok. More and more, I am seeing TikTok videos make their way onto the other platforms because they are so funny and something new and unlike what people are used to seeing on the other channels.

Would your organization be okay with you sharing a joke or a pun? There are tons of jokes, especially dad jokes, floating around on social media. If you are worried about objectionable content then stick to clean dad jokes or innocent yet corny kid jokes.

Don't be afraid to solicit humour from your community. Ask them to make you laugh. Ask them for a joke but you can always say to keep it clean. Don't stop with jokes. Ask them to share the last image taken on their phone without context. Share a picture, ask them to caption it and acknowledge the winner somehow, perhaps with corporate swag. The point is to try stuff. Not every joke is going to land but you can even be self-deprecating when it doesn't. People will appreciate the effort and you being self-aware.

Wendy's

I can't talk about humour and being human without mentioning Wendy's. They have taken humour to a whole new level. The social media team has swagger and looks for opportunities to poke fun at competitors and mix in some snark on occasion. It got to the point where people actively tweet to the corporate Twitter account just to get some of the snarky comments.

On the surface you would think, 'Who would want to be insulted by a restaurant chain's Twitter account?' but plenty of people do and Wendy's was happy to oblige. Some of their best snark responses have made it into the mainstream media so it is definitely working for them.

The secret to their snark is just that – a secret. Wendy's would not allow the people behind the snark and the account to speak to the media. They wanted to keep their secret sauce, pardon the pun, a secret.

Behind the brand

People want to know that there are people behind your logo. Some organizations have the folks managing their social accounts sign off with their names as a small gesture to humanize them. That's a great start but more can be done.

Showing images and videos behind the scenes showing collaborations, team building and the work that goes into delivering the products or services all work to building your brand and showing just who is involved.

Instagram is one particular channel where behind the scenes content garners high engagement and works really well for building an employer brand. That kind of content helps with recruitment and gives future employees a taste of your culture.

Get people on camera to share a day in their work life. Have them provide work testimonials. Let some of your newest hires describe their particular experience during the interview and hiring process.

Showcase employees who have reached work milestones or received recognition for their work or contributions within the company or their community. You can recognize and celebrate them for things outside of work. Some employees are competitive athletes or serve in the military outside of work and could be celebrated for it.

Allow or empower your employees to personalize their interactions with customers. Financial advisors send birthday cards every year to their clients. Think of something equivalent in social media. Let them respond with a gif or a video message. If a representative can solve a customer's problem by recording something on their phone or doing a crude screen recording then let them. The goal is to solve the customer's problem, not to delay a response to edit a video to ensure only properly branded content gets distributed.

The pandemic has shown us that people will forgive production value for immediacy and access. Talk shows from the hosts' homes are perfect examples of that. Do not get hung up on making something perfect. To use a Silicon Valley reference, just ship it.

Speak human

You can't write a chapter about bringing humanity to social media without talking about talking like a human. The earlier example from Boeing showed that the company defaulted to corporate-speak as a reflex. That just doesn't work in social media. People will not think that there are people behind the logo if the accounts do not talk like a human being.

To be fair, there are situations such as with crisis communications or related to regulations or compliance like a press release from a publicly traded company where every word must adhere to certain protocols. Outside of those situations, there is little to stop you from speaking in more common everyday language.

The pendulum does not need to swing in the other direction towards slang and pop culture references that not everyone will understand. It is about avoiding jargon or language that is too specific to an industry or something like that where people less familiar would be challenged to know what it means.

This approach should translate to your copy. Simple. Short. Succinct. Hemingway may have been on to something. If you can say it with three words instead of five then do it. When Twitter was limited to 140 characters, we had to get creative. Yes, that meant specific acronyms and shortcuts just for that platform but tweet threads and the new character limit of 280 have alleviated some of that.

Platforms like Facebook, LinkedIn and Instagram allow for longer copy. That does not necessarily mean you should. People remain time-starved with diminished attention spans. Add to that the fact that social media is mobile-centric and you face some challenges getting people to engage with your content.

Making your copy simple and accessible with the expectation that it will likely be read first on a mobile phone should increase the likelihood that it will be read at all. While there are exceptions when copy takes on a longer format as it sometimes does on Instagram, keep longer content for your blog or a LinkedIn article.

Speaking like a human does not have to be relegated just to the written word. We have already noted how prevalent video is on every platform. While most video, excluding TikTok, is watched without audio, you can still strive to speak like a human through the words you choose to say on camera that will also end up incorporated into the video's caption.

Short videos are being used more and more to provide provocative and valuable information in snackable bits. They can also be used to entice the viewer to seek out the longer form versions from which the clip was derived. No matter the length, the words spoken, like the words written, should be simple and free of as much jargon as possible.

Having said that, there may be an opportunity for your written or spoken word to explain the jargon or common language of your industry and make it accessible to your target audience. Providing educational and informative content is fundamental to content marketing so this would certainly be a reasonable thing to do but you want to make sure that you do not leave them more confused than when they began.

Social media marketing is filled with jargon and acronyms. Even memes often have to be explained on occasion. Those of us who work in the digital bubble have to regularly remind ourselves that what we know first-hand is not necessarily common knowledge to those with whom we are communicating. We all need to slow down sometimes and make sure that our messages are getting across.

Social media is constantly evolving and changing and so are related language and terminology. For example, UGC stands for user-generated content. This is a term that began in and because of social media. Not everyone would know the meaning of the acronym at first glance. As a digital marketer, I have to be patient and show understanding for my audience that is likely less familiar with the many terms and acronyms I use daily. That doesn't even include the technologies and methods involved either. I have to be careful not to overwhelm them. Their unfamiliarity can make them reticent. They may be reluctant to engage if there is a barrier to their understanding.

Err on the side of over communicating. Make sure they know that it is okay to ask questions and make sure your answers are clear and easy to understand. Do not pile jargon on top of jargon. Feel free to record yourself and/or a screencast to explain something. Sometimes seeing and/or hearing you provides more context to what is being said and can increase understanding.

Endnote

1   R Martin. Personalized customer service gives Samsung a big viral push, *Marketing*, 29 August 2012, marketingmag.ca/advertising/some-honest-csr-love-gives-samsung-a-big-viral-push-60887/ (archived at https://perma.cc/H23F-GPUJ)

15

Bringing it all together

This part of your social media journey is coming to an end but your travels will continue. The social media we know and use today will continue to evolve. TikTok is the social media platform on the rise now. What will be the bright new shiny thing in 2025? I am not sure either but no matter the platform or the time period the general approach to formulating and executing a social media strategy has not changed.

I want to recap that approach as I bring this book to a close. I have broken things into 10 parts that I will delve into with greater detail. They are still a summary so be sure to check back to the main chapters for more details for each topic and area.

Fundamentals

I do not know whether you are in a new social media role at your organization, an entrepreneur trying to figure out where and how social media could help market your business or you are trying to improve your current social media activities. Regardless, the fundamentals remain unchanged.

Whether you are starting from scratch or inheriting an existing social media strategy, you need to be clear on your objectives. Are you trying to raise awareness? Reduce customer service costs? Generate leads? Reduce the cost of acquisition? Conduct competitive analysis? Manage brand reputation? A combination of two or more of those?

What is being asked of you and who is asking? What does social media success look like to them? What are the overall corporate objectives that they are focused on? That will certainly have some bearing on where you will need to focus your time and energy. What is the general feeling towards social media? Definitely needed? Trivial? Somewhere in between? The internal attitude towards social media will give you a sense of where support lies and where potential roadblocks will occur.

If social media has been in place for a while then what has happened to that point? Are there any signs of success? What factors helped or hindered that success? What has been the catalyst for you finding yourself in your current circumstance? Competitive pressures? Staff changes? Shift in focus? Where do you fit in relation to all of the other corporate objectives and related activities? Is there alignment with any other area that could foster support and collaboration?

I know that I am asking a lot of questions but that is what has to happen in the early stages. When formulating a strategy you have to conduct some situational analysis. That means asking a lot of questions to assess the situation. You have to be clear about where you are starting and with what resources and support. You need to understand the context for social media. If the organization is facing challenges and they are looking to social media to help then that could mean unrealistic expectations and undue pressure to achieve and surpass objectives.

Once you have your situational analysis sorted, you can begin to develop and refine your strategy plan in pursuit of the identified objectives. Your strategy will be dictated by those defined objectives. A strategy for raising brand awareness will defer from one for lead generation. Working back from your objectives, you can lay out your plan with defined tactics, timelines and measures of success. You will need to make sure that they align with the process and priorities for the organization's other measures of success. Without those, you will find it challenging to track your progress and keep stakeholders apprised of where you are in relation to the plan.

You can only move as fast as the organization can handle so be prepared to adjust your pace accordingly. The organization may have a mismatch between their objectives and the pace by which they are accustomed to operating. Have you ever been in a situation where goals are set and delays happen that are out of your control yet the goals and the time set to achieve them do not get adjusted? Don't be surprised if it happens again.

What do you have?

Go on any adventure and your planning includes doing an inventory of the gear and supplies you already have. It is the same with your social media adventure. What is already in place? What is working? What isn't? How do you know?

If you are fortunate to be taking on a situation where social media has been running for a while then there should be historical data that will prove helpful to determine what is working, what isn't and where. Which channels are doing best and with what kind of content and formats?

How much content already exists that has not been used or can be repurposed? How easily can new content be developed from existing sources? Will it be easy to take over management of the channels and content planning or does there need to be a transition?

Operationally, what is in place? What is being used to manage social media posts? How are analytics being captured? Is brand monitoring in place? Who is creating content and how? How many staff resources are currently involved and who does what? It may be too early to tell but are the right people in the right roles? Are resources shared with other teams or departments? What is in-house versus outsourced?

How far are your objectives from where you are now? If you are confident that the tools and resources that are currently in place are sufficient to achieve your objectives, then that is great. However, if you believe that what you have will only get you so far, then you will need to start building a case to get more resources. No matter whether it is software, services and/or people, you will need more budget.

What is your sense of how your social media stacks up against other organizations to which you are comparing yourself? Are there any standouts? Sometimes you have a situation where nobody is doing a great job. They all seem to be just doing the minimum to keep the lights on. I have seen that on numerous occasions. It tends to set the bar low to over achieve.

Basically, it comes down to what tools, content and people you have in place and how much of each category. Some things are more costly than others. Some scale more easily than others but, when it comes to people, their capacity is finite. What is the optimal combination of tools, content and people for what you face immediately and for where you need to go?

Do the software tools you have in place scale? Meaning you have an upgrade path that aligns with your requirements to meet your objectives. If you are going to have to switch horses then when would be the best time? Now or later and what are the cost implications? It will not just be the cost of the software if you have to switch. You may have overlapping billing cycles. Your team may require training and support. Business continuity will be at risk too.

While you may have determined how much content already exists or can be repurposed, you will want to know what the organization's production volume capabilities are. If some or all of your content production is outsourced then what is their capacity and, if it were to be increased, what would be the cost implications?

What do you need?

Your situational analysis should help you determine where your budget is best allocated. Do you need impact on near- or long-term objectives? Maybe at the stage you are at, applying budget to tools that scale is the best use of your resources. Staff tend to be more expensive than software so the budget for staffing may have to come later.

Do you have a collection of tools and services involved in your social media management or is it an all-in-one solution? There are a number of suppliers for the latter that exist but an all-in-one may not meet all of your requirements. You will need to determine if your current tool set or tech stack meets your needs.

Maybe your primary focus is getting a handle on management and scheduling while brand monitoring is secondary. What kind of posting volume are you dealing with or anticipating? Most social media management solutions base their pricing on the number of connected social accounts and users with a few occasionally incorporating monthly social post limits too. You might get by just addressing your connected social account requirements and add users as needed later.

Conducting a content audit will give you a sense of your existing content inventory. How much is usable and how much can be repurposed? What formats do you have and what formats have proven to perform best? Are capabilities in place to continue to produce content in sufficient volumes, frequency and formats? For example, video may be your top-performing content type but all of your video content production was outsourced to an external service provider. Can you bring production in-house with existing tools? If not, what are the cost implications for outsourcing and increasing production volume?

One thing that has happened in social media is that there has been an explosion of tools to create and manage social posts, conduct research and analysis, and monitor your brand through social listening. Many of these tools come at a very low monthly fee or discounted annual fee. Some are even free to start, but you have to pay for more functionality.

This tool proliferation has led to more empowerment and capability for every social media manager. For example, Canva has made basic graphic design possible for millions of people who were never formally trained as graphic designers but need to put visual graphics together for their social channels quickly and cheaply.

No disrespect to graphic designers and videographers. They have their place and you can utilize them for more important content. In the meantime, you can cover a lot of ground with free and near free tools provided you have resources in place who know how to use them. Why incur content production costs if you don't have to? Furthermore, having in-house capabilities means faster production and turnaround time, especially if internal stakeholders require changes.

You may end up with tools for management, production and analytics. Combining two or more of them could be possible but be sure to look into the trade-offs, if any, for doing so. Savings in the short term may prove costly in the long run if you run into issues of scale or time.

Who do you want?

Just as there are some all-in-one software tools, there are people who have all the required social media capabilities all rolled into one. If you have one or more of those people already in place then count yourself lucky. They are rare but organizations are looking for and, in fact, nearly demanding that people come with deep and broad digital skills.

They may have a variety of digital skills and experiences but which ones are most important to you? Do you need more of a strategist or more capabilities related to execution? Do you want them to be good at writing? Do you want a copywriter, a blogger or both? Familiar with constructing and executing paid campaigns? Conduct research and analysis and be able to distil insights into a report or presentation that anyone can understand? What about video editing and/or graphic design?

Build a skills matrix so that you can inventory skills and capabilities similar to your content inventory. You will be able to see where gaps exist and determine if they can be filled with training, hiring or outsourcing.

Just because someone can do something does not mean they want to do it for the rest of their life. This may be an opportune time to talk to your existing resources to match their strengths with what they want to do and what you need done. Having happy members of your team will be more productive and reliable. Furthermore, it will make it easier to delegate tasks that you need off your plate while avoiding any resentment from them. You can't scale if you can't delegate.

Be prepared to offer training and involve the customer success reps from the vendors you work with to help enhance your team's skills and provide support. It is in their best interest to help you and your team so take advantage of the available resources. This may be the shortest path to upskilling your team.

As a side note, I often do check-ins with my customer success reps to make sure that we are getting the most out of their solution, hearing about updated features, gaining access to beta features ahead of others and just having the opportunity to ask questions. These check-ins also go a long way to fostering a strong client–vendor relationship that has proven helpful over the years when I need a favour regarding pricing, technical support and more.

Prioritize your resources and any potential training around what you need most. What are the most common and frequent activities? Conducting an audit may not happen every day but creating and scheduling content does. Make sure you configure your resources and their related skills accordingly.

If you anticipate that your skills requirements will evolve over time then put together a training timeline, identify who amongst your team is to be trained and, if necessary, identify what needs to be outsourced and when. If you are not going to run campaigns that often then perhaps that is something that makes sense to outsource. Keep in mind that it does not have to be a permanent thing.

Platforms like LinkedIn, Facebook, Instagram and Twitter offer free certifications to enhance your skills and enable you to build and run paid campaigns. The certifications are designed to help you help them achieve their revenue goals, but you get the knowledge directly from the source through self-driven courses you can take online whenever and wherever you want.

Getting started

You have your content, tools and team in place. You know how much content you have so build a quick and dirty content calendar to see how long your existing content will last. Marry that with key events, both internal and external, for the coming months that would drive content. Leave some slack in the system to respond to ad-hoc content requests and adjustments.

Develop a preliminary posting schedule for optimal reach and performance based on available data but track everything over time in order to adjust if necessary. Leverage the historical knowledge of your team to inform the strategy and any changes necessary.

Involve your vendors as soon as is necessary to keep you on track for meeting your objectives. Make sure they know what you are trying to accomplish. Give them a sense of accountability if that is possible. They will want to help you succeed. Depending on the level of involvement, look for the opportunity to generate a case study with them. You will get enhanced support and it might even expedite reaching your goals.

Move quickly but don't break things. This isn't Facebook. You want to plan as much as possible while still allowing yourself the flexibility to try stuff. The more you plan and schedule ahead the more time you have for analysis, content creation and refining your strategy.

Using your existing content as a jumping off point, develop a content plan for at least the next 90 days. This will be less about what is to be posted on a given day and more about the type of third-party content you research and curate based on topic and the content you create based on the themes and topics that have been determined for that period.

Maybe you have a series of blogs that build on one another. That takes planning but it will make writing easier, especially if research is required. The research is utilized for more than one blog. Less time but more value. Look for these types of opportunities to gain efficiency with your content.

Speaking of efficiency. How much of your existing content can be repurposed with little to no changes? Are there blogs from last year that can be updated and shared again? What content, if any, can be considered evergreen? If you have some then it can be shared again and kept in rotation, avoiding the 'one and done' problem that persists with content and, instead, squeezes more value out of every piece of content.

As part of your repurposing efforts, what other formats can you use for your content? Which blogs can be turned into animated gifs or graphics with powerful quotes? The goal is to work smarter with your content, not harder. Strive to get five pieces of content from every blog. That is not just about the number of pieces of copy for social posts but the number of distinct pieces of content in different formats. You may not get there with every blog but it is worth trying.

Early wins and obstacles

You know your objectives. You have put together your strategy and begun to execute. Now what? Similar to any change management initiative, you need to achieve some early wins to show progress towards your goals. People do not have that much patience. If a long period passes without anything tangible being achieved, support for the strategy will wane.

People lose sight of the vision if a lot of time has passed since they had a sense that their work was getting the organization closer to the goal. Small wins early and often give a sense of progress and validate the contributions from your team are having an impact.

During your situational analysis, you may have seen some red flags related to operations and/or people. Some of those flags may still be evident as you are getting underway. Politics often percolate below the surface. Maybe it is something more obvious and non-political like a lack of content, insufficient tools or too few skilled resources.

You may not be able to surmount every obstacle. Determine which ones do not matter, which ones can be addressed immediately and which ones will take time to overcome. Prioritize any of the ones that fundamentally stand in the way of you achieving your objectives. If other people are involved then see if common ground can be found so that your respective objectives can be achieved.

I know that seems like something that is more easily said than done. I am not trying to be flippant. As mentioned previously in this book, social media is more often than not about change and culture. Scheduling tweets is secondary. People are resistant to change and your implementation of the social media strategy can't feel disruptive or like they are being steamrolled over with social media.

It has been said that culture eats strategy for breakfast. If the organization's culture is accepting of the need to digitally transform itself then that is fantastic. If there are resistors and naysayers among the staff then they may be a drag on your ability to get things done.

Getting some early wins and minimizing obstacles will help address their concerns about change and make them feel like contributors to the organization's overall success. Those who tasked you with achieving those objectives will also need to be kept apprised of your progress. Stakeholder management is a bigger part of a social media strategy than most people realize.

We meet with stakeholders every month to review analytics, discuss wins and fails, and identify what adjustments to strategy and priorities should be made. We rationalize which channels to focus on and which to maintain. We talk about the content calendar overall and the small ad-hoc adjustments to be made.

Do not to allow too much time to pass between updates to stakeholders. You want them onside and that is not possible unless you keep them informed. They will never have the same depth of knowledge about your social media activities. You need to tell them what they need to know, why it is important and what it means to the strategy and achieving their objectives.

Never send analysis to stakeholders without a summary in plain language. Highlight what they should know. Identify any influencing factors and note what action, if any, is being taken to refine the strategy, mitigate risks and address anything impacting execution of your strategy.

Milestones and review

It is safe to assume that as part of your strategic planning you had to have a timeline and note what milestones would be achieved and when. People want to know what was accomplished with each leg of the journey.

You may have specified some big, hairy, audacious goals (BHAGs), some modest ones or a combination. Regardless of the type, as each one is reached you need to socialize the achievements throughout the organization to keep stakeholders updated and to avoid any loss of support.

This is also the time for review. Were the milestones reached according to the plan and timeline? Were they ahead of schedule or delayed? What factors were involved that helped or hindered? What changes, if any, need to be made for the next phase in pursuit of the next set of milestones?

We spent several months working on an Instagram strategy and implementation plan only to hear about changes to the Instagram platform just days before we were to start. These changes to the platform would not delay the launch but would mean refinements to some of our tactics and measures of success.

Unanticipated events and changes in social media are par for the course so you have to plan but, at the same time, you have to be agile so you can respond quickly. Some changes may take longer to implement so you will have to adjust your expectations accordingly and inform stakeholders too.

Recalibrate and go

Once you have completed your review and assessed what changes need to be made then you need to recalibrate your strategy, your tactics and your day-to-day activities accordingly. That does not mean sweeping changes but refinements or adjustments based on your learnings.

Assuming you had your performance measurement processes and tools in place then it should be pretty straightforward to determine what changes are necessary and where. If your engagement is not where it needs to be or your audience growth is not on track to reach your targets then you need to take action.

Do you need to change your content strategy in terms of type of content, frequency of posting and/or incorporate paid campaigns to get more engagement and visibility for your content? Will paid promotion or an influencer marketing campaign help get audience growth back on track?

You may not be able to implement every change at the same time. Roll them out in such a way that the organization and the current team can handle without further disruption or delay to achieving your objectives. The key is to set the changes in motion.

Build momentum

With every milestone being reached, a review should occur and a recalibration should take place but the focus should be maintaining the momentum despite the need to implement changes to your strategy and tactics.

Testing, measuring and adjusting will be ongoing activities. You may stop doing some things because they are not producing the desired results or they are taking time and resources away from other areas that could use them. You may want to do more of other things that are showing signs that they are having the kind of impact you want.

Social media engagement can turn on and off like a light switch but persistent effort to engage your audience with consistent content production and sufficient frequency of posting, perhaps with some paid support, can build an engaged audience and sustain it over time.

It is a cliché but social media truly is a marathon and not a sprint. It takes months to see growth and impact with constant tweaks along the way. Using another cliché, you have to get the flywheel spinning and keep it spinning.

There will be quieter periods during holiday and vacation periods where engagement will dip but do not let that deter you. Stay the course and keep active. Do what works and either change or drop what isn't working.

You need to have somewhat of an 'always on' approach. Campaigns, organic or paid, come and go but your community is there every day so you need to be too. Campaigns receive increased focus and effort for short periods of time but your social media operations have to be maintained before, during and after campaigns.

Too often I see organizations run campaigns and then go silent. Some time passes and they run another campaign followed by silence. The campaigns worked hard to build and engage a community so then why do brands walk away until the next campaign?

An agency friend of mine shared an anecdote about a chocolate bar brand whose brand manager applied their budget to build a community on Facebook of fans of that particular chocolate bar. Music was incorporated too, making for a very vibrant community. Fast forward to the end of the budget cycle and the brand manager announced that they would be moving on because their budget had been spent. This new and lively community was being abandoned and would have to fend for itself. Of course, with no one to actively manage the community, it petered out.

Don't be that chocolate bar brand. You are better off being active on a few platforms you can maintain than spreading yourself too thinly with no ability to build communities. How many LinkedIn groups or Facebook groups have you seen or been a part of that are absolute ghost towns? Every person who started them had the best intentions but it is like hosting a party. You have to be there all the time. If you are not prepared for that kind of commitment then do not even start. It will look better on you if you didn't start then have a group, page or social account that you abandoned.

Business as usual

As you move through the timeline of your strategy plan and momentum has been built, you should be starting to see and feel the organization setting into a bit of a groove. Assuming you did a thorough job with your content planning then you should be turning more to recurring activities that maintain your momentum.

Perhaps you will implement a regular cycle or cadence for content curation, development and planning. For some clients we research content weekly but our content plan and associated calendar is for at least a month. Our bloggers typically create a plan for a blog series spanning three months so they can be more efficient with their research.

Figure out what works best for you and your resources. There will be factors like your own organization's cycles or external factors like seasons and holidays that will impact your planning so bear them in mind.

What do you need to address daily, weekly, monthly, quarterly and annually? We celebrate wins and talk about clients and deliverables every week. We report metrics monthly, quarterly, at the half year mark and annually.

Over and above all that we do planning, implementation and metrics reporting for campaigns. You will need to manage the added demands of campaigns so that there is little to no disruption to business as usual.

Combine as much of the work as possible. Do bulk content research. Do bulk scheduling. Create content in bulk whenever possible. Doing as much as you can in batches or in bulk will leave you in a better position to respond to changes and ad-hoc requirements from stakeholders.

We can plan a calendar for a month or more for a client but then something happens in the media or one of their executives gets an interview or gives a presentation and we need to respond to their request to address these events on their social channels. It is easily dealt with if everything else has been dealt with through proper planning.

We have had periods of heightened activity and intensity with a bit of chaos mixed in but you can't let it become the status quo. Don't think that throwing more people at the situation should be your first response. That can prove costly.

We know that a small group of well-trained social media managers with scalable tools can do a better job at managing the volume of work involved than just adding less-skilled bodies that are doing most things manually or in a less efficient way.

Spend more time on processes, workflows and the tools to support them. Regularly check with the team to hear from them about what is working, what isn't and what to succeed. They know first hand what is working and what isn't so create an environment where they feel comfortable being candid with their input.

I love the phrase 'a fool with a tool is still a fool'. I can be easily influenced by the latest thing that will supposedly do something better, faster, cheaper or a combination thereof. I have to remind myself to be careful not to put too much on my team. I want them to feel supported and not overwhelmed. You can't keep throwing new things at them, tools or otherwise, without giving them sufficient time, training and support.

I have witnessed social media team members be forced to use tools they hate or that they have not been properly trained on. That kind of situation does not point to success. Changing out tools can be costly so you need to be certain it is warranted. Maybe refresher training or leveraging the customer success rep to be readily available will help alleviate any anxiety or stress.

Getting to a comfortable state of business as usual means having the right tools, processes and people in place. What you had at the beginning may not be what you need to maintain things. With every milestone achieved and review that occurs, rationalize what you have in place.

Where do you need to make any adjustments? Can you promote someone to be a team lead and delegate more responsibilities to them? Do you need to cross-train resources so they can back each other up when people are on vacation or sick? I have had to deal with that issue and those days can be stressful when you are filling in for someone and you are not as familiar with their daily activities.

It could be that spending more time and money on professional development will have the greatest impact. The social media space is constantly changing. The course I teach has students every semester adding to their skill sets in an effort to remain competitive.

There are lots of resources available (see the resources section) so it doesn't necessarily mean that members of your staff have to take a course. They may just need time and your support to do some online certifications. Ask them what they need and want to see, what you can do to give it to them.

While ultimately you want to get to a state of business as usual, you want to avoid becoming complacent. It is not about putting your social media activities on autopilot. You cannot lose sight of what you are doing and why. There will be dips in performance. Some content will be lacklustre and fail outright. That is to be expected.

You must remain diligent. Focus on the metrics. Assuming your organization tracks its performance on an ongoing basis, so should you. Setting and forgetting it will mean your social media strategy will experience the same fate as an abandoned Facebook group.

I have used clichés and metaphors so I am not going to stop now. Think of your social media strategy as a garden. You plan and prepare before you plant your seed. Once you have done your planting, you weed, prune, water and protect it from insects. Assuming all goes well, you harvest the fruits of your labour and start all over again.

With each season you take the learning from the previous one and try to improve upon it. What worked on social media six months ago may no longer work now. Facebook used to get fantastic organic engagement but now you can't even dream of starting a new company page without setting aside a budget for paid campaigns to get it off the ground.

Visibility on social media is becoming more challenging as each platform grows and social media overall continues to grow in popularity and in time spent. We are fighting for people's attention. I am not suggesting that you should give up if it is that challenging. I just want you to go in with your eyes wide open regarding the current dynamics in the space and what will be expected of you to achieve success.

I have been on LinkedIn and Facebook for over 15 years. I have been on Twitter for over 13 years. Snapchat and Instagram for probably five years. They have all changed over time. There have been ebbs and flows. Some have come. Some have gone.

While it has been said that change is constant and that is definitely true, when it comes to social media, what remains constant is engagement. People continue to engage with content that makes them feel something. As I write this, there is a tremendous amount of heightened emotion happening online related to the pandemic, vaccine passports and the politicization of wearing a mask.

Social media can bring about change. It can influence thoughts and emotions. Sadly, in recent years it has also fostered trolling, racism and hate. Hopefully, by the time you read this we have moved beyond the polarization we have witnessed and experienced and returned to business as usual.

Engagement should still be the priority and there is nothing wrong with inciting debate. It's just that it should be constructive debate. I might be being too pollyannaish when I say that but I remain hopeful.

I have consumed a truly ridiculous amount of information, laughed more than I would have ever imagined and surprisingly felt more emotions than I ever could have predicted because of my time spent working in social media. My experience may not have been exactly the same as someone else but the last thing you liked, commented on or shared on social media was most likely because it made you feel something and that isn't necessarily a bad thing. Feeling something means you're alive.

RESOURCES

There are numerous apps, tools and services available to help you successfully execute your social media strategy. I have compiled categorized lists to help you navigate through the social media solutions landscape. Please note that some may appear on more than one list because of their features and/or capabilities. Others may only apply to one or a few of the social platforms so be sure of your requirements. Inclusion on the lists is not an endorsement. I simply wanted to provide a comprehensive list of what is available here, but we will strive to regularly update the resources page for the website related to the book.

However, the space changes quickly and often and some of those listed may have been acquired, rebranded or shuttered by the time this book is published. Others may have cropped up that are actually better so be prepared for that too.

Some of those listed are free while some operate on the freemium model where they provide a free version but encourage upgrading to more feature-rich versions. Many are inexpensive even if they are not free. As you move into more enterprise-grade solutions, you get into higher costs, but hopefully you can make a sufficient business case to secure budget allocation.

Social media management solutions

Agorapulse	Hubspot	Metigy
Buffer	Iconosquare	NapoleanCat
ContentCal	Khoros	Nuvi
CoSchedule	Lately	Oktopost
Creator Studio	Later	Post Planner
Crowdfire	Loomly	PromoRepublic
eClincher	MavSocial	Ripl
Falcon	MeetEdgar	Salesforce Social Studio
Hootsuite	Meltwater	SEMrush

Sendible

Social Hub

Sprout Social

SocialBee

SocialOomph

Tailwind

SocialChamp

Social Pilot

Tweetdeck

Social Flow

Sprinkler

Zoho

Content discovery/curation

Anders Pink

GoogleAlerts

Samplify

Audiense

Leiki

Scoop.it

Buzzsumo

LinkedIn

SocialAnimal

ContentStudio

Miappi

StumbleUpon

DrumUp

Pocket

Swayy

Facebook

PostPlanner

Trapit

Feedly

PublishThis

UpContent

Flipboard

Reddit

Zest

Visual design tools

Adobe Spark

Designs AI

Limitless Designs

Animaker

Desygner

Lucidpress

Artboard Studio

Digifloat

Luminar AI

Artify

Doka Photo

Over

Bannersnack

Easil

Pablo

Bee

Flipsnack

PaintShop Pro

BeFunky

FotoJet

PhotoADKing

Canva

Fotor

Photopea

Crello

Fotoram

Photoshop

Colorcinch

Genially

PicMonkey

DesignBold

Gravit Designer

Piktochart

DesignCap

Infogram

Pixelied

Design Wizard

Inkscape

Pixlr

PixTeller

PiZap

Placeit by Envato

Polarr

QwikBanners

RelayThat

Shutterstock Editor

Snappa

Stencil

Tailor Brands

Tyle

Vectr

Venngage

Visme

Xtensio

Youzign

AI copywriting tools

Anyword

ClosersCopy

CopyAI

Copysmith

Frase

GoCopy

Grammarly

Headlime

Jarvis AI

Lately

Niches$$

Outranking.io

Rytr

Shortly AI

Smartwriter

Snazzy AI

Topic

Wordsmith

Wordtune

Writesonic

Video creation tools

Adobe Premiere Pro

Adobe Spark

Animoto

Biteable

Boosted

Camtasia

Capto

Filmora

Hippo Video

Impresso

InVideo

Lumen5

Magisto

MiniTool MovieMaker

Moovly

Movavi

Offeo

Powtoon

Prezi

Promo.com

Renderforest Video
    Maker

Rocketium

Screencastify

Semrush

Videolicious

Vidnami

Viddyoze

VidToon

Wave.video

WeVideo

Wibbitz

Social listening tools

Agorapulse	Keyhole	Sendible
Brand24	Khoros	Socialbakers
Brandmentions	Meltwater	Sprinklr
Brandwatch	Mention	Sprout Social
Cision	NetBase	Zignal Labs
Critical Mention	Nuvi	Zoho Social
Falcon	Salesforce Social Studio	
Hootsuite	Semrush	

Social media analytics

Agora Pulse	Hootsuite	Post Planner
Audiense	Lately	Quintly
Buffer	Loomly	Rival IQ
Buzzsumo	MavSocial	SEMrush
Crowdfire	MeetEdgar	Sendible
eClincher	Meltwater	Socialbakers
Falcon	Metigy	Sprinkler
Google Data Studio	NapoleanCat	Sprout Social
Hootsuite	Oktopost	Zoho

Blogs, podcasts and online courses/certifications

Blogs

Agorapulse	CopyBlogger	PRDaily
Buffer	Hootsuite	Seth Godin
Buzzsumo	LinkedIn Marketing Solutions	Six Pixels of Separation
Content Marketing Institute	MarketingProfs	Social Media Examiner
Convince and Convert	NeilPatel.com	Social Media Explorer

Social Media Today

Spin Sucks

Sprinklr

Sprout Social

TopRank Marketing

Podcasts

Akimbo: A podcast from Seth Godin

B2B Growth

Behind the Numbers: eMarketer Podcast

Big Technology Podcast

Content Creatives Podcast

Content Matters

Content Sells

Copyblogger Podcast

Copywriter Club

Copywriters Podcast

Digital Marketing Podcast

Explicit Content Podcast

Growth Experts

Leveraging Thought Leadership

Marketing Over Coffee

Marketing School with Neil Patel and Eric Siu

Marketing Smarts from MarketingProfs

Maximize Your Social Influence

Pivot

Six Pixels of Separation

Social Media Lab by Agorapulse

Social Media Marketing Podcast

Social Pros Podcast

Spin Sucks

Sway

The Content Strategy Podcast

The Customer Engagement Lab

The Customer Experience Podcast

The Drum Network

The GaryVee Audio Experience

The How of Business

The Marketer's Journey

The Psychology of Copywriting

The Virtual CMO

This Old Marketing

Today in Digital Marketing

Courses and certifications

Agorapulse Academy

Facebook Blueprint for Facebook and Instagram

Hootsuite Academy

LinkedIn Marketing Labs

Snap Focus for Snapchat

Sprout Social Agency Certification

Twitter Flight School

YouTube Ads Certification

My tech stack

When it comes to selecting your own social media tools and services, it is going to come down to objectives, requirements and budget. Let's look at each of these more closely and how they influenced what I put together for my company's tech stack.

Objectives

A lot of your social media efforts can be managed natively on each platform but if your strategy requires efficiency and scalability then you will need to consider a social media management solution of some kind.

Are you looking to raise awareness, drive engagement, increase referral traffic, achieve or surpass sales targets or a combination? The more defined your overall sales and marketing objectives are then the easier it will be to determine which solution(s) will help you achieve them.

You might find yourself looking for a Swiss Army knife-type of solution that has a lot of features and functions so that you are getting essentially everything you need from one supplier. That is a sound idea but be clear about your objectives and requirements. You want to ensure you do not lose sight of them during your research and evaluation and mistakenly select a solution that does many things well but comes up short in a few areas that you may not realize until it is too late. I have found that the more complex or feature-rich the solution is the more trade-offs or compromises that have to be made.

Some solution providers continue to improve their solutions through development or acquisition, with the latter approach helping them to leap-frog the competition and add functionality that may have been slow to develop internally if they are resource constrained. This also gives them an opportunity to research and acquire the best-in-breed in the industry and remain competitive.

Requirements

If you are managing social media accounts for a single organization then your requirements are not going to be the same as an agency that is managing potentially hundreds of social media accounts. Your idea of scaling social media will most certainly differ from that of an agency.

How many accounts will you need to manage? Will you have multiple people involved in social media management and, if so, will you need to assign tasks? What kind of content development and approval process do you have or require and how does that impact your requirements? Something as simple as saving a social post as a draft for approval may be of utmost importance to you.

What kind of resources do you have now versus what you will have at some point in the future? Do you need to choose to handle the immediate tasks with a mind to scaling for the future? What are non-negotiable requirements versus nice-to-haves? How many other stakeholders are involved and how much influence do they have?

Analytics, calendar, listening, centralized inbox and integrations with key social platforms, third-party tools and services may also be on your wish list. Have a checklist to guide your evaluation and selection process. Get input from your team if they will be the primary users. Get demos and ask lots of questions. Check out reviews and ask other people who have used what you are considering. Conduct trials or pilots if possible, to test things in a real-life situation – yours.

Budget

You can manage your social media natively on most platforms. However, that doesn't necessarily make people comfortable, especially if that means a company Instagram account is being managed from one employee's phone. A social media management solution of some kind will be required to ensure ownership and proper governance by the organization.

Lots of solutions exist that are free or low cost. The free ones usually have limited functionality or capabilities. You tend to hit those limits pretty quickly if you are trying to manage numerous accounts and/or higher volumes of content.

The typical things that drive up costs are the number of users, the number of social accounts and the number of posts per month. As well, you need to be clear about what you mean by social media management. Do you primarily need to schedule posts or do you need to conduct listening and be able to communicate with customers? Those situations will impact what solution you need and how much it will cost.

You can start off with something simple like Buffer as purely a scheduling solution but move up to more robust functionality with Buffer or move over to a Sprout Social, Hootsuite or Agorapulse. If you are truly in need of an enterprise-grade solution at some point then you may want to look at Sprinklr but then you are getting into a substantially higher cost.

Do you need to keep costs within a monthly or annual budget? Some solutions offer discounts if you purchase an annual subscription upfront but you will want to be certain before you make that kind of commitment. If requirements may change that have cost implications, then you may want to keep things flexible so that you do not incur certain costs unnecessarily. Furthermore, you can start with lower monthly pricing and then move up as your requirements change or grow.

Over several years we went from managing 50 social accounts for clients to 250 so our tools and budgets had to change with them. We need to scale while still being efficient. I would be lying if I didn't say that there was some pain. We tried to keep the pain away from clients. They didn't need to know as long as there was no disruption to how we supported them.

Try to share costs where possible with other departments or lines of business. Consider sharing costs with another company if they are willing to share the cost burden. I have done it with partner firms in some cases and everybody wins.

I do not get a referral or affiliate fee for mentioning Appsumo but consider subscribing to their email and even paying the annual subscription to get discounts off the tools and services they promote. You can often find emerging tools being offered at severe discounts or lifetime licences for a one-time fee. Sometimes, you can find an inexpensive solution that meets your needs and your budget. I have managed to build up quite a tool kit that way. Other sources such as *Entrepreneur Magazine* and Mashable promote similar affiliate offers so keep an eye out for them too.

What I did

My situation is likely different from yours. I run an agency managing multiple clients and hundreds of social media accounts. I spend more money per month on social tools than most people or organizations ever would. My needs are different. It wasn't always that way. It grew over time so we had to adapt. Thousands are spent per month on tools and services to serve our clients and manage the volume of social media activities happening every month while maintaining a small team.

There are powerful all-in-one solutions out there that will help you get the job done without the need for anything else. If you find one that works based on features, budget or both then look no further. My requirements differ from most who are not running an agency but focused on the social media activities of one organization – theirs.

I have tried, on more than one occasion, to find an all-in-one solution to meet my requirements but, inevitably, I would come up short when it came to capabilities or budget. The solutions were feature-rich but I always seemed to find a shortcoming that I just couldn't ignore or overlook. If it wasn't a feature issue then it was often a budget issue. I would find it surprising to be blatantly clear with a vendor regarding my budget requirements and still receive a quote that was, in some cases, ridiculously higher than expected. They seemed to think the features of their offering would be enough for me to justify suddenly adjusting my budget upward to meet their quote.

I have been in the social media space for over a decade and I have seen solutions come and go. I may be unique in that I am very curious and am constantly looking at emerging solutions and trying out new tools even if they are in beta. I have found that if you show interest early and support new entrants that they remember you and often reciprocate the support. I have received things for free, at a reduced price and pricing grandfathered as my needs changed just because of the collaborative relationship I had established with them.

I know that may not be an option for you or something you would be interested in doing. Perhaps it is more conducive to an agency. I simply mention it here because this approach has helped me gain access to solutions early and at a lower cost, enabling me to scale, remain competitive and offer services and support to clients that they could not otherwise get on their own.

As a result, I have tended to choose solutions that are purpose built. That means I find myself in a situation where, depending on client needs, I have used or am still using such things as scheduling solutions (Buffer, Agorapulse, Sprout Social), social listening solutions (Nuvi, Meltwater, BrandMentions, Awario), analytics solutions (Rival IQ, Buzzsumo, Sprout Social, Audiense), several content research and curations solutions (Fee-dly, Buzzsumo, UpContent, Anders Pink, Social Animal) and more. Yes, it means that I and members of my team have to be familiar with a number of different solutions but time and time again we find ourselves providing more robust analytics, research and support than our competitors. It simply comes down to the value we strive to deliver and the associated cost.

That has been my approach. I don't expect anyone to follow it but if, by explaining it, you find yourself being more scrutinous in your evaluation and selection process and potentially save some time and money then I have already helped you.

INDEX

Note: Page numbers in *italics* indicate figures